W9-ARG-770

Victory for the Vote

Victory for the Vote

The Fight for Women's Suffrage and the Century that Followed

Doris Weatherford

Foreword by Nancy Pelosi

Mango Publishing

Coral Gables

Published by Mango Publishing Group, a division of Mango Media Inc.

Developed and edited by MTM Publishing
Publisher: Valerie Tomaselli
Executive Editor: Hilary Poole
Adjunct Writer: Beth Scully

Part One originally published as *A History of the American Suffragist Movement* (ABC-CLIO, 1998; MTM Publishing 2005).

Cover Design: Valerie Tomaselli and Roberto Núñez
Cover Photo: Library of Congress
Back Cover Photo: Valerie Tomaselli
Layout & Design: Roberto Núñez

For permission requests, please contact the publisher at:
Mango Publishing Group
2850 S Douglas Road, 2nd Floor
Coral Gables, FL 33134 USA
info@mango.bz

For special orders, quantity sales, course adoptions and corporate sales, please email the publisher at sales@mango.bz. For trade and wholesale sales, please contact Ingram Publisher Services at customer.service@ingramcontent.com or +1.800.509.4887.

Victory for the Vote: The Fight for Women's Suffrage and the Century that Followed

Library of Congress Cataloging-in-Publication number: 2019954753
ISBN: (print) 978-1-64250-053-0, (ebook) 978-1-64250-054-7
BISAC category code HIS058000, HISTORY / Women

Printed in the United States of America

To the great army of women (and men) who fought for women's rights, including the vote, and are continuing the fight today.

Table of Contents

Foreword

by Nancy Pelosi,

Speaker, U.S. House of Representatives

One hundred and seventy-one years ago, 300 women and men gathered in Seneca Falls, New York, and shook the world with a simple proclamation: "We hold these truths to be self-evident: that all men and women are created equal." With those words, the women of Seneca Falls ignited a relentless, generations-long struggle by America's women to secure what is rightfully ours: the sacred right to vote.

Yet, for more than 70 years after, the full promise of equality would be denied to America's women. When the Nineteenth Amendment finally passed, the headlines said "Women Given Right To Vote"—but women were not given anything; they struggled for the right to vote. For decades, in the face of overwhelming challenges, brave women protested and picketed, marched and mobilized, were beaten and jailed, and finally won the right to vote. It is on their shoulders that we all stand today.

Doris Weatherford's inspiring book, *Victory for the Vote: The Fight for Women's Suffrage and the Century that Followed*, reminds us all that the trailblazing suffragists did not wait for change, they worked for change! This important book not only tells the story of the trailblazing suffragists of Seneca Falls; it also shares the stories of women of color whose heroism in the fight for women's suffrage is too often unsung, but who are finally taking their rightful place in American history.

As Speaker of the House, it has been my priority to ensure that the halls of the U.S. Capitol reflect the full diversity of our history. It was my honor to bring a bronze bust of Sojourner Truth to rest under this dome of our democracy in commemoration of her immeasurable contributions to the cause of equality and those of all the women of color who fought for suffrage. This book stands as another fitting tribute to their sacrifice.

The story of America's suffrage did not end with the passage of the Nineteenth Amendment. Decades after our nation declared that "the right of citizens of the United States to vote shall not be denied or abridged by the United States or by any State on account of sex," women would have to fight for another right: the right to take our seat at the decision-making table.

When I first arrived, there were only 25 women in Congress. Back then, women weren't considered a threat to the established, male-dominated power in Washington. When I ran for a leadership position that had been held by men for more than 200 years, the men asked, "Who said she could run?" Yet, the women of the House refused to sit on the sidelines. We knew our purpose and we knew our power—and we used it to make progress, demanding not only a seat at the table, but a seat at the head of the table.

When, as Democratic Leader, I went to my first meeting at the White House with President George W. Bush and House and Senate leaders, I realized that I was at a meeting unlike any other I—or any woman—had ever been to. As an Appropriator and as a Member of the Intelligence Committee, I attended meetings at the White House many times. But this was different.

As President Bush graciously welcomed me, all of a sudden, I felt very closed in to my seat. There I was with Sojourner Truth, Susan B. Anthony, Elizabeth Cady Stanton, Lucretia Mott, Alice Paul: all the suffragists who fought so hard for the right to vote. And as they sat with me on that chair, I could hear them say, "At last we have a seat at the table." And my first thought was "We want more!"

Today, remarkably, in the same Congress that will mark 100 years since women won the right to vote, we serve with more than 100 women Members—and with a woman Speaker! There is nothing more wholesome for our democracy than the increased participation and leadership of women in politics and government.

The women of the 116th Congress have made history, and now, they are making progress. Just like the suffragists of the past, the trailblazing women of the 116th Congress are fighting to ensure that every freedom, every liberty, and every right belongs to every American—including the right to be heard at the ballot box, which is the mainstay of our democracy. The suffragists' cause continues in our fight against blatantly partisan, morally wrong voter suppression efforts that target communities of color.

Today, much more remains to be done to bring our nation closer to its founding promise of equality. We must defend and strengthen the progress we have made on equal pay for equal work, affordable childcare, quality healthcare, and other pillars of health and economic security for women and families—and to do that, we need every woman to be able to exercise her right to vote.

As we celebrate the 100th anniversary of the Nineteenth Amendment, we must channel the same pioneering spirit of America's suffragists and rededicate ourselves to the important work left to be done to ensure that all can enjoy the blessings of liberty in America.

Since my dear friend, the Honorable Geraldine Ferraro, wrote the original foreword to Part One of this book just over twenty years ago, much progress has been forged in the fight for equality. But it is my hope that twenty years from now, the foreword to this wonderful book will be written in a time when even more progress has been forged—and that it will be written by a woman in the White House!

Victory for the Vote will help encourage that change, educating America about the struggle for suffrage and engaging and empowering the next generation of history-makers and game-changers to make a difference. Together, we must continue our progress for women and for the cause of equality—because, when women succeed, America succeeds!

Part One

THE FIGHT FOR THE VOTE

Chapter One

In the Beginning, 1637 to 1840

It was a tiny ad placed in an obscure newspaper. The *Seneca County Courier*, a weekly paper delivered to farms in the cold country of upstate New York, ran just three sentences in its edition for July 14, 1848. The simple announcement invited women to a discussion of "the social, civil, and religious rights of women."

This little news release shook the earth. From the tiny town of Seneca Falls in 1848, a mighty flood of disruptive ideas reached around the world and into the twenty-first century. The global expansion of human rights for women—the notion that women are full human beings and that women's rights are human rights—began here, in a little country church that we, the recipients of hard-fought victories, thoughtlessly have allowed to be destroyed. Ideas live on after buildings go, however, and the voices of these women still echo with words we need to hear.

Why Seneca Falls, New York? Why July 1848? The answer, of course, is that ideas find their time and place in people. The unpretentious circumstances of many women's lives, however, often obscure the power of their minds. We may find it difficult to believe that culture-changing concepts can emerge from a tea table in a country kitchen, but the humble truth is that it was Seneca Falls because Lucretia Mott visited Elizabeth Cady Stanton there. It was 1848 because it was the first time that these busy mothers could manage to get together after their vow to do so in 1840. And the other truth is that both of these women were not only brilliant, but also possessed extraordinary courage.

It is altogether typical of the history of American women that it was their moral sense, their mutual effort to do good for others, that drew Mott and Stanton together. For them and for many other women, the cause of women's rights long would be subordinated to other moral crusades, especially that of abolishing slavery. The Seneca Falls meeting was, in fact, directly rooted in other meetings, especially the 1840 World Anti-Slavery Convention in London.

There were other moral and intellectual roots. More than 200 years before Seneca Falls, a woman named Anne Hutchinson defied the dominant leadership and exercised her right to free speech. In 1637, the theocrats who ran the newly founded colony of Massachusetts tried and convicted Hutchinson of sedition because her religious ideas did not agree with theirs. Her brand of feminine spirituality was proving more popular than their harsh theology, and, when prominent young men exhibited their respect for this female leadership, Hutchinson was banished. At age 46, heavily pregnant for the twelfth time, she accepted exile rather than surrender her independent ideas. It literally cost her life; a few years later, Hutchinson and most of her children were killed by Algonquins in the Long Island Sound area where she had settled after banishment from the safety of Boston.

Although shamefully few Americans know it, an even more powerful case for female participation in the exchange of ideas was made by Hutchinson's friend Mary Dyer. The only person courageous enough to protest when Hutchinson was excommunicated from their Boston church, Dyer returned to England in 1652; there, she converted to the newly founded Society of Friends, more commonly called Quakers. While she was abroad, Massachusetts and Connecticut passed laws banning Quakers, and Dyer was exiled from both colonies upon her 1657 return. Although she could have remained safely in more liberal Long Island, she defied convention—and the pleading of her husband and sons—

Anne Hutchinson preaching in her house in Boston. (Library of Congress)

to repeatedly return to Boston to preach her vision of a loving, egalitarian God. On June 1,1660, the theocracy of Massachusetts, which was both church and state, hanged Mary Dyer.

The Quaker beliefs that she professed soon became America's most important intellectual root of female freedom. Founded in England by George Fox, the Society of Friends quickly established itself in America. Women were important participants in the Quaker movement from the beginning: the group consistently committed itself to the idea of human equality. From the beginning, Quaker women were considered to have an inner light from God just as men did, and they were equally entitled to express moral and spiritual ideas. Nor were their views limited to the quiet of Quaker meeting houses; women were ordained and engaged in street preaching just as men were.

As Quaker culture evolved, especially in Pennsylvania, female leaders developed schools, hospitals, and other charitable organizations, and they controlled financial decisions on these enterprises. Older women also exercised strong powers over younger women, including resolving such personal issues as whether or not a young woman should accept a particular marriage proposal. Obviously, voting of a sort was inherent to such decision making, but because Quakers in general did not participate in secular government, their internal egalitarianism did not necessarily translate into a movement for political equality.

Quakers also were exceptional in seeing American Indians as full human beings—although even Quakers assumed their own religion to be the correct one. They sent missionaries to convert the natives, and, like virtually all other newcomers, took little heed of the political models offered by native societies. In some of those societies, especially the tribes of the northeastern Iroquois Confederacy, women were powerful. In many tribes that practiced farming, the culture was matrilineal. This was a crucial distinction from Europeans, for it meant that children took their mothers' names and traced their families through the maternal, not the paternal, lineage. Thus, it was impossible to be a bastard, and the European shame of illegitimacy was unknown. Beyond that, matrilineal societies rejected the newcomers' patriarchal view of women as the property of their fathers and husbands. In the Iroquois tribes that northeastern settlers encountered, for instance, a newly married man went to live with his wife's family, and his children belonged to that clan, not to his. Personal possessions were relatively rare, but those that did exist were passed on through the mother's line, not the father's. If a marriage did not work out, couples easily separated, and the man went home to his mother.

Moreover, in many tribes, women held genuine political and military power. Women in the Iroquois Confederation, for example, traditionally controlled the fate of captives: they decided if a prisoner of war was to be killed, tortured, held for ransom, or adopted into the tribe. Although Pocahontas lived farther south, her famous intercession on behalf of John Smith thus can be seen as the native rule, not the exception. In the southeast, Cherokee women sometimes participated in actual combat and earned the title of "War Woman." During Massachusetts warfare in 1676, the Pocasset band of Wamponoag was led by a woman named Wetamoo, whose head was displayed on the Taunton town square when only 26 of her 300 men survived the battle.

Indian women held their own councils and participated in treaty-making with whites—much to the annoyance of a number of white writers. Indeed, in the same year of 1848 that whites held their first women's rights convention, the Seneca tribe of the Iroquois Confederation adopted a new constitution. Under its provisions, both men and women elected judges and legislators, and all major decisions had to be ratified by three-fourths of the voters and by three fourths of the clan mothers. Despite this, historians deem this period to mark a decline in the status of Seneca women: after their men interacted with European men, Seneca and other native women would continually lose traditional rights as their cultures adopted the white example.

Few Americans, however, were aware of these alternative societal structures, and almost none were willing to emulate the "savages"—or even the egalitarian ideas of their Quaker missionaries. Nevertheless, there were other female political leaders in mainstream colonial America, many of whom have been forgotten and remain unrecognized even by modern feminists. Lady Deborah Moody, for example, led the first English settlement of what is now Brooklyn when she took followers of her religious ideas there in 1643. They left Massachusetts because of disagreements with Governor John Winthrop, who called Lady Deborah "a dangerous woeman [sic]." Like Anne Hutchinson, her home was attacked by Native Americans. But Moody not only survived, she stayed there, holding steadfast to political and religious liberty. She also paid the natives for their land and went on to build an enlightened community.

Other charismatic religious women led similar settlements, making themselves, in effect, political leaders. Jemima Wilkinson, who called herself the "Publick Universal Friend," took some 300 men and women into the wilderness of western New York in 1788, where her commune established peaceful relationships with its Seneca neighbors. "Mother" Ann Lee was even more successful. She immigrated from England just before the outbreak of the American Revolution, and, distrusted by both sides, was imprisoned for the pacifism she preached. Within a decade, her original eight disciples expanded to several thousand; eventually, the Shaker movement that she founded developed economically successful colonies in 18 states.

It was not coincidental that rebellious women—Hutchinson, Dyer, Moody, Wilkinson, Lee, and others—took refuge in New Netherland and its later version, New York. The Dutch who settled there in 1626 not only were religiously tolerant, they also were exceptionally egalitarian in their treatment of women. Colonial Dutch women retained their maiden names, which were recreated each generation with a father's first name used as a girl's surname. Married women not only had property rights, but also, commonly, prenuptial agreements. Most significantly, Dutch women engaged in a great deal of commercial enterprise, even after marriage.

Margaret Hardenbroeck, for example, owned a shipping line, exporting furs and importing merchandise from Holland; despite two marriages and five children, she frequently sailed across the Atlantic on business. Polly Provoost also was an importer; she attracted customers by laying America's first sidewalk outside of her business. Annejte Loockermans Van Cortlandt paved the first street in America; her daughter, Maria Van Rensselaer, eventually controlled a 24-square-mile Albany fiefdom. Among the first public expenditures in New Amsterdam was the construction of a house for the colony's midwife, Tryntje Jonas; her daughter, pioneer settler Annetje Jans, farmed 62 acres of land along Broadway, and her granddaughter, Sara Roeloef, was employed as an interpreter among English, Dutch, and Algonquin speakers. Although none of these women voted or held office, a historian of early Manhattan described Van Cortlandt's home as "one of the centres of the petticoat government that so often controlled the affairs of the Colony."

The least covert, most undeniable political power exercised by a colonial woman was that of Catholic Maryland's Margaret Brent. Although from a noble family, she emigrated when Lord Baltimore granted her a tract of land as an inducement. Presumably he saw her as more talented than two of her brothers, for she led them, a sister, and servants to Maryland in 1638. Remaining determinedly single, she owned thousands of acres of land. When the governor, Lord Baltimore's younger brother, lay dying, he granted his power of attorney to her, and she ran the colony after his death. After Lord Baltimore, comfortable back in England, complained about one of her decisions, Maryland's legislative assembly backed her judgment call, not his: without Mistress Brent, they averred, "All would have gone to ruin."

English-speaking colonial women, of course, benefited from the examples of seventeenth-century Queen Mary and especially the highly successful Elizabeth I, followed in the next century by Mary II and Anne. The English idea that a woman was capable of being the supreme monarch was rarely replicated on the European continent, Spain's Isabella notwithstanding, and the status of women in French and Spanish colonies reflected this lesser place. Nor did the Catholic Church of France and Spain offer women roles analogous to those of Protestant women, especially Quakers. Although Spain's Catholic colonies were North America's first and priests held significant roles in them, more than two centuries would pass before the first Spanish sisterhoods arrived.

Spanish colonial women did enjoy some social freedoms that Anglo women lacked—dancing, drinking, smoking, gambling, wearing more comfortable clothing—but any aspirations to educational and political equality were more difficult. As late as the nineteenth century, for example, Catholic women in California were actively discouraged from even reading.

In contrast, reading was fundamental to Protestantism. Especially in the Puritan colonies of New England, girls were taught to read so that they could properly inculcate religious principles in their children. It is therefore wholly appropriate that the nation's first written feminist theory came from its original Puritan settlement, Salem. It was the work of a intellectual giant whose name should be well known, but again, few Americans are familiar with Judith Sargent Stevens Murray.

A childless sea captain's wife, Murray had time to think. In 1784—almost a decade before English Mary Wollstonecraft published the much more famous *Vindication of the Rights of Women*—she wrote on the need for improved female self-esteem, "Encouraging a Degree of Self-Complacency, Especially in Female Bosoms." The thoughts she expressed are still being rediscovered by women today:

> Will it be said that the judgment of a male of two years old is more sage than that of a female of the same age? I believe the reverse is generally observed to be true. But from that period what partiality! How is the one exalted and the other depressed.... The one is taught to aspire, and the other is early confined and limited.

Murray eventually collected her essays into three books, the sales of which were promoted by George Washington, and at least one critic has compared her work with that of Noah Webster. Yet after her 1820 death in the wilderness of Mississippi, where she had gone to live with a daughter she bore by her second husband, Judith Sargent Murray's brilliant mind was soon forgotten.

A better-known writer of the same era is Mercy Otis Warren. Perhaps her work is remembered both because it was less feminist and because she was well-connected to male leadership. The wife and the sister of governmental officials, Warren had a political insider's view of the tumultuous days of the American Revolution; indeed, she played her own significant role in bringing on the rebellion by anonymously publishing satires of the British. While her chief purpose in writing was political in the usual sense of the word, Warren also included asides that made feminist points. "Hateall," for example, a character in one of her plays, not only represented British brutality toward colonists, but also was a blatant misogynist. In a tavern scene, he boasted that he married only to win his wife's dowry and then "broke her skirts." His recommendation for a "rebellious dame" was "the green Hick'ry or the willow twig."

Although both Warren and Murray called for greater respect for women, they nevertheless published much of their work under pseudonyms, and neither ever suggested the vote for women or even demanded clearly defined rights to property, custody, or other legal empowerments. Abigail Adams, who never published, was more assertive about political inclusion of women in her voluminous correspondence with the era's important men.

Future president John Adams acknowledged that it was his wife's property management ability that allowed him to spend his life in politics, and their records make it evident that she was the business executive of the family. And yet, although John had great respect for Abigail and their marriage was ideally companionate, he laughed off her most famous call for female freedom. When he met with the Continental Congress in Philadelphia, she wrote from their farm near Boston in March 1776—well before July's Declaration of Independence. "I long to hear you have declared an independency," she said, "and, by the way, in the new code of laws which I suppose it will be necessary for you to make,"

Abigail Adams (Library of Congress)

> I desire you would remember the ladies and be more favorable to them than your ancestors. Do not put such unlimited power into the hands of husbands. Remember all men would be tyrants if they could. If particular care and attention are not paid to the ladies, we are determined to foment a rebellion and will not hold ourselves bound to obey any laws in which we have no voice or representation. That your sex are naturally tyrannical is a truth so thoroughly established as to admit of no dispute, but such of you as wish to be happy willingly give up the harsh title of master for the more tender and endearing one of friend.

Her husband's reply was amused; rolling eyes and a quizzical grin seem to suffuse his words. Not only did he treat her demand for respect as cute, he could not even grant that these creative thoughts were her own:

> As to your extraordinary code of laws, I cannot but laugh. We have been told that our struggle has loosened the bands of government everywhere–that children and apprentices were disobedient, that schools and colleges were grown turbulent.... But your letter was the first intimation that another tribe, more numerous and powerful than all the rest, were grown discontented.... Depend on it, we know better than to repeal our masculine systems.... I begin to think the British as deep as they are wicked at stirring up Tories, Canadians, Indians, Negroes, Irish, Roman Catholics, and, at last, they have stimulated the women to demand new privileges and threaten to rebel.

Abigail Adams's and Mercy Otis Warren's feminist arguments were clearly subordinate to their mainstream political ideas, for it was the success of the new nation that motivated the majority of the words they wrote. Yet the rhetoric of freedom—as John Adams reluctantly acknowledged—inevitably encouraged rebellion among the less privileged. It was simply impossible to proclaim a Declaration of Independence that spoke of "life, liberty, and pursuit of happiness" and of "the consent of the governed" without inspiring hopes that those words might mean what they say.

Perhaps these women of the Revolutionary Age influenced the political climate more than is easily traced, for the same era did produce the first actual voting rights for women. In 1776, the first official year of the Revolution, New Jersey implicitly granted the vote to its women when it adopted a constitution that enfranchised "all free inhabitants." English-speaking women, however, had long experience with gender-neutral language that did not actually mean to include them. In Virginia, too, similar gender-neutral language implied an enfranchisement of which women remained unaware. When Hannah Lee Corbin wrote her brother, General Richard Henry Lee, in 1778 to protest the taxation of women without representation, he replied that Virginia "women were already possessed of that right"—something that seems to have been news to her.

Not surprisingly, such ambiguous and unpublicized enfranchisement meant that few women actually cast ballots. Surprisingly, almost a decade after the Revolution's end, its spirit still prevailed: in 1790, the New Jersey legislature confirmed that it indeed had meant what it said by adding the words "he or she" to its election codes. The amendment's sponsor was Joseph Cooper, a Quaker accustomed to voting women. More remarkable is the fact that only three of his male colleagues voted against this precedent-setting legislation.

New Jersey women voting, late eighteenth century. (Library of Congress)

The act was little publicized, though, and few women knew of this fundamental change in their status. Especially because many Quaker women refused to participate in secular government at all, the legalism made little difference for nearly a decade. In 1797, however, women in Elizabethtown marched together to vote against a legislative candidate who was backed by the male power structure. They nearly defeated him, and politicians began talking about repealing women's franchise. Newspaper editors backed the ruling cabal, ridiculing the female voters in print and intimidating them from casting ballots in the future. Like John Adams's view that the British had planted rebellious thoughts in his wife's mind, editorials portrayed the Elizabethtown women as the opposition's dupes—either ignorantly misled or forced to the polls by scheming, domineering husbands. That women were capable of both forming their own political views and organizing a coalition was a thought that these newspaper men simply could not entertain.

A decade later, in 1807, New Jersey women lost their vote, with the repeal sponsored by the Elizabethtown man they had nearly defeated. A recent campaign over whether a new courthouse would be located in Elizabethtown or Newark became his excuse for the repeal. The race was hotly contested, and there were newspaper allegations that women were so ignorant, corrupt, or obtuse that they "voted again and again." The guilty party, however, was likely to have been men and boys disguised as women who cast multiple ballots. That women were disenfranchised for reasons of corruption and fraud is greatly ironic, because one of the strongest arguments against suffrage in the following decades was that women were naturally pure and should not engage in anything so dirty as politics.

As the new republic developed, ideologies of individual liberty expanded. This was, after all, the first nation in the Western world without a divine-right personage at its head, the first in which citizens openly averred their intention to govern themselves, and the vote continually expanded as state governments grew from colonial ones. Disenfranchised males, including non-property holders, Catholics, Jews, and free blacks, were granted suffrage. Especially after frontiersman Andrew Jackson won the popular vote in the presidential elections of 1824 and 1828, the "common man" ideals of Jacksonian populism were assured.

This rise of democracy, however, would continue to exclude the female half of the population. The only actual enfranchisement of women during the Jacksonian era was in Kentucky in 1838, when widows were allowed to cast ballots in school elections—but only if they had no children currently in school. The exclusionary provisions made it clear that Kentucky's men did not believe that their wives, sisters, mothers, and daughters were able to make informed judgments: even when a woman was allowed to vote because there was no man to cast a ballot in her stead, she apparently could not be trusted to vote reasonably if an issue actually might touch her personal life.

Yet it was, of course, for their own lives that women—like men—wanted the vote. They wanted to improve educational opportunities, especially for girls; they wanted to protect property that they earned or inherited; they wanted custody of their children when a man was abusive. And some of them wanted grander, less personally necessary political change; many women did think of themselves as their brothers' keepers, as the most likely embodiment of purity and morality.

This moral realm was the one in which they felt most comfortable, and indeed, one of the things that kept them out of politics for so long was the difficulty of convincing both women and men that moral imperatives often are best implemented through government. In the case of ending slavery, for example, only government could achieve their goal. The same was true of the temperance movement, because laws regulating the sale of alcohol and other addictive substances could only be enacted by political bodies.

Although women long would be severely constrained even in their traditional realms of moral and educational improvement, the era again showed signs of slow progress. In 1817, in the same rural New York area where Ann Lee and Jemima Wilkinson had led religious movements, Deborah Pierce published *A Scriptural Vindication of Female Preaching, Prophesying, or Exhortation.* The following year, Bostonian Hannah Mather Crocker published another innovative piece, *Observations on the Real Rights of Women.* With this work, Crocker redeemed some of the harm done to women by her grandfather, Reverend Cotton Mather, whose writing on witchcraft helped produce the hysteria that had led to 19 executions and more than 140 arrests in the infamous Salem witch trials in 1692. Far more thoughtful and less mystic than he, Crocker was the mother of ten—and yet she found time to read the work of English feminists, especially Hannah More, and to follow up on the theories of Judith Sargent Murray, especially concerning the negative effects of educating boys and girls differently.

Emma Willard (Library of Congress)

Although it is unlikely that they knew of each other, Emma Willard was thinking the same thoughts. In 1818, the same year Crocker's work was published, Willard presented to the New York legislature *An Address... Proposing a Plan for Improving Female Education.* The lawmakers were shocked by her intention to teach math and science—especially anatomy—to girls, but the working-class town of Troy, New York, saw the good sense behind Willard's innovative curriculum and raised taxes to build the school. An amazingly quick success, it demonstrated a great public desire for serious female education. Willard's model was soon adopted elsewhere, and the Emma Willard School continues today.

Willard's most significant early emulator was Mary Lyon, who built a work/study institution of higher education for women, Mt. Holyoke Seminary, in western Massachusetts in 1834. Those who knew Lyon said that they recognized immediately that they were in the presence of a genius, and her words certainly indicate an innate grasp of the subtlety of politics. "The plan," she wrote to a friend of her ideas for this school, "should not seem to originate with us, but with benevolent gentlemen." Lyon literally went from farm to farm, raising $15,000 for her school in two years. When criticized for this unladylike method of implementing her dream, she confidently replied, "I am doing a great work; I cannot come down."

But Lyon spoke to people one-on-one; except for Quakers and others willing to be seen as on the radical fringe, women did not speak in public. Even Emma Willard's famous "address" was written, not spoken. It was considered scandalous for a woman to speak to a "promiscuous audience"—an audience composed of men and women. Nor was this simply a societal taboo, but, in the view of almost everyone at the time, it was a commandment from God. St. Paul's words in First Corinthians are unequivocal: "Women should keep silent in the churches.... If there is anything they desire to know, let them ask their husbands at home. For it is shameful for a woman to speak in church" (1 Cor. 14:34–35). Because virtually all of the era's cultural activity was church-related, very few women ever learned to speak in public. The subliminal message from Anne Hutchinson and Mary Dyer doubtless rang across the decades as a warning that speech could mean death.

Stage fright could not have been more real for the pioneers who broke this taboo. Clarina Howard Nichols, a Vermont newspaper editor of sufficient political power that, in 1852, she was invited to speak to the state's senate on married women's property rights, was nonetheless so frightened that she showed the symptoms of a heart attack. Nichols later wrote that she only barely managed to calm the "violent throbbing" in her chest to finish her speech, and her "voice was tremulous throughout." She was supported by a local judge, who, with incredible kindness, had gone door-to-door the previous day, encouraging women to sit in the gallery. When the speech was over, they ran down the gallery stairs and said, "We did not know before what Woman's Rights were, Mrs. Nichols, but we are for Woman's Rights." Another showed her vicarious anxiety: "I broke out in cold perspiration when...you leaned your head on your hand. I thought you were going to fail."

The public-speaking taboo reflected more than a little class bias: working women in the textile mills of Lowell, Massachusetts, headed by labor leader Sarah Bagley, had addressed a legislative committee in 1845 with little public criticism. These working-class women were less concerned about accusations of unladylike behavior, and it is important to remember that their testimony focused on their legal needs as workers, not on their needs as women. Presumably because men in the mills also would benefit from labor reforms, public speaking by these women appeared acceptable.

One woman stands out above all others of this era for insisting on her right to free speech. Frances Wright, a wealthy Scot who spent much of her life in the United States, violated the taboo with complete abandon. She made her first trip to the U.S. in 1818, and the travelogue she published was Europe's first widely read book on the new nation. She returned again in 1824 and sailed around the Gulf of Mexico and up the Mississippi, where she established a colony for freed slaves near modern Memphis. Not surprisingly, the economy of this remote place could not support them, so Wright financed and personally escorted some 30 blacks to a new home in Haiti.

Frances Wright (Library of Congress)

As early as 1829—decades prior to other feminists—Wright traveled the country on a paid lecture tour. Especially in the Cincinnati area where she eventually settled, she attracted large and generally respectful crowds, with men actually more likely to support her radical ideas than women. Not only an abolitionist and a utopian, Wright also unhesitatingly attacked organized religion for the secondary place it assigned women; most shockingly, she advocated the empowerment of women through divorce and the use of birth control. She married in France in 1831 after bearing her lover's child. A true internationalist, she crossed the Atlantic five times in the 1840s alone. In 1851, a fatal accident deprived feminists of Frances Wright's leadership, but decades later, they paid tribute to her by placing her picture first in the first volume of their *History of Woman Suffrage.*

A second well-known feminist did not engage in public speaking but did charge money for "conversations" in her home. New Englander Margaret Fuller's writing was at least as influential as Wright's; she was a close friend of the era's most famous literati, including Emerson, Thoreau, Hawthorne, Bronson Alcott, and others. They chose her to edit the group's innovative journal, *The Dial,* and she went from there to the *New York Tribune,* where she carved out a position as the nation's first professional book reviewer. Like Frances Wright, Margaret Fuller bore a child abroad before she married her lover, an Italian revolutionary; also like Wright, an early death cut short the contribution she could have made to the women's rights movement. The young family drowned in a shipwreck while returning to America.

Margaret Fuller (Library of Congress)

Fuller's most important feminist work was *Woman in the Nineteenth Century,* published in 1845. Her national reputation brought readership to the book, and it was a factor in creating the ferment of ideas that led to the Seneca Falls Convention three years later. Like Frances Wright, however, Fuller was at least a century ahead of her time, especially in her advocacy of "free love," the era's term for sexual liberation.

In the nineteenth century, more people lived unconventionally than is generally recognized today. By the time of the Seneca Falls meeting, the United States had at least 40 functioning utopian communities—what we might call "cults" today—with alternate lifestyles that usually included communal property, vegetarianism, and other health reforms, as well as sexual behavior that ranged from abstinence to communal sex. The Oneida community of rural

New York probably was the most radical; its men were required to use birth control, and, even today, some of their "complex marriage" practices would be deemed not only scandalous, but criminal.

The era's morally driven women, of course, were more than a little ambivalent about Wright and Fuller and the harm that this radicalism did to their shared cause of abolishing slavery. Those who hoped to influence a public that still believed in slavery as both economically necessary and divinely sanctioned could not afford the distraction and credibility loss that would result if they associated themselves with advocates of "free love." Some abolitionists, however, were prescient enough to understand that, whatever the intentions of reformers, the public inevitably would link the agitation for women's civil rights with that of blacks. Already at this embryonic stage of the movements, they understood that the best approach was to work for justice for both women and blacks, without forcing the two into a false competition.

Lydia Maria Child was one who had both causes on her mind: in 1833, she published an anti-slavery classic, *An Appeal in Favor of That Class of Americans Called Africans*. Just two years later, she wrote *The History of the Condition of Women*. These books were so controversial that Child went bankrupt. Subscription cancellations for her previously successful children's magazine arrived in droves; it was America's first, in which Child wrote classics such as the lyrics to "Over the River and Through the Woods." The image that she had built as the author of bestselling *The Frugal Housewife* (1829) was destroyed, and she was ostracized by former Massachusetts friends.

Lydia Maria Child (Library of Congress)

For a while, Child maintained the household income by adopting an early commuter-marriage lifestyle; she edited the *National Anti-Slavery Standard* from New York, while her husband worked as a journalist in Washington.

The tie between racial and gender liberation also was spelled out by Sarah Grimké. In 1838, just one year after becoming an active abolitionist and a decade prior to the Seneca Falls meeting, she published *Letters on the*

Equality of the Sexes and the Condition of Women. At the time, she and her sister Angelina were becoming famous (or notorious, depending on one's point of view) for their courageous stand against slavery. Born into a wealthy slaveholding South Carolina family, the sisters moved north, converted to Quakerism, and began writing and speaking against slavery. The only white Southerners ever to be leaders in the cause, their Massachusetts speaking tour was the first by female abolitionist agents. During the summer of 1837, the Grimkés attracted hundreds of listeners, both men and women, every day. In Lowell alone, 1,500 came; in smaller towns, people stood on ladders peering into overcrowded churches.

Once again, it was speech, more than the written word, that made the Grimkés objects of scorn. Even the Society of Friends rebuked Sarah, not for speaking as such, but for raising the controversial subject of slavery at the society's 1836 national convention. The next year, Massachusetts ministers of the Congregationalist denomination (the intellectual heirs of Puritanism) issued a pastoral letter denouncing the sisters' speaking tour. "We invite your attention to the dangers that at present seem to threaten the female character with widespread and permanent injury," the clerics read from their pulpits. "The appropriate duties and influence of woman are clearly stated in the New Testament."

Mary S. Parker of Boston was one of the women who would ignore the Massachusetts ministers' admonitions; in May 1837, she went to New York to preside over the Women's Anti-Slavery Convention. Arguably the first national organization of women, this initial meeting attracted 200 delegates from nine states, some of them free blacks including, among others, Julia Williams, a member of the Boston Female Anti-Slavery Society. A permanent organization grew out of it, but, when the women assembled in Philadelphia the next year, the City of Brotherly Love greeted them with immense hostility. After a howling mob made it impossible for them to continue their business, presiding officer Maria Weston Chapman led the women out of the hall with a white woman holding the hand of each black woman, something that she had done three years earlier when similar men threatened the Boston Female Anti-Slavery Society. So frequently attacked for her views that she said she was afraid to walk alone because of the "odious" comments Bostonians made to her, Chapman nonetheless displayed singular courage and leadership as did the black activists who marched with her. After the women's dramatic exit, the mob set fire to the building.

It was from these female anti-slavery societies that women went to the World Anti-Slavery Convention held in London in June 1840. The previous month, a serious split had developed in the American Anti-Slavery Society when its founder, William Lloyd Garrison, appointed Abby Kelly to the society's business committee. Garrison was impressed by Kelly's commitment to the cause; she had given up her teaching job to endure the most hostile of conditions while lecturing against slavery. During a tour the previous year, she was slandered, physically attacked, and refused hotel rooms. Despite this demonstration of commitment, many male abolitionists objected to a woman in a leadership position. At the May convention, "clergymen went through the audience urging every woman…to vote against the motion." The contradiction of asking women to vote in this case but not in others did not escape ironic comment from feminists, and Garrison's appointment of Kelly prevailed. Some of the losers, however, could not accept majority rule, and they vented their frustrations in London the next month.

Also sailing across the sea were the female delegates: Lucretia Mott led five Philadelphia women "in modest Quaker costume"; the three from Boston were "women of refinement and education" and they were joined by "several still in their twenties." Among them was Elizabeth Cady Stanton and her husband Henry, who went to the abolitionist meeting on their honeymoon. Much later, in the first volume of the *History of Woman Suffrage*, she would recall:

> The American clergymen, who had landed a few days before, had been busily engaged in fanning the English prejudice into active hostility against the admission of these women into the Convention.… The excitement and vehemence of protest and denunciation could not have been greater.

While the women watched in silence, some of the male American delegates made strong arguments for their inclusion. George Bradburn, a Massachusetts legislator, orated for a half-hour: "What a misnomer to call this a World's

Convention of Abolitionists when some of the oldest and most thorough-going Abolitionists in the World are denied the right to be represented!" Toward the end of the day's debate, he sprang to his feet exasperated and used words that are almost incredible for a politician of any era:

> "Prove to me, gentlemen, that your Bible sanctions the slavery of women–the complete subjugation of one-half the race to the other–and I should feel that the best work I could do for humanity would be to make a grand bonfire of every Bible in the Universe."

Along with others, Bostonian Wendell Phillips zealously advocated the women's cause. He pointed out that the American men could not "take upon themselves the responsibility of withdrawing the delegates...[whom] their constituents...sanctioned as their fit representatives." In response to the most frequently offered argument for excluding women—that a mixed group would be offensive to the host country—Phillips retorted:

> In America we listen to no such arguments. If we had done so we would never had been here as Abolitionists. It is the custom there not to admit colored men into respectable society, and we have been told again and again that we are outraging the decencies of humanity when we permit colored men to sit by our side. When we have submitted to brick-bats, and the tar tub and feathers in America, rather than yield to the custom...shall we yield to the parallel custom or prejudice against women in Old England? We can not yield this question if we would; for it is a matter of conscience. But we would not yield it on the ground of expediency. In doing so we should feel that we are striking off the right arm of our enterprise. We could not go back and ask for any aid from the women...if we had deserted them.

The feminist arguments were of no avail. The vote to refuse to accept the credentials of the female delegates passed by an overwhelming majority. The women were fenced off behind a curtain, where they could hear but could not be heard or seen. None of the men cared enough about the principle to surrender his credentials—except for William Lloyd Garrison, who arrived too late for the debate. "Brave, noble Garrison" sat "a silent spectator in the gallery" during the ten-day convention. "What a sacrifice," Elizabeth Cady Stanton wrote, "for a principle so dimly seen by the few, and so ignorantly ridiculed by the many!" Wendell Phillips, in contrast, assured the other men that he had "no unpleasant feelings." Stanton concluded bitterly:

Wendell Phillips (The Free Library of Philadelphia)

> Would there have been no unpleasant feelings in Wendell Phillips' mind had African American Frederick Douglass and Robert Purvis been refused their seats? And had they listened one entire day to debate on their...fitness for plantation life, and unfitness for the forum and public assemblies, and been rejected as delegates on the grounds of color.

The sadness of her conclusion still echoes. Although she commended Phillips's leadership, his easy acquiescence to the status quo upset the young Stanton greatly, and it changed forever her view of even good men. Although much in love with her groom of exactly one month, she was forced to acknowledge: "it is almost impossible for the most liberal of men to understand what liberty means for woman."

Chapter Two

"Let Facts Be Submitted to a Candid World": 1840 to 1848

At the end of the long debate that banned them from the Anti-Slavery Convention in 1840, Lucretia Mott and Elizabeth Cady Stanton "wended their way arm in arm down Great Queen Street." During the next nine days, they "kept up a brisk fire" of words aimed at "the unfortunate gentlemen" who shared their hotel, one of whom packed his luggage and "withdrew after the first encounter." Not eager to return to the convention and sit behind a humiliating curtain, Mott and Stanton spent much of their time walking in the June splendor of London's parks, where they "agreed to hold a woman's rights convention on their return to America."

But life got in the way. Lucretia Mott was one of the busiest women of her era, for there was little of Philadelphia civic life in which she was not involved. By the time of the World Anti-Slavery Convention, she and merchant James Mott had been married for 29 years. He was highly supportive of his unusual wife; she was not only the mother of six, but also had been an ordained Quaker minister for almost two decades. An ardent abolitionist, she spoke in black churches as early as 1829. Moreover, she took it upon herself to boycott

Lucretia Mott (Library of Congress)

everything produced with slave labor, which meant finding substitutes for such staples as cotton, sugar, coffee, and rice.

When they met in England, Lucretia Mott had been married for longer than 25-year-old Elizabeth Cady Stanton had been alive. Stanton graduated from Emma Willard's Troy Female Seminary, and then became involved in abolitionist activity, where she met journalist Henry Stanton. He was so impressed with her that he agreed to omit the bride's traditional vow of obedience from their May wedding—and they immediately sailed for London.

After losing the debate, the Motts and Stantons adopted the utilitarian view that it was better if one partner of their marriages was represented at the convention than none, and the women thus had plenty of time to spend together. Lucretia Mott became a true inspiration for Elizabeth Cady Stanton: "I felt at once a new-born sense of dignity and freedom," Stanton would write later, for Mott "seemed like a being from some larger planet." James Mott similarly provided a model for Henry Stanton.

Elizabeth Cady Stanton and one of her children, 1876.
(From the archives of the Seneca Falls Historical Society)

The Stantons traveled in Europe until November, and then Henry studied law with Elizabeth's father, a judge in Johnstown, New York. While she bore the first three of their seven children, he passed the bar and they moved to Boston. During four wonderful years there, she met many inspirational women, including abolitionists Maria Weston Chapman, Lydia Maria Child, and Abbey Kelly Foster—whose husband was so feminist that he cared for their child when she went on lecture tours. In 1847, however, the Stantons again moved to a town where Henry would have fewer attorney competitors: Seneca Falls, New York.

It happened that Lucretia Coffin Mott had relatives nearby. Her youngest sibling, Martha Coffin Wright, lived in Auburn, New York. Mott was much more religious than Wright—who had been expelled from the Society of Friends for her first marriage to a non-Quaker who died young—but the sisters shared a commitment to liberal ideas. Like most women of their era, their lives were dominated by their anatomy: in July 1848, Martha Wright was pregnant with her seventh child. Her attitudes were unconventional enough that she taught her sons needle skills. One of them, she said, "had knit a bag to put his marbles in."

Mott stayed with Wright when she came to western New York for the annual meeting of the Society of Friends, and Stanton met them for a tea party at the home of Jane Hunt, who, with her husband Richard, was considered "a prominent Friend near Waterloo," New York. They were joined by Mary Ann M'Clintock, also a Quaker and a mother; her husband, Thomas, would later assist the women with their activism.

Desperately unhappy in Seneca Falls after the excitement of life in activist Boston, Stanton poured out her woes to her old soulmate Lucretia Mott, and, as Stanton would later write, they "at once returned to the topic they had so often discussed…the propriety of holding a woman's convention." With encouragement from the other women, they "decided to put their long-talked-of resolution into action, and before twilight deepened into night, the call was written, and sent to the *Seneca County Courier*." When it appeared in the paper a few days later, it read:

> WOMAN'S RIGHTS CONVENTION–A Convention to discuss the social, civil, and religious condition and rights of women, will be held in the Wesleyan Chapel, at Seneca Falls, New York, on Wednesday and Thursday, the 19th and 20th of July, current; commencing at 10 o'clock A.M. During the first day the meeting will be exclusively for women, who are earnestly invited to attend. The public generally are invited to be present on the second day, when Lucretia Mott, of Philadelphia, and other ladies and gentlemen, will address the convention.

The women gathered on Sunday morning at Mary M'Clintock's home (minus Jane Hunt) to write the documents that would form the agenda for discussion at the meeting—and, as it turned out, set the agenda for American women for more than seven decades. Had they known the gravity of the cause upon which they embarked, it is possible that they would not have undertaken it: none of the women who met around the parlor table lived to see the achievement of their goals.

At the end of her life, M'Clintock regretted that she was unable to have done more for the cause, but Stanton pointed out the importance of M'Clintock's influence within her own family: her son-in-law, Dr. James Truman of the Pennsylvania School of Dental Surgery, led the fight for the admission of women to dentistry in the 1870s.

According to Stanton, the women were "quite innocent of the herculean labors they proposed," and they systematically set about the task of preparation for the gathering. Joined by Amy Post, Catherine A.F. Stebbins, and others—including husbands and children—they first perused documents from meetings they had attended for the causes of temperance, abolition, and even peace. All, however, "seemed too tame and pacific for the inauguration of a rebellion such as the world had never before seen." Indeed, there was no precedent. From family roles (and unspoken family violence) to the dearth of educational and employment opportunities to the almost complete lack of legal rights and much more, women had problems that no male agenda had ever begun to envision, let alone address.

Finally they hit upon the right format: the nation's Declaration of Independence, which was then 72 years old. Ironically, it would turn out to be exactly another 72 years later, in 1920, when women finally received full enfranchisement. The women's Declaration of Independence thus fell at a precise midpoint of a female version of American history. Of course, those who wrote the 1848 Declaration of Sentiments had no way of foreseeing this long future. Instead, they set about their task with inspiration and even the good humor that comes with the excitement of doing something that will surprise and possibly shock. Stanton wrote later:

> It was at once decided to adopt the historic document, with some slight changes such as substituting "all men" for "King George." Knowing that women must have more to complain of than men under any circumstances possibly could, and seeing the Fathers had eighteen grievances, a protracted search was made through statute books, church usages, and the customs of society to find that exact number. Several well-disposed men assisted in collecting the grievances, until,

with the announcement of the eighteenth, the women felt they had enough to go before the world with a good case. One youthful lord remarked, "Your grievances must be grievous indeed, when you are obliged to go to books in order to find them out."

In just three days, these remarkable women had decided to hold a "convention"—without the delegate selection process that precedes most such gatherings—and made all the arrangements for planning it, publicizing it, and preparing an agenda for it. Their declaration was as dramatic as the more famous one Thomas Jefferson and his colleagues had prepared. Elizabeth Cady Stanton was analogous to Jefferson as the document's chief author. With no resources beyond paper, pencil, pens dipped in inkwells, and their powerful intelligence, they framed their thoughts as eternal truths.

The declaration was ready for discussion when "the eventful day dawned at last," but those in charge on the morning of July 19, 1848, felt a last-minute panic: the doors of the Wesleyan Methodist church in Seneca Falls, where the meeting was to be held, were firmly locked. One of Stanton's nephews—the son of her sister Harriet Cady Eaton and "an embryo Professor of Yale College"—was boosted through a window and opened the chapel from the inside.

Meanwhile, crowds headed through the town. On a Wednesday morning in July, when they could have been cultivating or mowing or doing any number of the tasks that had to be packed into summer weekdays, some 300 people (of an approximate 8,000 living in Seneca Falls) chose instead to participate in this wildly unusual meeting. Women walked or, in many cases, persuaded their husbands to hitch up the horses to take them to town. The latter was so often true that dozens of men were present, and the leaders decided to ignore their own newspaper announcement that said the first day's discussion would be limited to women. Because so many men were at the church, the women quickly decided that they could remain. In this reversal of their original plans, the women's rights movement accepted an important principle from the beginning: feminism is not necessarily defined by gender.

Confronted by an unexpectedly large crowd, most of the women rapidly felt the inadequacy of their leadership training. Because of the taboo against public speaking by women and because, outside of the Quaker meeting house, and a handful of female anti-slavery societies, there were no women's organizations, none had experience in parliamentary procedure or the fundamentals of running a meeting. They "shrank from the responsibility of organizing the meeting and leading the discussions," Stanton said, and held "a hasty council around the altar." Because experienced men were "already on the spot," they decided that "this was an occasion when men might make themselves pre-eminently useful." Men could "take the laboring oar through the Convention."

This engraving from *Harper's Weekly* parodies the 1848 Seneca Falls Convention. (Library of Congress)

Lucretia Mott, who was "accustomed to public speaking in the Society of Friends, stated the objects of the Convention," while her husband James, as Stanton later described him, stood "tall and dignified, in Quaker costume" as he presided. Frederick Douglass, a decade out of slavery and a recent resident of Rochester, joined in leading the discussion. Mary M'Clintock was appointed secretary—but she did not limit herself to secretarial duty; both she and her sister Elizabeth M'Clintock read "well-written" speeches. Stanton displayed her early talent in doing the same, while Martha Wright "read some satirical articles she had published in the daily papers answering the diatribes on women's sphere." Among the male presenters was Ansel Bascom, a recent delegate to a state constitutional convention, who thus was well qualified to speak to women's property rights. Samuel Tillman, a young law student, had researched a "most exasperating" set of English and American statutes related to women, all of which demonstrated "the tender mercies of men toward their wives, in taking care of their property and protecting them in their civil rights."

The meat of the convention was debate on the Declaration of Sentiments. After two days, "the only resolution that was not unanimously adopted was the ninth," the one favoring the vote for women. Even longtime liberal Lucretia Mott did not favor this resolution, because she agreed with those who "feared a demand for the right to vote would defeat the others they deemed more rational, and make the whole movement ridiculous." Elizabeth Cady Stanton and Frederick Douglass, however, insisted that without this fundamental right to participate in government, the principle of equality for women would never be taken seriously. After long discussion, the resolution "at last carried by a small majority." The document was signed by exactly 100 participants: 32 men and 68 women. Just one of them, 19-year-old Charlotte Woodward, would live to see the centerpiece of the declaration achieved: only she was still alive to vote in 1920.

Although they talked for two days in Seneca Falls, "there were still so many new points for discussion," according to Stanton, that the excited participants planned a follow-up meeting for the big city of Rochester. It was to be held just two weeks later, on August 2, 1848. This time the Committee of Arrangement was composed of Amy Post, Sarah D. Fish, Sarah C. Owen, and Mary H. Hallowell—none of whom had worked with the original planners. So untapped were these women's talents, however, that the Rochester organizers had no trouble setting precedents of their own.

The meeting, which was scheduled for the city's Unitarian Church, was "so well advertised in the daily papers" that when the day came, it "was filled to overflowing." The women's personal growth also was exponential; they had gained enough confidence that they undertook the parliamentary offices at this meeting. James Mott was present and ready to preside again, but the night before the meeting, Amy Post, Sarah Fish, and Rhoda DeGarmo undertook to persuade Abigail Bush to assume the leadership. According to Bush, her old friends "commenced to prove that the hour had come when a woman should preside, and led me into the church." Much later, she would say: "No one knows what I passed through on that occasion. I was born and baptized in the old Scotch Presbyterian church. At that time its sacred teachings were, 'If a woman would know anything let her ask her husband.' " Somewhere, however, she found courage.

Amy Post called the packed house to order and nominated Abigail Bush for president, with Laura Murray as vice president, and three women—Elizabeth M'Clintock, Sarah Hallowell, and Catherine A.F. Stebbins—as secretaries. Elizabeth Cady Stanton later wrote that she, "Mrs. Mott, and Mrs. McClintock [sic] thought it a most hazardous experiment to have a woman President, and stoutly opposed it." The original leadership was "on the verge of leaving the Convention in disgust," Stanton said, "but Amy Post and Rhoda de Garmo assured them" that a woman "could also preside at a public meeting, if they would but make the experiment." Those in attendance voted, a majority agreed, and Abigail Bush took the chair. "The calm way she assumed the duties of the office, and the admirable manner in which she charged them," Stanton admitted, "soon reconciled the opposition to the seemingly ridiculous experiment." Bush humbly summarized, "from that hour I seemed endowed as from on high to serve."

Still, some of the secretaries were so inexperienced at using their voices that they could not be heard. In a time before microphones, the crowd cried for increased volume so that they could participate. Finally, Sarah Anthony Burtis, a teacher and a Quaker accustomed to public speaking, volunteered. She "read the reports and documents of the Convention with a clear voice and confident manner, to the great satisfaction of her more timid coadjutors."

Men once again were involved, including Frederick Douglass and a "Mr. Colton," who traveled the long distance from eastern Connecticut to remind the audience that "woman's sphere was home." Lucretia Mott's response to him indicated her exceptional awareness of seemingly every aspect of her world: she embarrassed Colton by pointing out that his church limited its Female Moral Reform Society to its basement and then only on the "condition that none of the women should speak at the meeting." These societies had begun in the 1840s, especially in Ohio and other non-coastal areas, to encourage men to drop immoral behaviors: some were even courageous enough to publicize the names of men seen visiting brothels. Mott's point was that Colton welcomed women to the anti-vice movement merely as listeners, even in a group ostensibly for women.

Another memorable aspect of this meeting was the appearance of a "young and beautiful stranger," who held the audience "spell-bound." It was near the close of the morning session when a "bride in traveling dress, accompanied by her husband, slowly walked up the aisle and asked the privilege of saying a few words." The newlyweds were going west, heard of the convention, and rearranged their train schedule so that they could come. During a 20-minute speech, Rebecca Sanford advocated female political participation; she ended by encouraging women to "hang the wreath of domestic harmony upon the eagle's talons."

Perhaps the most important person to appear at this meeting, however, was Ernestine Rose, who had long labored for women's rights in isolation. Born as Ernestine Susmond Potowski in Poland, she had gone to court at age 16 to insist on receiving her inheritance from her mother; after emigrating and marrying an Englishman, she arrived in New York in 1836. Within months, she began working to ensure property rights for American women. There were just five signatures on the first petition that she sent to the New York legislature—and those she obtained only "after a good deal of trouble." Rose explained, "Some of the ladies said the gentlemen would laugh at them; others, that they had rights enough; and the men said the women had too many rights already." Undaunted, her efforts put American-born women to shame: from 1837 to 1848, when she came to feminists' attention at the Rochester convention, Ernestine Rose addressed the New York legislature five times. Supported in her travels by a feminist husband, she had lectured on women's rights in Ohio and lobbied the legislature of frontier Michigan.

Ernestine Rose circa 1850. (Schlesinger Library on the History of Women in America)

The Rochester convention also brought attention to economic needs, as several speakers reported on women's working conditions. The upper-middle-class women in attendance, the only ones with sufficient leisure to organize such meetings, found disgraceful "the intolerable servitude and small remuneration paid to the working-class of women." Once again, however, more time was spent on religious issues, especially on the interpretation of biblical injunctions regarding a woman's place. The question of taking a man's name at marriage also was debated; Elizabeth Cady Stanton reminded the others that this practice was neither divinely ordained nor universal.

After three sessions before a large and receptive audience, the convention adopted resolutions that were shorter and more concrete than those of Seneca Falls. The first called for the vote, and another commended Elizabeth Blackwell, who recently had become the world's first female student in a traditional medical school. But the majority were based on women's economic needs, focusing on taxation without representation, property ownership, and the inheritance rights of widows. Most meaningfully, the convention called upon the audience to be better employers: "Those who believe the laboring classes of women are oppressed ought to do all in their power to raise their wages, beginning with their own household servants."

The strongest language centered on the right to retain one's own earnings. "Whereas," the document proclaimed, "the husband has the legal right to hire out his wife to service, collect her wages, and appropriate it to his own exclusive and independent benefit…reducing her almost to the condition of a *slave*…. [W]e will seek the overthrow of this barbarous and unrighteous law; and conjure women no longer to promise obedience in the marriage covenant."

Amy Post moved for the adoption of the resolutions, and with only "two or three dissenting voices," they were accepted and the meeting adjourned. The significant differences from the Seneca Falls resolutions showed that the movement's leadership already was learning a lesson in pragmatism: they saw that, more than the intellectual and legal arguments that motivated so many of them, the average woman instead was moved on pocketbook issues. "Though few women responded to the demand for political rights," Stanton said of the Rochester meeting, "many at once saw the importance of equality in the world of work."

As Stanton suggested, not everyone was brave enough to respond to the call. Some of the signers of the Seneca Falls declaration withdrew their names within weeks, as soon as a derogatory volcano erupted in the press. It was largely Amelia Jenks Bloomer who served as the unintended publicity agent for the Seneca Falls convention—and, later, as a chief target for the barbs of cartoonists.

Although her name (or more aptly, her husband's name) became synonymous with pants worn by women, Amelia Bloomer had been a rather conservative schoolteacher until she married a more liberal man. Her husband, Dexter Bloomer, owned the *Seneca County Courier*, and she often wrote for it. The couple also served as postmaster and postmistress for Seneca Falls.

Bloomer attended the historic convention but did not sign the declaration. She was there primarily as a reporter, and it would be several years before Bloomer became an advocate of voting rights. Her chief interest was temperance, and, in January 1849, she began her own paper, *The Lily*. It focused on ending the abuse of alcohol, with women's rights incidental to that, and soon circulated beyond state borders. Adding more than a thousand subscribers per year, *The Lily* would bring women's needs to a national audience.

Amelia Bloomer (Library of Congress)

Prior to that, however, other journalists learned of the unconventional convention from the Bloomers' *Seneca County Courier.* Train service had come to Seneca Falls in 1841, seven years prior to the convention, and in a time before syndicated press services, journalists met the trains and read each other's papers to discover the news. On learning of the Seneca Falls Convention, most editors responded with an incredulity that still conveys a mental picture of men rubbing their eyes in disbelief—but they rapidly spread the story. A Massachusetts paper, the *Worcester Telegraph,* was one of the more objective, although editorial amazement at the women's audacity suffused its commentary:

> A female Convention has just been held at Seneca Falls, N.Y.... The list of grievances which the *Amazons* exhibit, concludes by expressing a determination to insist that woman shall have "immediate admission to all the rights and privileges which belong to them as citizens".... This is *bolting* with a vengeance.

In an era when it was almost impossible to distinguish between news coverage and editorial opinion, James Gordon Bennett, publisher of New York City's widely read *New York Herald,* was unusual in putting his name on his report about the Seneca Falls convention. In a long argument with himself, Bennett offered a bit of encouragement for every point of view and ended with a surprising conclusion:

> This is the age of revolutions.... The work of revolution is no longer confined to the Old World, nor to the masculine gender. The flag of independence has been hoisted, for the second time, on this side of the Atlantic; and a solemn league and covenant has just been entered into by a Convention of women at Seneca Falls, to "throw off the despotism under which they are groaning"....
>
> The declaration is a most interesting document.... The amusing part is the preamble.... It complains of the want of the elected franchise.... We do not see by what principle of right the angelic creatures should claim to compete.... Though we have the most perfect confidence in the courage and daring of Miss Lucretia Mott and several others of our lady acquaintances, we confess it would go to our hearts to see them putting on the panoply of war, and mixing in scenes like those....
>
> It is not the business, however, of the despot to decide upon the rights of his victims; nor do we undertake to define the duties of women. Their standard is now unfurled by their own hands. The Convention of Seneca Falls has appealed to the country. Miss Lucretia Mott has propounded the principles of the party. Ratification meetings will no doubt shortly be held.... We are much mistaken if Lucretia would not make a better President than some of those who have lately tenured the White House.

The editor gave the meeting more credence than some of its participants: Bennett assumed that the world would soon be debating the declaration's principles in "ratification meetings," and his musing on the possibility of a female president was not even a notion that the women themselves had begun to envision. Newspaper circulation of the declaration meant that its ideas traveled around the globe far faster than its rural authors ever could have expected.

The Rochester convention, held in a much larger city, naturally elicited more editorial comment, most of it negative. According to the *Rochester Democrat,* "The great effort seemed to be to bring out some new, impracticable, absurd, and ridiculous proposition, and the greater its absurdity the better." The *Rochester Advertiser* took an unusual approach: its editor appeared to hope that the women's gatherings would go away if he yawned: "to us they appear extremely dull and uninteresting, and, aside from their novelty, hardly worth notice." Despite the efforts in the Rochester meeting to direct attention to women's economic needs, one of the state's most populist newspapers was also one of its most annoyed. The *Mechanic's Advocate,* published in the capital of Albany, was uncharacteristically conservative in its reaction when women were the issue. After an internal debate with its better nature, its editorial essentially ended up saying that even if changes were needed, the upheaval would be so great that it was not worth the effort:

> The women who attend these meetings, no doubt at the expense of their more appropriate duties, act as committees, write resolutions... make speeches, etc....
>
> Now, it requires no argument to prove that this all is wrong. Every true hearted female will instantly feel that this is unwomanly.... Society would have to be radically remodeled in order to accommodate itself to so great a change.... But this change is impracticable, uncalled for, and unnecessary.... It would be of no positive good, that would not be outweighed tenfold by positive evil.

An out-of-state paper, the *Public Ledger and Daily Transcript,* apparently was unaware of Lucretia Mott and other Pennsylvanians who initiated the feminist agenda. Its editorial began with smug congratulations to "our Philadelphia ladies," who not only possessed "beauty, but are celebrated for discretion and modesty.... Whoever heard of a Philadelphia lady setting up for a reformer, or standing out for women's rights?" Seemingly blissfully ignorant of the long records established by the city's women in the Society of Friends and other reform groups, the paper continued mockingly, "Boston ladies contend for the rights of women [and] the New York girls aspire to mount the rostrum.... Our Philadelphia girls prefer the baby-jumper...and the ballroom." The unsigned editorial concluded by revealing a profound masculine egocentrism: "A woman is nobody. A wife is everything."

The *Lowell Courier* displayed a similarly regressive attitude, even though this Massachusetts textile town employed thousands of women who entertained no thoughts of babies and ballrooms. Most Lowell mill workers were unmarried women who lived in company housing; many were highly literate, for they had the opportunity to read, join study clubs, and even publish their own writing in industry-sponsored publications. Blind to this audience, however, the Lowell editor assumed his satire would please: "They should have resolved," he said of the conventions, "that it was obligatory also upon the [men of the house] to wash dishes, scour up, be put to the tub, handle the broom, darn stockings, patch breeches...look beautiful and be fascinating."

It was a thought that the *Rochester Daily Advertiser* found surprisingly plausible. Although Henry Montgomery titled his editorial "The Reign of Petticoats" and began with satirical commentary about "the beautiful and feminine business of politics," he ended up with a most unconventional endorsement:

> Can not women fill an office, or cast a vote, or conduct a campaign, as judiciously and vigorously as men? And, on the other hand, can not men...boil a pot as safely and as well as women? If they can not, the evil is in the arbitrary organization of society.... It is time these false notions and practices were changed.... Let the women keep the ball moving, so bravely started by those who have become tired of the restraints imposed upon them.

The end of summer did not end the publicity. "There is no danger of this question dying for want of notice," Elizabeth Cady Stanton wrote in the *National Reformer* on September 14:

> Every paper you take up has something to say about it.... For those who do not yet understand the real objects of our recent Conventions at Rochester and Seneca Falls, I would state that we did not meet to discuss fashions, customs, or dress, the rights or duties of man, nor the propriety of the sexes changing positions, but simply our own inalienable rights.... There is no such thing as a sphere for a sex. Every man has a different sphere, and one in which he may shine, and it is the same with every woman; and the same woman may have a different sphere at different times.

Stanton explicated her point with the examples of Angelina Grimké and Lucretia Mott. Grimké had gone "the length and breadth of New England, telling the people of her personal experience of the slave system," and her testimony had moved the public in a way "unsurpassed by any of the highly gifted men of her day." She then married and chose to remove herself from public life. "Her sphere and her duties have changed," Stanton wrote, but both portions of her life had value. Mott, in contrast, devoted the first part of her life to children and home, and now, "her husband and herself, having a comfortable fortune, pass much of their time in going about and doing good." Like men, Stanton argued, women are naturally capable of many "spheres" and of making different choices at different points in life.

Stanton also reached out from their tiny town to larger and more diverse circulation sources. By far the most important of the papers that supported the women's agenda was Horace Greeley's tremendously popular *New York Tribune.* Although he later would quarrel with suffragists and retract much of his support, in these early days, he encouraged women, including the first credentialed female physician, Dr. Elizabeth Blackwell. He opened the *Tribune's* pages to Stanton, and she used Greeley's paper as an opportunity to respond to the verbal assaults that most journalists made. Elizabeth Cady Stanton—who never would be recognized as the philosopher that she actually was—mailed out her brilliant argumentation and transformed her world.

Chapter Three

"The Spirit of a Snake" and the Spirit of Success, 1848 to 1860

After the excitement of 1848, the women's movement drew a collective breath and allowed 1849 to pass quietly. In 1850 came a second explosion of women's rights conventions, and from that year, the revolution would be permanent. That year the movement went national, expanding out of New York with conventions in Ohio and Massachusetts.

Frontier Ohio may seem an odd place to follow the Rochester meeting, but several factors made it logical. It was a haven for young people dissatisfied with life in the staid East, making a new start in what was still considered the West. Second, because only the Ohio River separated it from slave territory on its southern border, the state became an early refuge for escaped slaves—and thus for abolitionists. Finally, Oberlin College, a hotbed of radical ideas, had operated there for almost two decades. The nation's first college to admit women and blacks when it began in 1833, Oberlin graduated abolitionist lecturer Lucy Stone in 1847, and more shockingly, had yielded to the persistent pleas of Stone's roommate, Antoinette Brown, to be admitted to its theology department. Both women, while still students, had "lectured at different places in the State" in 1849.

Just as Seneca Falls hosted its famous convention because Elizabeth Cady Stanton lived there, the site of Ohio's 1850 convention was chosen largely because it was home to Josephine Griffing and other abolitionists. Salem, in eastern Ohio between Akron and Pittsburgh, was known as an "underground railroad" town, welcoming to escaped slaves. It was also the base of the *Anti-*

Slavery Bugle. Griffing frequently wrote for this widely circulated paper; its owners, Oliver and Mariana Johnson, were committed to women's rights as well as to abolition. When the abolitionist and women's rights causes began to diverge in the Civil War era, Griffing would concentrate on the first cause; the postwar Freedman's Bureau was largely her brainchild.

The year was as meaningful as the site, for 1850 saw the adoption of the Fugitive Slave Act, which demanded the return of all escaped slaves to their previous owners. One of the cruelest pieces of legislation Congress ever passed, the act forced people of conscience to choose between what was legal and what was morally right. Because geography made Ohio a likely route to freedom, it had enacted similar laws earlier, which Salem abolitionists defiantly violated. They were encouraged by Abby Kelly, who was one of the first to travel through the state denouncing "the black laws of Ohio"; indeed, one feminist pioneer dated "the agitation of Woman's Rights" in Ohio from Kelly's lectures in 1843. Finally, the state planned a constitutional convention for 1850. Ohio women who had learned through the national press of the 1848 meetings in New York decided, in the words of their report for the first volume of the *History of Woman Suffrage,* "if the fundamental laws of the State were to be revised and amended, it was a fitting time for them to ask to be recognized."

The women's convention was planned for April 19 and 20, 1850, in Salem's Second Baptist Church. At 10 a.m. Emily Robinson gaveled it to order and turned the podium over to Mariana W. Johnson, who read "the call" that stated their aims. They were there "to concert measures to secure to all persons the recognition of equal rights…without distinction of sex or color." Participants were invited "to inquire if the position you now occupy is one appointed by wisdom, and designed to secure the best interests of the human race."

Abby Kelly (Library of Congress)

Although these women had no parliamentary experience, they showed none of the timorousness of Seneca Falls and filled organizational positions with women. They created a business committee of six, chose three secretaries, and named three vice presidents to assist the president, Betsey M. Cowles. Ohio women felt fortunate to have Cowles as their leader: she was establishing a reputation as one of the state's outstanding educators. A teacher since 1825, she had remained single, and, in 1834, organized a Young Ladies Society for Intellectual Improvement. She helped introduce the new concepts of kindergarten and Sunday school, and a few months after she chaired the convention, Cowles began work in the prestigious position of superintendent of girls' elementary and secondary schools in Canton, Ohio.

The secretaries read greetings from Lucretia Mott, Elizabeth Cady Stanton, Lucy Stone, and others unable to attend. A speech that Mott had made in Philadelphia the previous December, "On Woman," was delivered, and the women proceeded to debate and adopt 22 resolutions without the least bit of timidity on the great question of demanding the vote.

Not only did women conduct this meeting, but they also did all of the debating: According to the report, "not a man was allowed to sit on the platform, to speak or vote. *Never did men so suffer.*" Betsey Cowles's school-teaching experience plainly showed, for the men "implored just to say one word; but no; the President was inflexible no man should be heard. If one meekly arose to make a suggestion, he was at once ruled out of order. For the first time in the world's history, men learned how it felt to sit in silence when questions in which they were interested were under discussion." In addition to their resolutions, the women adopted a "Memorial" to the upcoming constitutional convention. They reminded the men who planned to rewrite fundamental law:

> Women have no part or lot in the foundation or administration of government. They can not vote or hold office. They are required to contribute their share, by way of taxes, to the support of the Government, but are allowed no voice....
>
> We would especially direct attention to the legal condition of married women.... Legally, she ceases to exist.... All that she has becomes legally his, and he can collect and dispose of the profits of her labor as he sees fit.... If he renders life intolerable, so that she is forced to leave him, he has the power to retain her children, and "seize her and bring

her back, for he has a right to her society which he may enforce, either against herself or any other person who detains her." Woman by being thus subject to the control, and dependent on the will of man, loses her self-dependence; and no human being can be deprived of this without a sense of degradation.

An even longer document was aimed at their sisters. In an "Address to the Women of Ohio," they developed an argument based on the ideas of Locke and Jefferson, and these unknown women followed the concept of natural rights that human beings have rights as immutable as the natural laws of physics to its logical conclusion:

This government, having therefore exercised powers underived from the consent of the governed, and having signally failed to secure the end for which all just government is instituted, should be immediately altered, or abolished.

"The legal theory is, marriage makes the husband and wife one person, and that person is the husband.... There is scarcely a legal act that she is competent to perform.... She can make no contracts.... She has no power over his person, and her only claim upon his property is for a bare support. In no instance can she sue or be sued...." [quoted from Professor Walker, author of *Introduction to American Law*] Women of Ohio!... Slaves we are, politically and legally.... If men would be men worthy of the name, they must cease to disfranchise and rob their wives and mothers, they must forbear to consign to political and legal slavery their sisters and daughters. And we women...must cease to submit to such tyranny....

Woman, over half the globe, is now and always has been chattel. Wives are bargained for, bought and sold.... Can antiquity make wrong right?... We appeal to our sisters of Ohio to arise from the lethargy of ages...and take possession of your birthright to freedom and equality.

"A favorable and lengthy report" of the meeting "found its way into the *New York Tribune* and other leading journals," and Ohio women did not seem to feel themselves as much the objects of scorn as New Yorkers had. Instead, they believed their convention "had accomplished a great educational work." This statewide meeting was quickly emulated with smaller local events. The leader of the follow-up activity was Frances Dana Gage, who had been unable to attend the Salem convention. Known as "Aunt Fanny," she was an established writer, who, in her own words, was "notorious" for "craziness." Nonetheless, Gage had a mainstream readership, which she risked for the mocked cause of women's rights, in such publications as the *Ohio Cultivator,* a farm magazine, and the *Ladies' Repository* of Cincinnati. With three others—"all the women that I knew in that region even favorable to a movement for the help of women"—she called a meeting for her southeastern Ohio town of McConnelsville in early May.

"Women dared not speak then," and even among this venturesome four, Gage stood alone in asking "for the ballot…without regard to sex or color." She drew up a petition to omit the words "white" and "male" from the state's constitution, and at the end of the day-long meeting, 40 of the 70 attendees signed it. Excited by this, the four planned another meeting in the Methodist church of nearby Morgan County for late May. They advertised it, and early in the morning of the appointed day, they "hired a hack" and rode 16 miles, where they discovered that they were "to be denied admittance to church or school-house." A sympathetic minister, however, was prepared for his colleagues' hostility: according to Gage, he "had found us shelter on the threshing-floor of a fine barn," where the women found "three or four hundred of the farmers and their wives, sons, and daughters" already assembled. "Many names were added to our Memorial, and on the whole, we had a delightful day," Gage summarized. She concluded ominously, however: "But to shut up doors against women was a new thing."

Gage and others worked hard, and the petitions they presented to Ohio's constitutional convention held a significant number of signatures. The one for "Equal Rights" in property laws and similar legislation was signed by 7,901 people. The one for the "Right of Suffrage," on the other hand, was still seen as a radical idea: only 2,106 signed it. The men of the constitutional convention, however, did not appear to take these thousands of petitioners with any seriousness at all. Rebecca Janney, a leader in Ohio's movement from its earliest days, summarized tersely: "The discussions in the Constitutional Convention were voted to be dropped from the records, because they were so low and obscene."

The young state of Indiana also held a constitutional convention in 1850. The women's movement was not yet organized there, but feminist Robert Dale Owen made their case for them. He doubtless was inspired by his wife, Mary Robinson Owen, a Virginian who had endured pioneer Indiana with him. When the Owens married in 1832, they wrote an unconventional compact in which Robert declared: "Of the unjust rights which…this ceremony… gives me over the person and property of another, I can not legally, but I can morally, divest myself." He also was influenced by his longtime colleague, Frances Wright. Both natives of Scotland, Wright and Owen worked together in a number of reform efforts, including a utopian community at New Harmony, Indiana.

When the constitutional convention met, he argued especially for the property rights of married women and widows, but without success. Perhaps inspired by the efforts that this man made for them, Indiana women began to organize themselves at an anti-slavery meeting the following year. The first Indiana women's rights convention was held in October 1851 in the Wayne County village of Dublin. "Such a Convention being a novel affair," reads their record in the *History of Woman Suffrage*, "it called out some ridicule and opposition," but the women were "so well pleased" that they immediately planned another. From 1851 through the end of the decade, Indiana women held annual conventions that were never distracted by jeering men as those in the East would be.

Often Ohio women came to Indiana to speak, especially the ever-popular Frances Dana Gage and the thoughtful Caroline Severance. Amanda Way was perhaps Indiana's primary leader at this time; a talented tailor and milliner, she was a bit unusual in the women's rights movement in that she never married. A Quaker, she had ties to Lucretia Mott and the temperance and abolitionist movements, and Way would take these causes with her as she moved west to Kansas and then California during the rest of the century. Another inspirational leader was Mary F. Thomas, a married woman with three young daughters who had learned of the women's movement while she lived in Salem, Ohio. At the first Indiana convention, she announced her intention to become a physician and by the 1856 convention, she was Dr. Thomas. Less than a decade after Elizabeth Blackwell was the first woman to graduate from a male medical school, Thomas completed her education at Cleveland's Western

Reserve College (now Case Western Reserve) and at Philadelphia's Penn Medical University.

She also managed to participate in most of Indiana's systematically scheduled and smoothly run conventions. The 1852 and 1853 ones were in the town of Richmond; 1854 and 1855 took them to the Masonic Hall in Indianapolis, but meetings returned for the rest of the decade to the small towns of Richmond and Winchester. The most hostile press was in the largest city: at the 1855 Indianapolis convention, "the reporters gave glowing pen sketches of the 'masculine women' and 'feminine men;' they described the dress and appearance of the women very minutely, but said little of the merits of the question or the arguments of the speakers."

With the New York and Ohio precedents set, Massachusetts hosted its first women's rights convention in autumn of the same year. Unlike the earlier meetings, however, this one was carefully planned months in advance. In May, at an anti-slavery gathering in Boston, nine women caucused in a "dark, dingy room" about a convention for their own civil rights. They scheduled the meeting for October 23 and 24, 1850, and chose the Massachusetts town of Worcester because of its central location. Most important, they decided to aim for a national, not merely a state, women's rights convention.

Paulina Wright Davis undertook most of the planning work. In 1835, as Paulina Kellogg Wright, she and her husband had organized one of the first anti-slavery meetings and endured a mob assault on their home in Utica, New York. He died in 1846, leaving her a widow wealthy enough to do something very unusual: with a female anatomical mannequin imported from Paris, she taught the basics of their bodies to the relatively few women who dared to explore this forbidden subject. A second marriage to jeweler Thomas Davis changed her name, and as Paulina Wright Davis, she organized the Massachusetts meeting from her home in Providence, Rhode Island.

Paulina Wright Davis (Library of Congress)

Davis had hoped to turn over the leadership of this first National Woman's Rights Convention to famous author Margaret Fuller, but after Fuller drowned in a July shipwreck, Davis decided to assemble a list of prestigious names to sign the meeting's "call." She sent "earnest private letters" to those she hoped would become endorsers, but even though she thought her call was "moderate in tone," it nonetheless "gave the alarm to conservatism." The response was painful: "Letters, curt, reproachful, and sometimes almost insulting," Davis said, "came with absolute refusals to have the names of the writers used." But other mail brought better news. While the "alarmed conservatives" missed a chance to enshrine their names in history, visionary people gladly signed. More than 50 women and 30 men, including famed philosopher Ralph Waldo Emerson, endorsed the convention. The first signer, Sarah Tyndale, inspired particular optimism; Davis termed her "perhaps more widely known than any other woman of her time." Tyndale had run what the *History of Woman Suffrage* termed one of Philadelphia's "largest businesses" for more than two decades. Davis especially appreciated this support, for Tyndale made a "great social sacrifice in taking up a cause so unpopular." Another hopeful opportunity for broadening the movement's base of support was an endorsement from Catherine M. Sedgwick, one of the era's most popular novelists.

On "the bright October days" of the convention, reads the women's report of their historic gathering, "a solemn, earnest crowd of noble men and women" assembled in Worcester's Brinley Hall. The meeting was called to order by Sarah H. Earl, a locally prominent woman married to the editor of the *Worcester Spy*. She conducted an election and turned the gavel over to Paulina Wright Davis. Four other officers were equally divided by gender, and the five people elected came from four states. The meeting was indeed national in tone, with sizeable delegations from nine states, but all of them were in the North, a fact that presaged the coming of the Civil War.

Gathered in Worcester were the people who would form the backbone of the women's movement for the rest of the century. From Vermont came newspaper editor Clarina Howard Nichols; from Philadelphia, Lucretia Mott and other Friends. From Ohio came the *Anti-Slavery Bugle* editors Mariana and Oliver Johnson, as well as two sisters of Dr. Elizabeth Blackwell. Ernestine Rose was among those from New York, while longtime abolitionists Parker and Sarah Pillsbury came from New Hampshire. The two people who came the greatest distances, Mary G. Wright of California and Silas Smith of Iowa, were the only representatives from those states. Massachusetts, of course, had far more participation than any other state; among its many luminaries were Abby Kelly Foster, William Lloyd Garrison, and several members of 18-year-old Louisa May Alcott's family. Frederick Douglass and Sojourner Truth "represented the enslaved African race."

Just as the Rochester meeting introduced women to Ernestine Rose, Worcester debuted several other suffragist stars. Like Rose, Lucy Stone had been speaking out on behalf of women for years prior to the conventions. She was Massachusetts's first female college graduate, but not only did Stone have to go to Ohio's Oberlin to earn this credential, she also had to support herself because her affluent father refused to pay tuition for a girl. Nearly 30 when she graduated, she turned down the "honor" of writing a commencement speech that even at progressive Oberlin would be read by a man. Stone followed Abby Kelly Foster's example and earned a precarious living as a paid lecturer for the American Anti-Slavery Society on the weekends, while on weekdays, she freelanced as a women's rights speaker. Like others on the abolitionist circuit, she learned to expect routine greetings from jeering mobs armed with rotten eggs and stones.

Her Oberlin classmate (and future sister-in-law) Antoinette Brown also attended the convention. Brown had just completed three years of work in Oberlin's theology department, but the college would not grant this sacred degree to a woman. No church was willing to ordain her, and she was spending her autumn wandering country roads in hopes of finding a congregation that would allow her to preach. Perhaps more than anyone, Antoinette Brown needed the solace and support of the network she found at Worcester.

Antoinette Brown (Library of Congress)

Another celebrity at the meeting was, sadly enough, much more famous then than now. Dr. Harriot K. Hunt had begun practicing medicine in 1835; Dr. Hunt did not have a medical degree, but it was not uncommon at that time for even male physicians to lack medical school credentials. Her healing techniques emphasized hygiene and did not include leeches, mercury, and other dangerous interventions that many physicians used. Hunt's reputation as a successful healer soon was established enough that she had a busy practice among Boston's finest families, especially with female patients who appreciated having a female physician whom they could trust.

In the same way that Harriot K. Hunt's remarkable history was allowed to die, modern women also are unfamiliar with Abby H. Price, but convention president Paulina Wright Davis evidently thought of her in the same category as Lucy Stone. In a report on the Worcester meeting, in a sentence immediately before one about Stone, Davis wrote: "Abby H. Price, large-hearted and large-brained, gentle and strong, presented an address on the social question." Davis added that the speech was "seldom bettered," but provided no details, for the euphemistic "social question" doubtless referred to prostitution and venereal disease.

"The debates on the resolutions," Davis said, "were spicy, pointed, and logical" and kept "crowded audiences through two entire days." The resolutions not only included the same "sex and color" phrase that was used at Salem, but spelled out this commitment further: "Resolved, that the cause we have met to advocate the claim for woman of all her natural and civil rights bids us remember the two millions of slave women at the South, the most grossly wronged and foully outraged of all women."

Although the network of women's advocates would still be referred to as "Woman's Rights Conventions" until after the Civil War, this meeting took significant steps to chart out a permanent, national organization. Paulina Wright Davis would chair a Central Committee with members from every state; other committees were Education, Industry, Civil and Political Functions, Social Relations, and Publications. Except for Publications, which was undertaken by William Henry Channing, the committees were chaired by women.

"Thus encouraged," Paulina Wright Davis summarized, "we felt new zeal to go on." Once again, the group did an amazingly good public relations job, and this time, it was particularly effective in Europe. "Many letters were received from literary women in this country as well as abroad," Davis enthused. She was especially happy about favorable publicity from Swedish Frederika Bremer, one of the world's bestselling contemporary commentators. Bremer, who would tour and write about America in the 1850s, "quoted from our writings," Davis marveled. "Our words had been like an angel's visit to the prisoners of State in France," where revolution recently had been suppressed.

The most significant attention came from the October 29, 1850, international edition of the *New York Tribune.* Among many who read it was English philosopher John Stuart Mill, one of the modern age's greatest thinkers. The next July, the prestigious *Westminster Review* followed up with a philosophical essay in which Mill explicated the ideas of the American women or so people thought at the time. The article, "On Enfranchisement of Women," began by discussing the American phenomenon:

> Most of our readers will probably learn, from these pages, for the first time, that there has risen in the United States…an organized agitation on a new question…the enfranchisement of women, their admission in law, and in fact, to equality….
>
> It will add to the surprise with which many receive this intelligence that…not merely *for* women, but *by* them….
>
> A succession of public meetings was held, under the name of a "Woman's Rights Convention," of which the President was a woman, and nearly all the chief speakers were women….
>
> According to the report in the *New York Tribune,* above a thousand persons were present throughout, and "if a larger place could have been had, many thousands more would have attended."
>
> The proceedings bear an advantageous comparison with those of any popular movement with which we are acquainted, either in this country or in America. Very rarely in the oratory of public meetings is…calm good sense and reason so considerable.
>
> The result…is probably destined to inaugurate one of the most important of the movements toward political and social reform…. The promoters of this new agitation take their stand on principles, and do not fear.

Mill later explained that the true author of the famous essay was Harriet Hardy Taylor. For two decades, she had been, he said, "the honour and chief blessing of my existence," but she was married to another man. After her husband's

1849 death, Taylor married Mill, but they had only a few years together before her sudden death. When he wrote his most famous work, *On Liberty* (1859), Mill acknowledged that "so much of it was the work of her whom I lost." It goes without saying that his 1869 publication, *The Subjection of Women,* also originated in the mind of this unknown female philosopher. Still later, Mill wrote to Paulina Wright Davis:

John Stuart Mill (Library of Congress)

> It gives me the greatest pleasure to know that the service rendered by my dear wife to the cause which was nearer her heart than any other, by her essay in the *Westminster Review,* has had so much effect and is so justly appreciated in the United States. Were it possible in a memoir to have the formation and growth of a mind like hers portrayed, to do so would be as valuable a benefit to mankind as was ever conferred by a biography. But such a psychological history is seldom possible.

Just as New York's Seneca Falls convention was followed by one in the city of Rochester, Ohio's 1850 event in Salem was a prelude to a larger one in Akron. Midwestern activism was renewed, and many of those who made history at Salem went to Akron on May 28 and 29, 1851. This meeting also heralded several women who would be among the most important suffragists for decades to come.

Frances Dana Gage, who had clearly established her leadership the previous year, presided. Gage also mentored several of the women there, including Caroline Severance, who eventually moved back East and became the founding president of the important New England Woman's Club. The conventioneers were also excited about the presence of Maria L. Giddings; she not only gave "a very able digest on the common law," but also had political connections, for her father "represented Ohio in Congress for many years."

The appearance of Hannah Tracy, later Hannah Tracy Cutler, at the convention demonstrated tremendous commitment, for she had overcome serious handicaps. After her father refused to allow her to attend the new Oberlin College, she married at 18 and had three children. She was pregnant with the last when her husband died, after pro-slavery men assaulted him while he was helping slaves escape. Widowed, she then went to Oberlin, ran a boardinghouse to support her family, and even found time to write original feminist theory: *Woman as She Was, Is, and Should Be* was published in 1846. Tracy graduated the following year, and by the time of the Akron convention, she had the plum job of principal of the "female department" of the new Columbus high school. Most women in such a position would not risk it with radical feminist activity, but her courage was fired by experience.

Pittsburgh's Jane Grey Swisshelm had learned similar courage. The publisher of the abolitionist *Saturday Visiter* [sic] at the time, she attended the prior year's Worcester convention and would go on to national leadership in Minnesota and in Washington D.C. but despite this apparent success, Swisshelm still had a miserable personal life. Until her tyrannical husband discovered that her literacy could earn her money, he had sometimes forbidden her to read; he used his legal right to her wages to sue her family for the time that she devoted to her ailing mother. Another six years would pass before Swisshelm managed to get him to file for the divorce that would liberate her: in 1857, she took her little daughter and fled to Minnesota.

A network of female support was clearly developing. Among the out-of-state women who sent letters of support to Akron were Amelia Bloomer and Elizabeth Cady Stanton of Seneca Falls, newspaper editor Clarina Howard Nichols of Vermont, and Nantucket Island native Lydia Folger Fowler, who became the second female graduate of a traditional medical school this same year. Dr. Fowler, a happily married woman without children, wrote *Familiar Lessons on Physiology* in 1847 to teach women about their bodies. During a lifelong Rochester career teaching obstetrics and gynecology, she set another precedent as the world's first female medical school professor.

Unlike the Salem convention, men were allowed to participate at Akron and at future Ohio meetings to the regret of some women who said in their report that "the sons of Adam crowded our platform and often made it the scene of varied pugilistic efforts." The convention also was the first with entertainment: a popular singing group, the Hutchinson Family Singers, was a big hit at reform assemblies for decades.

Far and away the most important aspect of the Akron meeting, however, was the historic speech of Sojourner Truth. Born into slavery under the name Isabella in the late eighteenth century, she was owned by Dutch-speaking people who lived about 50 miles north of New York City. By her teenage years, she had been sold three times and was scarred from beatings she suffered when she did not understand orders in English.

Sojourner Truth (Library of Congress)

In 1827, a year before New York implemented its gradual emancipation plan, she ran away to a Quaker family. They not only sheltered her, but even supported her in a legal battle: amazingly enough, her son Peter, who had been sold in violation of New York law, was returned from Alabama. Feeling "tall within," she set out for New York City. She left the Society of Friends, she said, because "they would not let me sing," and developed her own deeply personal faith: "God himself talks to me."

After a disastrous time in a New York commune that ended up with her successfully fighting a murder charge, she took the name of Sojourner Truth in 1843 and set out to preach. In traveling through New England, she came to the attention of William Lloyd Garrison and other abolitionists. When she arrived in Akron in 1851, she recently had published her autobiography, which she dictated to a white woman, Olive Gilbert. Sales of the *Narrative of Sojourner Truth* would support her for the rest of her life, as she continued to move throughout the United States, living in Kansas during its tumultuous pre–Civil War years and finally settling in Battle Creek, Michigan.

Although she was listed as an attendee of the 1850 Worcester convention, the Massachusetts women who created its record for the *History of Woman Suffrage* did not see fit to discuss this black woman at any length in their convention report. Instead, it was Ohio's "Aunt Fanny," Frances Dana Gage, who detailed the appearance of Sojourner Truth at the Akron meeting:

> The ladies of the movement trembled on seeing a tall, gaunt black woman in a gray dress and white turban, surmounted with an uncouth sun-bonnet, march deliberately into the church, walk with the air of a queen up the aisle, and take her seat upon the pulpit steps. A buzz of disapprobation was heard all over the house, and there fell on the listening ear, "An abolition affair!" "Woman's rights and niggers!"....
>
> At my request, order was restored, and the business of the Convention went on.... All through these sessions old Sojourner, quiet and reticent...sat crouched against the wall on the corner of the pulpit stairs.... At intermission she was busy selling the "Life of Sojourner Truth," a narrative of her own strange and adventurous life. Again and again, timorous ones came to me and said, with earnestness, "Don't let her speak, Mrs. Gage, it will ruin us. Every newspaper in the land will have our cause mixed up with abolition and niggers, and we shall be utterly denounced." My only answer was, "We shall see when the time comes."
>
> The second day the work waxed warm. Methodist, Baptist, Episcopal, Presbyterian, and Universalist ministers came in to hear and discuss the resolutions presented. One claimed superior rights and privileges for man, on the ground of "superior intellect;" another, because of the "manhood of Christ".... Another gave us a theological view of the "sin of our first mother."
>
> There were very few women in those days who dared to "speak in meeting;" and the august teachers of the people were seemingly getting the better of us, while the boys in the galleries, and the sneerers among the pews, were hugely enjoying the discomfiture, as they supposed, of the "strongminded." Some of the tender-skinned friends were on the point of losing dignity, and the atmosphere betokened a storm. When, slowly from her seat in the corner rose Sojourner Truth,

who, till now, had scarcely lifted her head. "Don't let her speak!" gasped a half a dozen in my ear. She moved slowly and solemnly to the front, laid her old bonnet at her feet, and turned her great speaking eyes to me. There was a hissing sound of disapprobation above and below. I rose and announced "Sojourner Truth," and begged the audience to keep silent for a few moments.

The tumult subsided at once, and every eye was fixed on this almost Amazon form, which stood nearly six feet high, head erect, and eyes piecing the upper air like one in a dream. At her first word there was a profound hush. She spoke in deep tones, which, though not loud, reached every ear in the house and away through the throng at the doors and windows. [In the following, Sojourner Truth's speech has been freed of the nineteenth-century dialect style that Gage used in recording it. Gage's occasional descriptive interjections into the body of the speech also have been eliminated.]

"Well, children, where there is so much racket there must be something out of kilter. I think that between the niggers of the South and the women at the North, all talking about rights, the white men will be in a fix pretty soon. But what's all this here talking about?

That man over there say that women needs to be helped into carriages, lifted over ditches, and to have the best place everywhere. Nobody ever helps me into carriages, or over mud-puddles, or gives me any best place! And ain't I a woman? Look at me! Look at my arm! I have ploughed, and planted, and gathered into barns, and no man could head me! And ain't I a woman? I could work as much and eat as much as a man—when I could get it—and bear the lash as well! And ain't I a woman? I have borne thirteen children, and seen most all sold off to slavery, and when I cried out with my mother's grief, none but Jesus heard me. And ain't I a woman?

Then they talk about this thing in the head; what's this they call it? ['Intellect' someone whispers near.] That's right, honey. What's that got to do with women's rights or nigger's rights? If my cup won't hold but a pint, and yours holds a quart, wouldn't you be mean not to let me have my little half-measure full?

Then that little man in black there, he says women can't have as much rights as men, because Christ wasn't a woman! Where did your Christ come from? From God and a woman! Men had nothing to do with Him.

If the first woman God ever made was strong enough to turn the world upside down all alone, these women together ought to be able to turn it back, and get it right side up again! And now that they are asking to do it, the men better let them! Obliged to you for hearing me, and now old Sojourner has got nothing more to say."

At Sojourner Truth's rebuke of the minister who made the point about "intellect," the audience's "cheering was loud and long." When she spoke to the story of Eve, "the first woman God ever made," Gage said that "almost every sentence elicited deafening applause." Sojourner Truth "returned to her corner, amid roars of applause, leaving more than one of us with streaming eyes, and hearts beating with gratitude. She had taken us up in her strong arms and carried us," Gage averred. "I have never in my life seen anything like her magical influence."

When the speech was over, "hundreds rushed up to shake hands with her," and Sojourner Truth's place as a celebrity suffragist was solidified. More than most men or women, black or white, she immediately understood the crucial link between women's rights and the anti-slavery cause; from the beginning, she could see that women's needs should not be trivialized nor forced to compete with those of blacks. Earlier than Susan B. Anthony and others who became famous, Sojourner Truth stood tall.

A Currier & Ives print of the Bloomer style, circa 1851. (Library of Congress)

Not all progress is political. Social change can be of at least equal significance, and one of the greatest issues of the 1850s became feminine apparel. Early in 1851, Elizabeth Smith Miller appeared on the streets of Seneca Falls wearing "Turkish trousers." An affluent and fashionable young mother, she came to visit her father's cousin, Elizabeth Cady Stanton. The full, almost skirt-like pants that Miller wore were based on a fashion introduced by

English Fanny Kemble, whose stage portrayals of Shakespeare's Juliet in the 1830s had made her one of America's first entertainment celebrities. Both Kemble's professional and personal life led her to feminism. She had given up her career for a South Carolina planter and soon found that the marriage was a disaster. The law was on his side in every disagreement, including their frequent fights over her sympathy for slaves. When she finally left him, it meant leaving her children, too; she did not see them for more than 20 years. She returned to the stage, and in the midst of what was likely personal turmoil, introduced the shockingly different apparel known as "pantalettes."

While Kemble was a trendsetter, primarily for reasons of style rather than practicality or health, there were others who advocated dress reform for more serious reasons. A thoughtful listener at the Worcester convention might have been moved to consider these ideas when a letter was read from French agriculturist Helene Marie Weber. After apologizing that "circumstances place it out of my power to visit America" for the October convention, she wrote:

> The newspapers both of England and America have done me great injustice. While they have described my apparel with the minute accuracy of professional tailors, they have...charged me with undervaluing the female sex and identifying myself with the other.... I have never wished...to be anything but a woman.... I adopted male attire as a matter of convenience in my business.... I have never had cause to regret my adoption of male attire, and never expect to return to a female toilette....
>
> There is no moral or political principle involved in this question.... [If] the superiority of male dress for all purposes of business and recreation is conceded, it is absurd to argue that we should not avail ourselves of its advantages....
>
> Women who prefer the gown should, of course, consult their own pleasure by continuing to wear it; while those whose preference is a male dress, ought not to be blamed for adopting it. I close...by recording my prediction, that in ten years male attire will be generally worn by women of most civilized countries.

Paulina Wright Davis received Weber's letter via Mildred Spofford, an American living in France, who assured the Worcester audience that the French feminist was "lady-like, modest, and unassuming." Her deviance in dress was understandable, Spofford urged, for Weber was "a practical agriculturist" who personally conducted "the entire business of her farm." Although just 25 years old, Weber also was "in the front rank of essayists in France," and had "a perfect command of the English language." She not only practiced her feminism in her apparel, but also wrote feminist theory: "She has labored zealously on behalf of her sex, as her numerous tracts on subjects of reform bear testimony," Spofford concluded. "No writer of the present age has done more."

One of the Worcester attendees who must have nodded his head in agreement with Weber's words was Gerrit Smith, Stanton's cousin and the father of Elizabeth Smith Miller. He had inherited a fortune through a family partnership with New York millionaire John Jacob Astor, and the Smith home in western New York near Seneca Falls was a haven for both runaway slaves and the era's most prominent liberals. Stanton later remembered his estate as a place where "one would meet the first families in the State, with Indians, Africans, slaveowners, religionists of all sects…each class welcomed and honored."

No one was a stronger advocate of dress reform than Gerrit Smith. Long after women had given up the fight, he argued for making this area a "battleground." To the end of his life, he believed that women would find greater political success if their appearance were not so strikingly different from that of men. He received isolated support for this reform, often from other men. As early as 1787, Philadelphia's Dr. Benjamin Rush, a founder of the nation's first medical school, had written, "I…ascribe the invention of ridiculous and expensive fashions in female dress entirely to the gentlemen, in order to divert the ladies from improving their minds…to secure more arbitrary and unlimited authority over them." Many others, especially physicians, echoed the same

Gerrit Smith (Library of Congress)

thought, particularly after the Gilded Age brought even more confining corsets and bustles.

Because Gerrit Smith could not model ideal feminine clothing himself, it was no surprise that his daughter did. Cousin Elizabeth liked the idea, too, and soon Seneca Falls was seeing a second revolution, more visual than the first. "I wore the dress for two years," Stanton recalled, "and found it a great blessing."

> What a sense of liberty I felt, in running up and down stairs with my hands free to carry whatsoever I would, to trip through the rain or snow with no skirts to hold...ready at any moment to climb a hill-top to see the sun go down, or the moon rise, with no ruffles or trails to be... soiled. What an emancipation from little petty vexations.

Her friend Amelia Bloomer already was on record: she had defended Fanny Kemble's "pantalettes" in one of the first issues of Bloomer's temperance paper, *The Lily*. Seeing the practicality of Miller's costume up close, Bloomer also adopted the style. When she wrote about it in *The Lily*, her name forever would be attached to the garment. To her chagrin, it was soon clear that many women were more interested in clothing than in temperance, and when she included sewing patterns, subscriptions soared. Horace Greeley's *New York Tribune* was quick to pick up this second hot story from Seneca Falls, and soon people around the globe were debating the merits of the "Bloomer Costume."

Although she had not intended to create this "furor," Bloomer wore the style for "some six or eight years." That she stuck with it longer than Stanton is probably due to the fact that the Bloomers moved from Seneca Falls to Iowa in 1853. Practicality always has priority over fashion in frontier situations, and it therefore was not surprising that among those Stanton listed as long-term bloomer wearers were "many farmers' wives."

Other women's rights leaders who experimented with the costume included Lucy Stone, the Grimké sisters, and Susan B. Anthony. For the latter women, the change was an especially daring one from the modest Quaker dress of their youth, but for all women, wearing the new style meant inviting controversy and worse. Preachers, in Gerrit Smith's words, ran "to the Bible, not to learn the truth, but to make the Bible the minister to folly" in preaching against the garment. Using scripture such as "male and female He created them," clergymen argued that it was sinful for a woman to dress like a man. Any outing in the new clothes became a trial. "People would stare," Stanton said. "Some men and women make rude remarks; boys follow in crowds, or shout from behind fences."

In the end, she and others decided to surrender their freedom of movement at least in part because the experiment was literally threatening to the men in their lives: when strangers jeered at the women, "the gentleman in attendance felt it his duty to resent the insult by showing fight." Elizabeth Smith Miller's husband especially suffered while trying to support his father-in-law's visionary ideas. "No man," Stanton said in praise of Charles Dudley Miller, "went through the ordeal with [such] coolness and dogged determination." The cousins called on him to escort them in sophisticated places as well as on country outings, and when Washington and New York City were just as hostile to the style as rural bumpkins, the women decided the battle was not worth it. Helene Maria Weber's prediction was wrong. Male attire was not "generally worn" within the century, let alone within the decade that she forecast. Gerrit Smith, however, would not give up. In 1855, he even refused to attend the annual women's rights convention over this issue. He railed to his Cousin Elizabeth about women's timidity: "I am amazed that intelligent women…see not the relation between their dress and the oppressive evils which they are striving to throw off."

Stanton replied with equal force. She had lived with the experiment of dressing like a man, but Smith had never considered what public reaction would be if he were to adopt any aspect of female apparel. She argued that image was exactly that: a matter of style, not substance, upon which no individual rights should be based. Moreover, women had no reason "to hope that pantaloons would do for us" any more good than pants did for black men. It was not acceptance of apparel that mattered, but acceptance of ideas.

While she "fully agreed that woman is terribly cramped and crippled in her present style of dress," this was not the battleground on which to win the war. She pointed out that New York women recently had achieved an emancipating property law, something far more important than a fashion victory. "Depend on it," Stanton wrote, "when men and women…think less of sex and more of mind, we shall all lead…higher lives."

Smith did not let the issue rest with his cousin; he wrote an article on the subject that Frederick Douglass published in his reform newspaper. When Frances Dana Gage read it, she responded with an angry letter to the editor:

> This article, though addressed to Mrs. Stanton, is an attack upon every one engaged in the cause.... He has made the whole battle-ground of the Woman's Rights Movement her dress. *We must own ourselves under the law first,* own our bodies, our earnings, our genius, and our consciences; then we will turn to the lesser matter of what shall be the garniture of the body.

Gage, Stanton, and others made a reasoned case for a pragmatic solution to their problem, and most women agreed. They logically concluded that the political battle was both more important than the social one, and that it was more likely to be won if women were not engaged in a war on two fronts. A few women, however, ignored both the movement's leadership and the derisive jeers of scoffers to continue to wear the garment.

Perhaps the most dedicated and successful was Lydia Sayer Hasbrouck. She adopted pants earlier than the more famous Elizabeth Smith Miller. Late in life, she was openly resentful that others, especially Amelia Bloomer, became celebrities while her much longer commitment went unrecognized. In 1849, two years before the dress-reform publicity from Seneca Falls, 22-year-old Lydia Sayer was refused admission to a New York female seminary because she wore pantaloons. This was a defining moment of her life, and the clothing choice became one of principle. Long after most feminists gave up the fight, Hasbrouck carried on. In 1856, she began a biweekly publication, *The Sibyl,* that attracted a sufficient audience to keep it in business for almost a decade. Her chief editorial concern was improved health from less confining clothing, a point of view doubtless reinforced by the fact that she married and bore three children during the decade of *The Sibyl.* She also took on the presidency of the hopefully named National Dress Reform Association in 1863. The Civil War might have offered an occasion for more practical clothing, but the association never grew into a power. Nonetheless, with a highly supportive husband, she carried on her crusade to impressive personal success: in 1880, Lydia Hasbrouck was elected to the school board of Middletown, New York.

She achieved this electoral victory despite decades of unabashed feminism, for she not only wore unconventional clothing, but also refused to pay taxes because she could not vote. Perhaps her story makes Gerrit Smith's point: Hasbrouck's appearance was more like that of a man, and her townspeople treated her with respect that was measurable in votes. The more conservatively dressed suffragists, meanwhile, were not elected to anything. Conceivably, their dress-for-success strategy was wrong.

During the 1850s, the women's rights movement grew in both sophistication and numbers. Its system of operations was refined so that techniques for public relations and coalition-building became routine. In well-reported meetings, resolutions were debated and publicized. Letters to the editor and other writings educated the public on women's issues through nationally circulated media. In addition, the movement increased the number of supporters who came to conventions, offered donations of time and occasional money, and, most importantly, went home to organize meetings of their own. Beyond that, the decade developed a base of committed, quality leadership that would serve through the century.

All of this was evident at the 1851 annual meeting. Seeing no reason to argue with success, the Second National Woman's Rights Convention was held under the same circumstances as the first: in Worcester, Massachusetts, in October, with Ohio's Frances Dana Gage as president. Celebrities new to the list of endorsers were Rev. Henry Ward Beecher, an extremely popular preacher, and famous educator Horace Mann. Conventioneers also were thrilled to hear a speech by Elizabeth Oakes Smith, a well-known novelist and *New York Tribune* columnist.

Once more, the convention's report said that "every session" of the two-day meeting "was so crowded at an early hour that hundreds were unable to gain admittance." Because of the throng who wanted to hear, the closing session was moved to City Hall, and even that venue was not sufficiently large. Much later, Elizabeth Cady Stanton would summarize, "in the whole history of the woman suffrage movement there never was at one time more able and eloquent men and women on our platform and represented by letter than in those Worcester Conventions."

In 1852, the Third National Woman's Rights Convention moved out of Massachusetts and back to the movement's original home of western New York. Held in Syracuse for an unprecedented three days, the September 8–10 meeting drew people from eight states and Canada. For the first time, the women charged one shilling for admission, but that did nothing to deter attendance, for "City Hall was densely packed at every session." The program "called out immense audiences, attracted many eminent persons…and was most favorably noticed in the press."

Despite the crowd, "the proceedings were orderly and harmonious throughout" under presiding officer Lucretia Mott. A nominating committee had recommended her "as permanent President," and the convention elected this faithful, oldest member of the original movement by acclamation. Ever modest, she "sat far back in the audience" and asked for a second confirming vote before accepting the chair. In so doing, she "rendered herself liable to expulsion" from the Society of Friends, because the admission fee that had been charged violated Quaker tradition. Just four years after Mott herself had considered a female president to be a dangerous experiment at the Rochester convention, she presided in the words of the *Syracuse Standard* "with an ease, dignity, and grace that might be envied by the most experienced legislator in the country."

Elizabeth Cady Stanton, who bore the fifth of her seven children in 1852, did not come to Syracuse. It was, however, the first convention for two other women who would form the backbone of the movement for the rest of the century: Matilda Joslyn Gage and Susan B. Anthony. With Stanton, they would be the three coeditors of the first three volumes of the *History of Woman Suffrage,* a history in which they were also, in Stanton's words, "among the chief actors." (The surnames of Ohio's Frances Dana Gage and New York's Matilda Joslyn Gage appear to be coincidental; if there was any family connection between their husbands, it was not close.)

At the time of the Syracuse convention, Matilda Joslyn Gage was 26 years old and married to a merchant who valued his brilliant wife; affluent and well-dressed, but frequently ill, she would be the mother of five. When she entered the Syracuse convention, Gage did not know a single other woman. She sat alone, "trembling" as she anticipated her first public speech, but she was determined to make it clear why she was there. Later, Gage wrote of herself: "She consulted no one as to time and opportunity, but when her courage had reached a sufficiently high point, with palpitating heart she ascended the platform, where she was cordially given place by Mrs. Mott, whose kindness to her at this supreme moment of her life was never forgotten."

Gage was the youngest person to speak, and the better-than-average education she received from her physician father was reflected in the comments she made. A natural historian from youth, she told the audience of outstanding female models from Silesia to Ireland and from astronomers to musicians. It was just the beginning of her career as the movement's chief historian and most thoughtful intellectual.

Matilda Joslyn Gage (Library of Congress)

By the time of the Syracuse convention, Susan Brownell Anthony was 32 and had spent more than a decade as a teacher in upstate New York, a career that she turned to when her father went bankrupt in the 1837 financial panic. When family finances were better in 1849, she came home and volunteered for the Daughters of Temperance. Ironically, this first national depression provided an economic opportunity for a number of future female leaders who otherwise never would have lived independently from their fathers and husbands.

Her parents and her sister Mary had gone to the 1848 Rochester convention and signed its resolutions, but, like Amelia Bloomer, Anthony was more interested in temperance than in women's rights. Although she had met Elizabeth Cady Stanton in 1850 through their mutual friend Bloomer, Anthony did not attend the women's rights convention either that year or the next.

The events that galvanized a change in her priorities occurred just before and after the Syracuse convention. In January 1852 she, Dr. Lydia Fowler, and other women were refused permission to speak at a temperance rally in Albany. As a Quaker, Anthony was accustomed to speaking; she left the event in protest, and soon organized the alternative Woman's New York State Temperance Society. Two more such insults deepened her awareness of the secondary place of women, even in liberal organizations: in 1853, she was not recognized as a delegate at the World's Temperance Convention in New York City and was forbidden to speak at a convention of the state teachers' association. The men of these organizations had learned nothing since women were banned from the World Anti-Slavery Convention, and they again chose to drive away their sisters in these causes.

More than most women, Susan B. Anthony saw things in political and organizational terms, and the Woman's New York State Temperance Society was just the first example of her forte in organizing women. Almost from the beginning, Anthony targeted female political power, expressed in groups, as fundamental to success. Seldom swayed from this straightforward approach, she would set aside temperance, abolition, and other reforms to place singular value on women's rights and within that area, she would spend her life aimed like an arrow on the vote.

Susan B. Anthony (Library of Congress)

This sense of purpose was evident in physician Harriot K. Hunt, who also attended the 1852 convention. That year, she began an annual effort to draw attention to the vote. Along with her tax payment, Dr. Hunt sent a proclamation to the "treasurer, and the Assessors, and other Authorities of the city of Boston, and the Citizens generally":

> Harriot K. Hunt, physician, a native and permanent resident of the city of Boston...begs leave to protest against the injustice and inequality of levying taxes upon women, and at the same time, refusing them any voice or vote.... Even drunkards, felons, idiots, and lunatics, if men, may still enjoy the right of voting to which no woman, however large the amount of taxes she pays, however respectable her character, or useful her life, can ever attain.

She pointed out that because women lacked the vote, women's priorities were rarely considered when the government spent the taxes they paid. If women had the vote, she said, they would encourage common sense in government: women would provide schools and colleges to "supply our girls with occupation" and "save them from lives of frivolity and emptiness," which, in turn, would create more taxpayers. Year after year, Hunt would file similar protests with her taxes.

The Syracuse convention was dominated by one aspect that boded ill for the future: the first confrontation between Protestant theologian Antoinette Brown and Jewish immigrant Ernestine Rose. In one of the many long speeches Brown made as she wrestled with contradictory biblical statements on women, she said in part: "The Bible…recognizes neither male nor female in Christ Jesus…. The submission enjoined upon the wife in the New Testament…is a Christian submission due from man to man, and from man to woman." By the end, Rose had had enough:

> When the inhabitants of Boston converted their harbor into a teapot… they did not go to the Bible for their authority; for if they had, they would have been told…"to render unto Caesar what belonged to Caesar" [and] "Submit to the powers that be, for they are of God." No! on Human Rights and Freedom…there is no need of written authority.

Others joined "the somewhat bitter discussion," which continued "for two days, calling out great diversity." At one point, "the Rev. Junius Hatch made so coarse a speech" that the audience "called out, Sit down! Shut up!" and the president "was obliged to call him to order." The convention's wisdom in their presidential choice was clear, for Lucretia Mott was exactly the right person to preside over this clash. Obviously personally devout, she also firmly believed in freedom of expression, and perhaps only she was capable of bringing the meeting to an amicable close.

The undercurrent of animosity between the traditional Christians and the freethinkers would erupt again in the future. Christian debaters who labeled their opponents as "infidels" took a terrible risk, because reporters were invariably present at women's rights conventions; the participants, after all, eagerly sought publicity and most editorialists were delighted to expand on the "infidel" idea. By labeling women's rights advocates as dangerous atheists, both press and pulpit could ignore the questions of justice that the women raised. Moreover, although increasing numbers of Catholic and Jewish people immigrated to the United States, Ernestine Rose long would remain the leadership's only Jew, and in the whole long history to come of the suffrage movement, there never would be a prominent Catholic woman. The "diversity" of opinion was, in fact, almost wholly within the context of Protestantism and not nearly so great as it might have been. This also applied to African American suffrage activists—women marginalized throughout the movement and only recently finding their place in the history of suffrage activism.

That the Syracuse convention ended in unity was perhaps due to the distraction of a different debate: whether or not the movement should organize more formally. For the 1850s, the question was largely answered with an overwhelming no. Mary Springstead "moved that the Convention proceed to organize a National Woman's Rights Society," but a letter from Angelina Grimké Weld argued differently, predicting that more formality would "prove a burden, a clog, an incumbrance, rather than a help." Ernestine Rose agreed that "organizations were like Chinese bandages" in their restrictiveness, and Harriot K. Hunt preferred "spontaneity," which she deemed "a law of nature." Lucy Stone made perhaps the strongest argument when she said they "had all been in permanent organizations, and therefore dread them."

Paulina Wright Davis demonstrated her skill at achieving resolution, and the convention adopted her motion that "persons in any or all of our States who are interested in this great reform" should call state and local meetings, "certainly as often as once a year." That was the way the movement would proceed until after the Civil War: without any bylaws, headquarters, official publication, or other accoutrements of formal organization. The cause would carry on, as Weld had suggested, "by the natural ties of spiritual affinity."

These natural ties were strengthened by Davis herself when, just six months after the convention, she began publishing *The Una* from her Providence, Rhode Island, home. Her February 1853 inaugural issue announced: "Our plan is to publish a paper monthly.... Our purpose is to discuss the rights, duties, sphere, and destiny of women fully and fearlessly." *The Una,* she said, "signifies truth." For three years, Davis and her assistant Caroline H. Dall provided a communication network for feminists. Along with such familiars as Stanton,

Stone, and Frances Dana Gage, *The Una* also featured mainstream writers such as Ohio author Hannah Tracy Cutler, educator and publisher Elizabeth Peabody, the *New York Tribune*'s Elizabeth Oakes Smith, and "Fanny Fern," the pseudonym of Sara Parton who was so popular that in 1855, the *New York Ledger* paid her a fabulous $100 weekly for just one column. Illustrious men wrote for *The Una* too, including literary critic Thomas Wentworth Higginson.

Besides publishing, the other standard method of spreading the women's rights gospel was through lecture tours. Fall 1853 featured a particularly adventurous one, when Dr. Lydia Fowler took leave of her New York City medical practice to join Vermont newspaper editor Clarina Howard Nichols in frontier Wisconsin. Nichols estimated that they traveled 900 miles, "speaking in forty-three towns to audiences estimated at 30,000 in the aggregate." They spoke to women's rights through the facade of temperance, with "Mrs. F." using her medical expertise on "the physiological effects of alcohol" and Nichols emphasizing the tragic link between alcohol abuse and women's lack of legal rights. Once again, male temperance leaders in Milwaukee were hostile to this assistance from women, but their opposition backfired, as Wisconsin women welcomed the lecturers. When men closed off lecture halls, the women found alternate space.

The Midwest also hosted its first national women's rights convention in 1853. Cleveland was the site of the Fourth National Convention, with attendees from eight Northern states. Presiding officers Lucretia Mott and Frances Dana Gage laid down firm rules at the beginning, and the 1,500 attendees conducted a meeting that was more amicable than the Syracuse one had been. Newspaper response was detailed and generally favorable, although the *Cleveland Plain Dealer* could not resist playing favorites: "the handsomest woman" was Antoinette Brown, and although "Mrs. Gage is not a handsome woman, you can see genius in her eye."

Among the noteworthy new speakers was Henry Blackwell, brother of Drs. Elizabeth and Emily Blackwell, who doubtless hoped to impress his future wife, Lucy Stone, by speaking "with great eloquence for nearly an hour." His chief point was that "the interests of the sexes are inseparably connected, and in the elevation of one lies the salvation of the other." That it was women who needed to be "elevated" and men who needed to be "saved" did not require spelling out.

Back East, a very different event occurred that year. Just prior to the Cleveland convention, New York City hosted the World's Fair. This prompted many organizations to call meetings for the same time and place; among them was what women's rights leaders would dub "The Half World's Temperance Convention." Antoinette Brown's "handsome" appearance was worth little among the men of the temperance movement, for once again, they excluded women, Brown specifically. Horace Greeley sarcastically reported on September 7, 1853:

> This convention has completed three of its four business sessions, and the results may be summed up as follows:
>
> First Day–Crowding a woman off the platform
>
> Second Day–Gagging her
>
> Third Day–Voting that she shall stay gagged.
>
> Having thus disposed of the main question, we presume the incidentals will be finished this morning.

The following Sunday evening, however, Brown preached to a New York City audience of 5,000. Even more significantly, the next week simple farm folk quietly registered their disagreement with the temperance leaders: on September 15, the First Congregational Church of Wayne County, New York, ordained Rev. Antoinette Brown. She was the first woman to be an official minister of a church in a mainstream American denomination.

In the weeks that followed, many expressed respect for her and the other women, including Susan B. Anthony, who were so unchivalrously turned away from the convention. Pointing out that Brown had been duly elected as a delegate by not merely one, but two, temperance organizations, more liberal ministers took on their colleagues: "If any man says that Antoinette Brown forced the subject of 'Woman's Rights' on that Temperance Convention," Rev. William Henry Channing fumed, "*he lies.* She never dreamed of asking any *privilege* as a woman; she stood there in her *right* as a delegate." Rev. Channing denounced his fellow pastors, calling them "*Reverend* for what?" He cited an onlooker at the temperance rally who inquired, "Are those men drunk?"

Attendees in front of the Crystal Palace at the World's Fair in New York City in 1853, when women and other activists gathered for a world temperance convention. (Wikimedia/Karl Gildemeister)

In addition to the uproarious temperance meeting, abolitionists and other supporters of controversial causes held meetings. By the end of the week, the right-wing newspapers of the city had rallied the men who felt threatened by all this change. Unfortunately, the last of these meetings was on women's rights. As so many people were in New York for other events, this gathering, although not the official annual convention, attracted the greatest crowd thus far: 11 states were represented, as well as England and Germany. Even with a 25-cent admission, every one of the 3,000 seats in the Broadway Tabernacle was sold out—but not everyone was there to be enlightened.

The event went down in feminist history as "The Mob Convention." By "hissing, yelling, stamping, and all manner of unseemly interruptions," men in the audience thwarted the convention's speakers. William Lloyd Garrison, Wendell Phillips, and other men were attacked in the same way that the women were. Determined orators took on the mob and persisted in rising above the din, occasionally with success. "Never before," said Horace Greeley's editorial, "have we heard Antoinette Brown, Mrs. Rose, and Lucy Stone speak with such power.... When Lucy Stone closed the discussion with some pungent, yet pathetic, remarks on the opposition...it was evident that if any rowdies had an ant-hole in the bottom of his boot, he would inevitably have sunk through it and disappeared forever."

The rowdies, however, did not disappear. They were there again the next day, and this time, Sojourner Truth took them on. In the words of her New York women's rights colleagues, she personified the mob's "two most hated elements," for "she was black and she was a woman, and all the insults that could be cast upon color and sex were hurled at her; but there she stood, calm and dignified, a grand, wise woman." When "the terrible turmoil" abated a bit, Sojourner Truth's powerful voice rolled out:

> Is it not good for me to come and draw forth a spirit, to see what kind of spirit people are of? I see that some of you have got the spirit of a goose, and some have got the spirit of a snake.... I was a slave in the State of New York, and now I am a good citizen of this State.... I know it [makes you] feel like hissing...to see a colored woman get up and tell you...about Woman's Rights. We have all been thrown down so low that nobody thought we'd ever get up again, and now I am here....
>
> We'll have our rights; see if we don't; and you can't stop us from them; see if you can. You may hiss as much as you like, but it is coming.

The mob quieted briefly to satisfy their curiosity about German Mathilde Anneke, who recently fled from the repressive aftermath of the 1848 revolutions in Europe. Ernestine Rose translated for her, and when she told the audience that Anneke "could hardly express her astonishment at what she witnessed" in the hall because it contradicted "what she had heard so much of freedom in America," the tumult again erupted, proving her point. Rose called for the police, saying that "we have a right to this protection, for we pay our money for it." She pointed out that the mayor

New York Tribune editor Horace Greeley (Library of Congress)

had "promised to see that our meetings should not be disturbed," but no police came.

As translator, Rose took over the platform from President Lucretia Mott, who, consistent with Quaker principles, refused to bring in the police. In the end, Dr. Harriot K. Hunt shouted out a resolution thanking Lucretia Mott "for the grace, firmness, ability, and courtesy" that Mott had demonstrated in the "arduous" task of presiding, and the convention adjourned. That it was a pious woman in Quaker dress who was so abused by these political thugs did not pass unnoticed, and, in the eyes of many, the mob's behavior backfired. "If it had been their earnest desire to strengthen the cause of Woman's Rights," Horace Greeley said later, "they could not have done the work half so effectively. Nothing is so good for a weak and unpopular movement as this sort of opposition." William Cullen Bryant, famed poet and editor of *The Evening Post*, also spoke out "against mob law and for the rights of woman." In the end, the "spirit of a snake" whiplashed and bit its own tail.

Upper-class life was becoming sufficiently genteel in the 1850s that wealthy families began taking summer vacations, a phenomenon that would not extend to most people until the next century. A new railroad network in this decade made travel something to be desired instead of merely endured, and Southerners especially began leaving the heat, humidity, and frequently fatal mosquitoes of plantation life for the cool lakes and mountains of the North. New York's Saratoga Springs was one of the nation's first resort towns, and, in the summer of 1854, Susan B. Anthony demonstrated her savvy by going where the affluent and influential were likely to be. She wanted to use "the fashionable season" to reach "a new class of hearers."

Initially, things did not go well for the would-be lecturer. Anthony acknowledged that she had "but little experience as a speaker," and worse, someone stole her purse. She had no money to pay the printer for the flyers she ordered to advertise the event, and some of the scheduled speakers sent last-minute cancellations. In this unhappy situation, she came upon vacationer Matilda Joslyn Gage, whom Anthony had met when they both were newcomers at the Syracuse convention. Gage provided the money that Anthony lacked and even overcame her terror of speaking to join the platform. They both were favorably reviewed in the press that followed—along with great detail on Gage's stylish clothes.

For the rest of the decade, women's rights advocates would spend some of each summer in Saratoga. Anthony honed her fundraising and networking skills there. In 1855, for example, she "announced that woman's rights tracts… were for sale at the door" after the speeches, and she told the audience that "they must take *The Una.*" Even though she was disappointed that *The Woman's Advocate* confined itself to economic issues and did not endorse suffrage, she also sold this new Philadelphia-based paper, which was run by Anna E. McDowell and an all-female staff. Saratoga was exceptional in its ability to support fundraising: in 1855 alone, Anthony sold 20,000 pamphlets on women's rights. Many of them ended up in the South, where they were often the only such information available. Twenty years later, for example, Elizabeth Cady Stanton met a Texas woman who said that her introduction to the cause had come through a Georgia friend who attended a women's rights rally in Saratoga and brought back tracts.

The resort also was a rare opportunity for fun: Charles F. Hovey, a faithful supporter of the liberated women, made it a "usual custom" to invite them for "a bountiful repast" at the lake, and he even took them sailing. Moreover, the first endowment that the women's movement received was from this man: when Hovey died in 1859, he left $50,000 for the promotion of this and other reforms.

Their Saratoga experience cemented a friendship between Matilda Joslyn Gage and Susan B. Anthony that culminated decades later with their coeditorship of the first three volumes of the *History of Woman Suffrage.* The third coeditor, Elizabeth Cady Stanton, also set a milestone in 1854: she sent an address to the New York legislature, along with 5,931 petition signatures for "the just and equal rights of women." With Susan B. Anthony doing the legwork, the petition-gathering effort continued through the rest of the year. Anthony's organizational abilities sharpened as she followed this plan through: while "getting petitions and subscribers to *The Una,*" she reported holding "conventions in fifty-four counties."

This pattern became a model for the way that Stanton and Anthony would work: Stanton used her powerful writing skills, while Anthony excelled at the fieldwork. Not only was this an expression of their individual fortes, but also, in the first years of their relationship, it was essential because Stanton was tied down with children. Anthony became a frequent visitor to Seneca Falls, and after the seven little Stantons were in bed, their mother and "Aunt Susan" sat by the fireside and plotted strategy. The relationship was well defined by this commonly used description: Stanton made the thunderbolts, and Anthony threw them.

While these two led the petitioning of the New York legislature, Caroline Severance did the same for the Ohio Women's Rights Association. The married women's property rights bill that she proposed in 1854 was not taken up, but Massachusetts women were successful in winning property rights this year, and that example would be quickly emulated elsewhere. It was Mary Upton Ferrin of Salem who was almost singlehandedly responsible for setting the Massachusetts precedent. From 1848, when she became aware of the legalisms that prevented women from writing valid wills, Ferrin spent six years educating Massachusetts women on their lack of rights and asking for signatures. "Many persons laughed at her," said her friends later, "but knowing it to be a righteous work, and deeming laughter healthful to those indulging in it, Mrs. Ferrin continued." Without any connection to the emerging women's movement, Ferrin "traveled six hundred miles, two-thirds of it on foot," to gather the petitions that culminated in the 1854 success. During the next few years, other states began similarly revising their laws.

Perhaps the most talked-of event of 1855 regarded a completely different facet of the movement: the innovative wedding of Lucy Stone and Henry Blackwell. Even though she was appreciably older than he, Blackwell courted her assiduously. He finally persuaded her to marry by suggesting not only that they emulate the Stantons and eliminate the bridal vow "to obey," but also that their ceremony include a protest against the laws on marriage that they would circulate in the press. Most significantly, he encouraged her to retain the name by which she was known. The precedent was so unusual that "stoner" became a commonly used nineteenth-century noun to denote a woman who kept her maiden name. Nonetheless, habits were

Lucy Stone (Library of Congress)

so strong that even women's rights documents invariably added a marital honorific, turning her into "Mrs. Stone."

The next year, Samuel Blackwell won his even longer courtship of Antoinette Brown, but unlike her former Oberlin classmate Lucy Stone, Brown took her husband's name. With this, the Blackwells—physicians Elizabeth and Emily, Henry Blackwell and Lucy Stone, and Samuel and Antoinette Brown Blackwell—became the century's most visibly feminist family.

Lucy Stone and Henry Blackwell were thus very much the stars of the 1855 national convention, which took place in the calmer clime of Cincinnati in October. Martha C. Wright presided in the absence of her sister, Lucretia Mott. Wright, one of the five who had planned the Seneca Falls convention, pointed out that in the few years since that convention, "the newspapers which ridiculed and slandered us at first are beginning to give impartial accounts of our meetings. Newspapers," she noted sagaciously, "do not lead, but follow public opinion." A last gasp of the dress reform movement provided a spirit of fun in Cincinnati, as well as an exercise in consciousness raising: while some of women wore bloomers, their "gentlemen" donned shawls.

The women tested themselves the next year by going back to the scene of the "Mob Convention," Broadway Tabernacle. Perhaps because it was late November and New York was not filled with fair-goers looking for a cheap thrill, the convention was orderly. Martha Wright called it to order, and Lucy Stone was elected president. "This is a day of congratulation," she said: "It is our Seventh Annual National Woman's Rights Convention," and in just a few years, "almost every Northern state has more or less modified its laws." She reeled off a systematic list of property rights changes in Maine, Vermont, New Hampshire, New York, and Rhode Island, and then verbally moved west:

> Ohio, Illinois, and Indiana have also very materially modified their laws. And Wisconsin–God bless these young States–has granted almost all that has been asked except the right of suffrage.... In Michigan, it has been moved that women should have a right to their own babies, which none of you ladies have here in New York.

She went on with even more astonishing news: the Nebraska House had passed a bill granting women the vote! That it was lost in the senate, Stone said, was "only because of the too early closing of the session." The full story, however, was a bit more complex. It was true that the territorial legislature of infant Nebraska displayed far more liberalism than was ever the case in the ossified East. Nebraska men, of their own volition and without any organized pressure, invited Amelia Bloomer, who had recently moved from Seneca Falls to Iowa, to address them in December 1855. The next month, the House followed up on her well-received speech and, by a vote of 14 to 11, passed "a bill to confer suffrage equally upon women." Some legislators, however, seemed surprised with themselves: in the words of a local newspaper, the *Chronotype,* on January 30, 1856, "its passage by the House of Representatives created a great deal of talk, and several members threatened to resign." Although the newspaper alleged that the upper chamber failed to follow the House "only for want of time," on the last day of the session, it also reported a long filibuster on a minor local bill, which no member bothered to interrupt. Nor were women's rights taken up at later sessions, and Amelia Bloomer's positive effect was apparently brief.

Stone was perceptive in blessing these "young states," which would prove to be consistently ahead of older ones in the future. She was wrong, however, on her other assumptions. Though understandable, it was naive of her to believe that the Nebraska Senate loss was merely a matter of timing. This was simply the first of many times when politicians would assure women that their cause was nearly won, expecting them to go away happy in the innocent belief that only a technicality prevented men from doing the right thing. Stone was even more wrong when she moved from politics to education: she predicted that "our demand that Harvard and Yale Colleges should admit women… waits only for a little time." As it turned out, a "little time" was more than 100 years. The midpoint of the twentieth century would be long past before these most conservative of institutions finally admitted women to their undergraduate colleges.

That these hopeful predictions were so badly off probably was due to the fact that the property rights issue was being won with relative ease. After the 1850s, women did not have to expend much effort on this aspect of their great reforms, and so it was understandable that their judgments on other issues would be falsely skewed by this quick success. The vote for women was another matter, however, and its singular relationship to democracy made that effort much harder.

Moreover, the 1850s were infused with a spirit of change in a multiplicity of areas: from vegetarianism and "water cures" to celibacy and "complex marriage" in utopian societies, it was an age of experimentation. When all of those ideas channeled into one major one—abolition—with the coming of the Civil War, the expansion of women's rights from property rights to other civil rights would stall.

A preview of the Civil War played out in Kansas during the decade. Whether this territory would become "Free Soil" or lead to an immense expansion of slavery was the great question. Devoted abolitionists moved there, and Southerners did the same. "Bleeding Kansas" was the result: through the 1850s, anarchy prevailed, as women and men suffered from politically motivated arson and murder.

Vermont's Clarina Howard Nichols was among those who went to Kansas to support the abolitionists, and along the way, she discovered that her women's rights reputation preceded her. She received many invitations to speak, including one at a constitutional convention in Topeka. Her husband's illness prevented her from accepting, and so the convention did not hear the case for including women as voters in the new Kansas constitution. Without any female advocacy, seven delegates, including the governor, nevertheless voted to eliminate "male" from the proposed enfranchisement clause of the state constitution in 1855.

Clarina Howard Nichols (Kansas State Historical Society)

Ohio, a "middle-aged state" compared with Kansas, came even closer to setting the precedent that instead would elude women for decades. While revising property laws in 1857, its senate cast a vote on female enfranchisement: in response to some 10,000 petitions gathered by Caroline Severance, Frances Dana Gage, Hannah Tracy Cutler, and other Ohio women, a committee endorsed the amending of the state constitution to give women the vote. On the floor, the senators tied 44 to 44, which meant that the amendment was not adopted. It was the first of many such legislative heartbreaks.

Decades would pass before suffragists again saw similarly close margins. As the 1850s drew to a close, everything focused on the issue of slavery, and then the war came. A careful student of history knows that a period of conservatism follows almost every war, and the century would end before there was a genuine revival of the spirit of the 1850s. One thing that favors reform, however, is the very fact that the future cannot be predicted: the actors in this great American drama did not know that their lives would end before their goals were accomplished, and so they carried on.

In 1856, women watched the first election with participation from the new Republican Party. The neophyte group was the antithesis of what it would be at the beginning of the twenty-first century: those who joined the Republican Party of the 1850s never labeled themselves "conservatives," but were instead unabashed radicals wholly dedicated to ending slavery. One of the ways in which the new party displayed its disposition for reform was the first promotion of a woman as part of a presidential campaign. Jessie Benton Fremont, wife of Republican candidate Charles Fremont, became the first to star as a potential first lady and the first to be denounced as excessively ambitious. Had she been male, perhaps she would have been the candidate herself, for as the daughter of Thomas Hart Benton, a longtime senator from Missouri, she knew and loved politics. The Republicans not only used her connections, but also made her an integral part of the campaign, including a smiling picture of "Our Jessie" on lapel buttons. Although the new party lost, Charles Fremont did surprisingly well without the endorsement of his stoutly Democratic father-in-law. Jessie Benton Fremont would linger on the political stage through the century, occasionally helping suffragists with financial contributions, but never risking her political insider position by openly joining them.

There was no national convention the following year, although there were so many state ones that the authors of the *History of Woman Suffrage* only realized this omission in surprised retrospect: "The year 1857 seems to have passed without a National Convention," they wrote. In May 1858, they met again in New York. Although the convention was slightly disrupted "by the rowdyism of a number of men occupying the rear part of the hall," it nonetheless was successful.

Among the newcomers was Sarah Remond, a black woman from Boston who had successfully sued the city in 1853, when a policeman knocked her down the stairs as she tried to integrate an opera audience. Remond would eventually settle in Europe, and her speeches there not only raised funds for abolitionists, but also were a factor in keeping European nations neutral in the Civil War.

Another convention speaker was Eliza Woodson Farnham, who was known for her innovative policies as supervisor of women in Sing Sing prison. Her speech on the "superiority of women" asserted that "woman's creative power during maternity" made her "second only to God himself." Farnham suggested that man should consider himself "as a John the Baptist, going before to prepare the world for her coming." In 1864, Farnham published a major feminist work, *Woman and Her Era,* in which she expanded on this thesis of the natural superiority of women.

Finally, Parker Pillsbury recommended that "the women hold their next Convention at the ballot-box, as that would do more good than a hundred such as these." If officials refused to give ballots to women, Pillsbury suggested that they "look the tax collectors in the face and defy them to come for taxes." Perhaps inspired by Phillips's words, as well as by the example of Dr. Harriot Hunt, Lucy Stone used 1858 to set another precedent: in the year between her pregnancies at age 39 and 41, she allowed her household goods to be impounded rather than accept taxation without representation.

Stone's prescient observation at the 1856 convention that the "young states" were leading the older ones was demonstrated again the following year. Out in Indiana, "an immense crowd assembled in the Houses of the Legislature" on January 19, 1859, to hear Dr. Mary F. Thomas read a petition signed by over a thousand Indiana citizens. It asked for "laws giving equal property rights to married women, and to take the necessary steps to so amend the Constitution of the State as to secure to all women the right of suffrage." Mary Birdstall followed up with a half-hour speech, and the legislature unanimously accepted the women's documents and requested copies for newspaper publication. The senators then departed, while the House acted as a committee of the whole. Not surprisingly, their parliamentary maneuvers left the women both stranded and confused: they referred the petition to the Committee on Rights and Privileges, which eventually reported "that legislation on this subject is inexpedient at this time."

In May, intrepid Indiana women were among those who returned to New York for the Ninth National Convention. This one-day meeting held in Mozart Hall has only brief records in the *History of Woman Suffrage*, which characterized the speeches as "short" and the atmosphere as "turbulent." Wendell Phillips, "who understood from long experience how to play and lash a mob," proved the star of the show: "for nearly two hours he held that mocking crowd in the hallow of his hand." He pointed out, among other things, that "the reformers—the fanatics, as we are called—are the only ones who have launched social and moral questions." Once again, this 1859 convention adopted resolutions that were "extensively circulated and sent to the Legislature of every state," but this time, there was little reward. "Owing to the John Brown raid and the general unrest and forebodings of the people on the eve of our civil war," the report concluded, their resolutions "commanded but little attention." (White abolitionist John Brown and 16 other white and black men were either killed in or executed for their raid on a federal arsenal at Harper's Ferry, Virginia, in 1859. The object of the raid was to obtain arms, promote a rebellion among slaves, and establish a free state for blacks.)

The distractions of the coming war made the Tenth National Convention the last of its type. Held in New York's Cooper Institute on May 10 and 11, 1860, it was called to order by Susan B. Anthony, while Martha Wright once again presided. Hecklers left this convention in peace, and excellent stenographers detailed the exact words of lengthy speeches that run for almost 50 pages of fine print in the *History of Woman Suffrage.* Unfortunately, they were not all amicable speeches.

Elizabeth Cady Stanton and Antoinette Brown Blackwell introduced competing sets of resolutions on marriage and the family, and the convention erupted into a repeat of earlier debates on the role of religion. This argument centered on divorce, with Stanton arguing that since marriage was a civil contract, divorce should be a civil right. Her resolutions even included a clause "that children born in these unhappy [marriages] are, in the most solemn sense, of unlawful birth the fruit of lust, but not of love." Reverend Blackwell, in contrast, viewed marriage as a sacred religious covenant that could not be broken by the state, and she centered her argument on a "true ideal of marriage." Ernestine Rose retorted that "the Rev. Mrs. Blackwell" thought only of "what marriage ought to be" instead of what it often was. Rose added that the newspapers were "filled with heart-sickening accounts of wife-poisoning," and pointed out that the murders could be avoided if divorce were possible. After many more words, some of them personally acrimonious, Wendell Phillips moved to table both sets of resolutions. Newcomer Abby Hopper Gibbons of New York City seconded, saying that she "wished the whole subject of marriage and divorce might be swept from the platform, as it was manifestly not the place for it" and then the convention debated that point. Phillips's motion eventually lost, and the convention dissolved into irresolution on this important question. Stanton never forgave Phillips for his lack of support, and when Horace Greeley wrote conservative editorials on the divorce question, it also marked the beginning of the end of her valuable relationship with him. The divorce debate also signaled the beginning of animosity between Stanton (and her ever-faithful supporter, Susan B. Anthony) and Rev. Antoinette Brown Blackwell (and her sister-in-law, Lucy Stone).

Mary Grew of Philadelphia asked both sides to overlook their relatively minor disagreements for the larger cause. Her words were more prescient than she knew, for she could not have foreseen how long the cause would be delayed and how vast the separation would be when she said, "Friends, we are about to separate:

> The word I would impress upon you all is this–it is always safe to do right.... Forget for a little while the sneers of the press and pulpit, the laugh of the fashionable lady, who calls you unladylike, and the scorn of arrogant men, who appreciate not your labors! You need not pay back the laughter and the scorn with scorn. Your work is too great, too high, too holy. Forgive them, and pass on! Rejoice to think that, in a few years, they, too, will rise up and thank you for it.... The only thing is to be sure we are doing right...and to leave the world better than we found it.

Chapter Four

The Battle Cry of Freedom, 1860 to 1876

No women, of course, were allowed to vote in the presidential election of 1876, but that election set the course for the nation—and its women—for the rest of the century. Even without the vote, the political work of anti-slavery women was clear in that election: from a scorned philosophy that invited physical assault just a few years earlier, abolitionism moved to center stage and won the election. On only its second try, the new Republican Party elected its candidate, even though the Illinois lawyer was relatively unknown and possessed very slim political credentials: Abraham Lincoln had served one undistinguished term in Congress back in the 1840s. Not surprisingly, he won with far less than a majority of the popular vote. The nation was so badly fractured, however, that the Democratic Party split into Northern and Southern wings, and a fourth, minor-party candidate (who was also from Illinois) actually polled more electoral votes than the ostensible Democratic nominee. Except for opposing its expansion, Lincoln won without taking a firm stand against slavery. Although he evaded this crucial topic throughout the campaign, the anti-slavery "radical Republicans" had no choice but to support his candidacy as the best that they could do.

For the South, it was more than enough. Lincoln's election signaled abolitionism to them, and the Democratic Party's "Solid South" immediately rumbled rebellion. South Carolina seceded from the United States in December, months before the new administration took office in March, and Georgia, Alabama, Florida, and other states soon followed. When Lincoln went from Illinois to Washington, assassination threats were so real that he needed armed escorts. Within days of the inauguration, guns began firing in South Carolina and the inevitable war was on.

To speak to the roles of women in that war would require another book, for the Civil War was a tremendous turning point in the history of American women. It was so long, bloody, and costly that, at the beginning of the twenty-first century, the nation has never again experienced anything like the horror of those four years. Every resource was needed, especially in the South, and traditional conceptions of ladyhood simply had to be set aside to meet pragmatic needs.

A scene from Harriet Beecher Stowe's *Uncle Tom's Cabin*, which galvanized anti-slavery feeling on the eve of the Civil War. (Library of Congress)

Women discovered capabilities in themselves that they never knew they had, and the feats of tens of thousands of women earned grudging respect from men. Many disguised themselves and fought on battlefields as men; thousands nursed gruesomely wounded men, often without pay and under appalling conditions. On both sides, women did the necessary work of farm and factory while men went to war. Both sides used women as spies, and in both, women routinely performed Quartermaster Corps duty in supplying the armies. A number of women earned recognition as valuable orators for recruiting soldiers and molding public opinion, and dozens of female writers did the same—

Harriet Beecher Stowe's *Uncle Tom's Cabin*, more than any other single factor, turned the Civil War into a crusade against slavery. Women also organized entirely new systems for a military that had not yet developed modern humanitarian techniques. Clara Barton undertook the world's first systematic accounting of missing and dead soldiers, while the U.S. Sanitary Commission organized tens of thousands of women into local units that raised some $30 million for hospitals—which, in turn, were staffed largely by women.

All this gave women an unusual opportunity for personal growth. The taboo against traveling alone, for example, seemed outdated when a woman needed to get on a train to find a husband who was missing in action or to retrieve a wounded brother from a prisoner-of-war camp. That the taboo against public speaking was over became clear in 1864, when 21-year-old Anna Dickinson proved such an inspiring orator that she was invited to address Congress with President Lincoln in the audience. The notion that women were incapable of managerial responsibility was overturned by women in both the North and South who ran the largest hospitals the world had ever seen—sometimes with a pistol at hand to control psychotic men or to prevent the theft of precious drugs. All of these challenges were learning experiences, and, when the war was over, women had not only new confidence and new skills, but also new national networks that could be used for political action.

But for the duration, direct political action became taboo, a ban that was imposed by the women's rights advocates themselves. Not only were most of them devoted abolitionists whose time had finally come, but also the leaders understood that winning the war and ending slavery were themselves huge challenges, and they knew they would be criticized if they diverted time and energy elsewhere. As women had done for centuries, suffragists put aside their own interests for those of others. In a clear and conscious way, the leadership of the movement accepted a suspension of activity during the war, and there would be no more women's rights conventions until the year following its end.

And yet women's needs were still real. Even though the nation was in crisis, personal lives could be in crisis too, and this point was brought painfully home to Susan B. Anthony soon after Lincoln's election. She was in Albany in December of 1860 when a woman wearing heavy veils appeared in the dark of night, begging for help. The stranger explained that her husband was a Massachusetts state senator, Dr. Charles Abner Phelps, and she was fleeing from him. She had made the mistake of confronting her husband with evidence of his infidelity, and he had responded by declaring her insane and having her committed to an asylum. For a year and a half, she endured the hellhole that such institutions were at that time until her brother—a prominent political person in his own right—finally intervened on her behalf. But her husband, of course, retained absolute rights over their children, and she was trying to get a 13-year-old daughter away from him.

On Christmas Day, Anthony helped Phelps and her daughter disguise themselves, and the three took a train to New York City. Arriving late at night, they tramped through snow to several hotels that refused to rent them a room. The taboo against women traveling alone was still sufficiently strong that hotel managers routinely assumed that unescorted women were prostitutes or guilty of other criminal behavior; in fact, this was the case, for the senator had reported his wife's criminal desertion and "kidnapping," and the police were looking for them. Finally, Anthony found shelter at the home of Abby Hopper Gibbons, a Quaker accustomed to shielding escaped slaves from the law.

Gibbons was also the person who had seconded Wendell Phillips's motion to kill the controversial divorce resolutions at the last women's rights convention. In hiding the Phelpses, however, she demonstrated an understanding of the reality of women's lives that escaped Phillips and other well-intentioned men. As soon as Anthony returned to Albany, Phillips and other male colleagues besieged her, urging her to turn over the fugitives to the authorities. Even William Lloyd Garrison, usually the most empathetic to women, pleaded with Anthony to reconsider what he deemed her "hasty and ill judged" decision to harbor a woman from her lawful husband.

The men feared the harm this would do to their anti-slavery cause. They did not wish to offend the senator; they could not see the woman's problem as anything except personal. They argued that Anthony was violating the law in refusing to surrender her and never appeared to see the illogic of their position: they had argued exactly the opposite in the analogous case of the Fugitive Slave Law. The same men who firmly believed that conscience should override law when the victim was an escaped slave insisted, in the case of a fugitive woman, that the law must be obeyed.

It was another lesson that Anthony never forgot. She stood firm against their inconsistent sense of logic and justice, and despite pressure from many old friends, from the law, and from both of the families involved—even Mrs. Phelps's own powerful family wanted her returned—Anthony never told where she took the fugitives that night. She maintained her silence for more than a year, but eventually the senator's detectives found the daughter and kidnapped her from Sunday school. A network of women, however, protected Phelps from extradition to Massachusetts. She moved in with Elizabeth Ellet, a historian and author of sufficient repute that the senator finally decided to leave his wife in peace.

As Elizabeth Cady Stanton summarized, "All with whom Mrs. P. came in contact for years afterward expressed the opinion that she was perfectly sane and always had been." The whole episode, of course, raised still another troubling issue for the movement to tackle: "Could the dark secrets of these insane asylums be brought to light," Stanton said, "we should be shocked to know the countless number of rebellious wives, sisters, and daughters that are thus annually sacrificed to...barbarous laws made by men for women."

Mrs. Phelps demonstrated not only her sanity, but also a keen intelligence; even the fact that this Massachusetts woman managed to track down Susan B. Anthony in Albany was impressive. Perhaps she reasoned out from the newspapers where supportive women might be found, for Anthony was in the state capital to work on the issue of divorce—a subject of tremendous importance to Phelps. Anthony was staying with Lydia Mott, whom Elizabeth Cady Stanton described as "a dignified, judicious Quaker woman." A cousin to James Mott, she was the unmarried head of a home that was "one of the depots of the underground railroad, where slaves escaping to Canada were warmed and fed." Her home also was a gathering place for political men. "Leaders from opposite political parties...met at Miss Mott's dinner-table," said Stanton, and it was through these connections that the women managed to get a divorce bill introduced in January 1861.

Once again, women's rights advocates showed their admirable ability to separate abstract issues of justice from their own experience. Lucretia Mott encouraged her husband's cousin in this effort, even though neither of them had any personal need for divorce reform. In the same letter in which she said that she and James "had a delightful golden wedding [anniversary], with all our children and children's children present," Lucretia Mott also argued for the right to dissolve an oppressive marriage. Although she used pious Quaker language, her views were radically feminist: "I have wished ever since parting with thee...to send thee a line," she said, and then went on to enthusiastically echo views she had read of during a British debate on divorce. One member of Parliament expressed Mott's opinion exactly when he said that women needed not only change in marital codes, but also "a total reconstruction of the whole system."

The proposed act was far from total reconstruction. It required anyone filing for divorce to have lived in the state of New York for a minimum of five years and then allowed only two grounds: at least three years of desertion or "cruel and inhuman treatment so great as to...render it unsafe to live with the guilty party." Even with these restrictions, however, the idea was still too radical, and the bill went nowhere.

In connection with their hearing on the divorce bill, New York women also held a state Woman's Rights Convention in Albany on February 7 and 8, 1861—but the war began two months later, and life would never be the same. "Those who had been specially engaged in the Woman's Suffrage Movement," reports Volume Two of the *History of Woman Suffrage,* "suspended their Conventions during the war and gave their time and thought wholly to the vital issues of the hour. Seeing the political significance of the war, they urged the emancipation of the slaves.... To this end, they organized a National League."

Once again, they began by meeting. In March 1863, Horace Greeley's *New York Tribune* published a lengthy "Appeal to the Women of the Republic," which was later issued in tract form. Signed by Elizabeth Cady Stanton and Susan B. Anthony, it invited "the Loyal Women of the Nation to meet in the Church of the Puritans" in New York on May 14. Again, when the appointed day came, "an immense audience, mostly women, representing a large number of the States, crowded the house at an early hour." Anthony called the meeting to order, and Lucy Stone was elected president. The other 15 officers elected were all women, and they came from eight Northern states ranging from Maine to California. Most were familiar names, such as Amy Post, who led the effort to elect a woman as president at the second woman's rights convention in 1848, but some, especially Massachusetts's Mary H. L. Cabot, were important new additions.

Decisions were made by debating a set of resolutions. Susan B. Anthony introduced them, beginning by addressing the still-hot issue of whether the Civil War would be fought for the union or against slavery. "There is great fear expressed on all sides," Anthony said, "lest this war shall be made a war for the negro. I am willing that it should be." She stuck to the accepted strategy of making abolitionism the first priority, and it was not until the fifth resolution that she briefly touched on women's rights. Even that, though, was too much for some. "There are ladies here who have come hundreds of miles," said Mrs. E.O. Sampson Hoyt of Wisconsin, "to attend a business meeting of the Loyal League of the North.... We all know that Woman's Rights as an ism has not been received with entire favor by the women of the country, and...women will not go into any movement of this kind if this idea is made prominent."

The audience agreed with her, not with Anthony. To most of the women, organizing a "Loyal League" meant demonstrating loyalty to the United States and to the Lincoln administration, not introducing other controversies. After "spirited discussion," the resolutions on supporting the war and ending slavery were accepted—but not the fifth resolution, which read: "there can never be a true peace in this Republic until the civil and political rights of all citizens of African descent and all women are practically established."

The vote did not end the debate, though. Experienced leaders of the women's movement would not surrender so easily, and one after another, they tried to move the conservatives. Ernestine Rose was the first, saying, "I...object to the proposition to throw woman out of the race for freedom." Veteran abolitionist Angelina Grimké Weld added, "I rejoice exceedingly that the resolution should combine us with the negro.... True, we have not felt the slave-holder's lash...but our *hearts* have been crushed." Lucy Coleman of Rochester responded to the Wisconsin woman who thought "it might be well to leave out women" with "No, no. Do you remember...here in New York an Anti-Slavery convention broke up in high dudgeon because a woman was put on a committee? ... This Loyal League—because it is a Loyal League—must of necessity bring in Anti-Slavery and Woman's Rights."

Lucy Stone, as the presiding officer, attempted to mollify both sides and yet managed to put the case for women strongly:

> Every good cause can afford to be just. The lady from Wisconsin...says she is an Anti-Slavery woman. We ought to believe her. She accepts the principles of the Woman's Rights Movement, but she does not like the way it has been carried on. We ought to believe her....

She seems to me to stand precisely in the position of those good people just at the close of the war of the Revolution.... Men said, 'Let us have a Union. We are weak; we have been beset for seven long years; do not let us meddle with the negro question'.... They persuaded others to silence. So they said nothing about slavery, and let the wretched monster live.

To-day, over all our land, the unburied bones of our fathers and sons and brothers tell the sad mistake that those men made when long ago they left this one great wrong. They could not accomplish good by passing over a wrong....

All over this land women have no political existence.... Our property is taken from us.... The babes we bear in anguish and carry in our arms are not ours. We come to-day to say to...our Government...'do not forget that you must be true alike to the women and the negroes.'

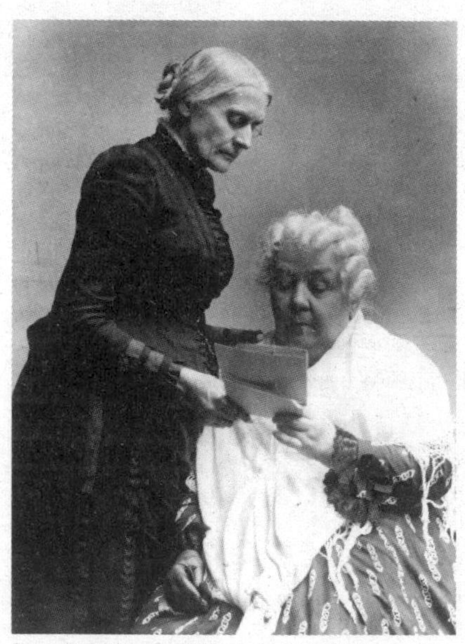
Susan B. Anthony and Elizabeth Cady Stanton (Library of Congress)

In the end, they adopted a resolution so vague that nearly everyone signed it: the women pledged "ourselves one to another in a Loyal League, to give support to the Government in so far as it makes the war for freedom." At an evening session, they adopted a lengthy address that was sent to President Lincoln. Elizabeth Cady Stanton was elected president of the new league, with Susan B. Anthony as secretary. Despite the failure of their dearest resolution, these two judged the meeting a success: "Many women spoke ably and eloquently; women who had never before heard their own voices in a public meeting discussed points of law and constitution in a manner that would have done credit to any legislative assembly."

It was not surprising that many at this meeting were confused as to its actual purpose, for there were several reasons beyond the obvious why Anthony and Stanton called it. The date alone was significant: the meeting was called in March, after Lincoln's Emancipation Proclamation in January had disappointed many of those who had supported his election. His attempt to please both abolitionists and those who argued that the war was about the union, not about slavery, resulted in a document that many viewed as outrageously cynical. The Emancipation Proclamation freed only slaves in enemy territory—where it could not be immediately enforced—and not those in the border states. Thus, the primary object of the petitions that the Loyal League would gather was to pressure Lincoln and the Congress to end slavery everywhere.

In addition to its political significance, the meeting's date also had personal meaning, for it marked an important change in Elizabeth Cady Stanton's life—and therefore in the life of the movement. The Loyal League began soon after the Stantons moved from Seneca Falls to the New York City area. Anthony and Stanton clearly intended the league to be a mechanism for carrying on the work of the women's rights movement, and they were delighted to have this great urban opportunity for organizing and access. That the league's majority differed from the leadership and nullified their only feminist resolution gave Anthony and Stanton little pause. They had enough political subtlety to understand that simply by organizing for any goal, women were organizing for themselves.

The existence of a conservative majority, however, was a good reason not to have many meetings that might contradict the leadership—the Loyal League had just two. Unlike the large women's rights conventions of the previous decade, Stanton and especially Anthony implemented league strategy through daily action in a larger, better funded national network. With support from Robert Dale Owen, who was living in New York City, they established headquarters at Cooper Institute. It marked the first time that any of the women involved in the movement had an office outside of her home. Susan B. Anthony earned a dependable salary for the first time, and the league paid Josephine Griffing and Hannah Tracy Cutler to act as field agents in the Midwest. A steering committee met weekly and during the first year raised and spent $5,000, one-fifth of it on postage.

Women in this era often employed their needlework and decorative skills on petitions, sewing together pages of paper or adorning rolled-up petitions with ribbons. In the Loyal League's case, their aim was to "roll up a mammoth petition, urging Congress to so amend the Constitution as to prohibit… slavery," and they literally rolled up the returned petitions by state, sealing the yellow paper "with the regulation red tape." The first 100,000 were collected in less than a year, and Massachusetts Senator Charles Sumner formally presented them to his congressional colleagues on February 9, 1864. The Loyal League carefully tabulated them by state and, within each state, by gender: women accounted for 65,601 signatures, while 34,399 men signed. The greatest number came from New York, Illinois, and Massachusetts, but even 36 U.S. citizens living in New Brunswick, Canada, signed. Collecting the signatures was not easy. According to an executive committee report, "many refused to sign because they believed slavery a divine institution," while others objected to women circulating petitions at all. At the same time that the league had to fight such attitudes on the right, some of their former colleagues on the left also disparaged the petition-gathering effort. "Old Abolitionists," said the report, "told us that petitioning…had become obsolete."

The Loyal League had a second national meeting in 1864 at the same time and place, but by the following May, the war was over. According to the count kept by Senator Sumner's office, 265,314 petition signatures had been sent by December 1865, when the Thirteenth Amendment that formally banned slavery was officially added to the Constitution. Many of the petitions had been collected at great personal cost: a "poor, infirm" Wisconsin woman, for example, who lost her husband and all of her sons in the war, was so dedicated to making their deaths meaningful by ending slavery that she "traveled on foot over *one hundred miles* in gathering *two thousand* names."

Knowing where to find such committed idealists is crucial to successful implementation of innovative ideas, and by the end of this process, the league had established a 2,000-member network of petition gatherers. Although the names and addresses of the hundreds of thousands of signers ended up in Congress and, later, at the National Archives, Anthony and Stanton kept other valuable records. They had "on file all the letters received from the thousands with whom we have been in correspondence," and they were politically astute enough to understand what a treasure trove that was for the future.

Even in the North, the war was so devastatingly disruptive that it was a year after its end before women organized another national meeting. The call for the Eleventh National Woman's Rights Convention announced a gathering at

New York's Church of the Puritans on May 10, 1866, and promised speeches by Ernestine Rose, Frances Dana Gage, Wendell Phillips, Elizabeth Cady Stanton, Lucretia Mott, Anna Dickinson, and Theodore Tilton, the editor of an influential journal, *The Independent*. The meeting was held in conjunction with the now unnecessary American Anti-Slavery Society. Because most of the activists were members of both groups, they formally renamed themselves "The American Equal Rights Association" and announced their intention to "include both classes of disenfranchised citizens."

Although the merger was supported by most, Wendell Phillips hinted of unhappy times to come when he argued against it. He was president of the American Anti-Slavery Society and lost his position at its dissolution, while the ever-popular, but aging, Lucretia Mott was elected president of the new association. Probably realizing that she was the best choice to blend the two groups, Mott accepted, but also made it clear that "feebleness unfitted her" and that she would lean heavily on the others. Therefore, when the group elected Elizabeth Cady Stanton as first vice president, they had reason to believe that she might well, in effect, head the organization.

Susan B. Anthony presented several resolutions that called upon Congress and the states to amend their constitutions "to secure the right of suffrage to every citizen, without distinction of race, color or sex." Including Congress was a new development, for, as Anthony said, "up to this hour, we have looked to State action." The war, however, had changed all that, and Anthony turned the conservatives' own argument against them: they had argued that the war was for the union, not against slavery, and had insisted that states had no right to secede from that union. Now Anthony followed that reasoning to its logical conclusion: "by the results of the war, the whole question of suffrage reverts back to the Congress and the U.S. Constitution." It was a major change of philosophy, and most of her listeners appeared not to grasp her quickly made point—especially when Anthony immediately went on to discuss her own state's upcoming constitutional convention. The resolutions were adopted without clear explication of Anthony's reasoning, and the seeds for misunderstanding were laid.

Attention went instead to the meeting's highlight, the presence of newcomer Rev. Henry Ward Beecher. The era's most popular preacher and the brother of Harriet Beecher Stowe, Beecher caused jubilation by unequivocally proclaiming himself in favor of the vote for women. In a portion of his hour-long speech, he said: "I declare that woman has more interest in legislation than man, because she is the sufferer and the home-staying, ruined victim. The household, about which we hear so much as being woman's sphere, is safe only as the community around it is safe."

Another progressive presence on the platform was Frances Watkins Harper, although Beecher's words were recorded with much more care than hers. A black woman born free in Baltimore, she had built a successful career as an author and lecturer during the 1850s. Briefly married and widowed, she would take her young daughter with her when she embarked on a four-year lecture tour of the South, where she rallied her newly freed sisters. Harper would be one of the cofounders, in 1895, of the National Association of Colored Women.

Abolitionist and suffragist, Frances Watkins Harper. (Wikimedia/State Library of North Carolina)

This first meeting of the American Equal Rights Association closed with Lucretia Mott reminding the audience of how far they had come, especially on the issue of slavery. "Let us remember," she said, "in our trials and discouragement, that if our lives are true, we walk with angels." As she spoke, the sun shone through the stained glass of the Church of the Puritans, and Theodore Tilton expressed the feelings of many when he said, "This closing meeting of the Convention was one of the most beautiful…which any of its participants ever enjoyed."

A Boston follow-up was held later in the month. Lucretia Mott did not make the trip, but sent her sister, Martha C. Wright, to preside. The only other leaders who went a second time were Wendell Phillips and Susan B. Anthony, who tangled again. For the first time, Phillips used the phrase that Anthony would come to abhor: "this hour," he said, "is preeminently the property of the negro." For the next decade, he and others would continually ask women to set aside their own interests for "the Negro's Hour." By that, of course, they actually meant black men: black women were of so little account, even among these liberals, that their exclusion from "the Negro's Hour" was taken as a given.

In a letter to the *Anti-Slavery Standard*—which was still in business long after the Thirteenth Amendment banned slavery—Frances Dana Gage expressed her outrage with Phillips's view:

> When the war-cry was heard in 1861, the advance-guard of the Woman's Rights party cried "halt!" And for five years we have stood waiting.... Not as idle spectators, but as the busiest and most unwearied actors.... We have, as our manly men assert, fought half the battle.... To save the four million negroes of the South, or rather to save the Republican party, seventeen millions of women...are proclaimed a disfranchised class.... Let us never forget his [the black man's] claim, but strengthen it, by not neglecting our own.

The issue became increasingly serious throughout 1866 and 1867, as Congress moved to add the Fourteenth Amendment to the Constitution. The intention of its sponsors was to ensure citizenship and civil rights to ex-slaves, but by then, women were making their case loudly enough that its drafters decided that the word "male" had to be included to make their intentions clear. It was a new thing: as New Hampshire abolitionist Parker Pillsbury said, "The word 'male' is unknown to the Federal Constitution." The point merited attention: the Constitution, especially in its First Amendment, spelled out important liberties such as free speech, free press, and the right to petition, without regard to gender. Everyone from Supreme Court justices to the lowliest female citizen assumed that these rights were not gender specific—as women had, in fact, demonstrated by signing hundreds of thousands of petitions. But many English nouns and pronouns are purposefully vague, with "man" and "human" and similar words applying or not applying to women as the interpreter chooses. What made voting different from these other constitutionally protected rights was that the Constitution allowed states to define their voters. Prior to the Jacksonian democracy of the 1830s, for example, states not only disenfranchised women and blacks, but also many white men on the basis of religion, property ownership, or other qualifications. What changed, as Susan B. Anthony had pointed out, was that the Civil War created a stronger federal role. The Thirteenth Amendment set an especially important precedent when the U.S. government, in effect, overruled state governments and banned slavery.

Now, in the discussion of the Fourteenth Amendment, the issue was enlarged: the federal government was about to define voters—a privilege heretofore reserved to the states—and insist that former (male) slaves be allowed to vote. That its sponsors felt forced to spell out women's exclusion by inserting "male" was in itself an ironic sort of progress, but it was far from satisfactory. The highest priority of the American Equal Rights Association for the next two years was keeping this four-letter word out of the U.S. Constitution.

The association met again in 1867, once more at the Church of the Puritans, and Lucretia Mott made an important symbolic gesture when she several times turned the gavel over to Robert Purvis, a black man. Mott also introduced "the venerable" Sojourner Truth, whose speech was so popular that the audience "called for her" twice more during the convention. A tremendous amount of progress had been made on racial attitudes in the 17 years since Frances Dana Gage overruled her audience and allowed Truth to speak, and it was Gage who followed up her points at this meeting. "Sojourner Truth gave us the whole truth in about fifteen words. 'If I am responsible for my deeds the same as the white male citizen is, I have a right to all the rights he has.' "

Gage went on to give examples of women's need for political independence based on her experience in the South during and after the war. Black women had told her, she said, "You give us a nominal freedom, but you leave us under the heel of our husbands, who are tyrants almost equal to our masters." She reported that black men—following the legal example of white men—had insisted on collecting their wives' income from the Freedman's Aid Society. "Men came to me," Gage added, "and wanted to be married because they said if they were married, they could manage the women and take care of their money...but the women came to me and said, 'We don't want to be married because our husbands will...whip us.' "

Charles Remond, the brother of Boston's Sarah Remond, also supported the women. Speaking as a black man, he objected to Wendell Phillips's "negro hour" strategy and said powerfully, "I repudiate the idea of expediency. All I ask for myself, I claim for my wife and sister. Let our action be based on everlasting principle. No class of citizens in this country can be deprived of the ballot without injuring every other class." That was the point of view the association adopted in a memorial they sent to Congress. It was signed by Lucretia Mott as president and Susan B. Anthony as secretary, as well as by three vice presidents who demonstrated the group's commitment to gender and racial unity: they were Elizabeth Cady Stanton, Theodore Tilton, a white man, and Frederick Douglass, a black man.

Lucy Stone and Henry Blackwell missed the 1867 convention because they were hard at work in Kansas. This new state was different from any other, for many of its residents had moved there in the 1850s as idealists who intended to stop the expansion of slavery into the western territories. It was reasonable, therefore, to hope that such committedly liberal men could see that the women who shared their pioneer difficulties also deserved to vote. So hopeful were some Eastern suffragists that Kansas would become their heaven on earth that some "even made arrangements for future homes…where at last [they] were to stand equal." The state already had sent one encouraging signal: during the first year of the war, Kansas women won the right to vote—but only in school elections. Limited though this was, it was the first suffrage success of the era, and it offered realistic hope that the precedent for full equality would be achieved here in the country's heartland.

While women's rights leaders played defense on the national level, trying to keep the word "male" out of the U.S. Constitution, they played offense in Kansas: the object was to remove "white" and "male" from its constitution. Twelve Kansas women had led the way by organizing themselves into a Woman's Rights Society in 1858. Vermont suffragist Clarina Howard Nichols, who moved to prewar Kansas, offered her experienced leadership, and after nearly a decade of letter-writing and petitioning, the women had some prestigious allies. The first governor after statehood, Charles Robinson, and other elected officials were strong supporters and successfully carried the women's argument in the January legislative session. The legislature put referenda on the ballot for the fall: the male electorate could choose to delete "white" or "male" or neither or both. While black men were more likely than women to win their enfranchisement, experienced activists agreed that Kansas might be the first state to grant women full voting rights. The chance seemed real enough to Lucy Stone and Henry Blackwell that they headed out to the springtime prairies. In a series of letters back East, the two displayed tremendous enthusiasm. Blackwell wrote to Elizabeth Cady Stanton on April 5 "Good news!… Our coming out did good. Lucy spoke with all her old force and fire."

His wife's letter a few days later was not as ebullient, but still optimistic. In reporting the "mean speech" of a lawyer who argued that "if I was a negro, I would not want the woman hitched to my skirts," Stone made it clear that women could expect the same "negro's hour" argument here that they got back East. On the other hand, she also cited a Wyandotte woman who "carried petitions all through the town for female suffrage, and not one woman refused to sign." The campaign's steering committee was headed by the wives of the governor and lieutenant governor, and Stone observed, "It is not possible for the husbands of such women to back out, though they have sad lack of principle and a terrible desire for office."

The sophistication of Stone's effort was well illustrated by her letter of April 20. She asked Stanton to take a "capital article by Col. [Sam] Wood"—a legislator so committed that he had babysat during an earlier women's rights convention—to their mutual friend Theodore Tilton for publication in his nationally circulated *Independent*. Stone cautioned, however, that if Tilton "hesitates," he should not get this exclusive; instead, she listed a string of competitors and told Stanton to send the article to them. Stone was clearly worried that Tilton might adopt the "negro hour" policy and editorially drop women in favor of black men: "If the Independent would…write for us, as it does for the negro, that paper alone could save this State."

Her husband remained as excited as a boy:

> Lucy and I are going over the length and breadth of this State speaking every day.… In an open wagon, with or without springs, we climb hills and dash down ravines, ford creeks…struggle through muddy bottoms, fight the high winds on the rolling upland prairies, and address the most astonishing (and astonished) audiences in the most extraordinary places.… Kansas is to be *the battleground* for 1867. *It must not be allowed to fail.*

In July, Rev. Olympia Brown was the first of the Eastern suffragists to respond to their pleas for help. Although no kin to Rev. Antoinette Brown Blackwell, Olympia Brown had been inspired by her, and in 1864—facing nowhere near the resistance Blackwell had endured a decade earlier—began a lifelong career as a Unitarian pastor. The fact that she kept her maiden name when she married in the next decade went almost unnoticed, and while mothering two children, Brown served pastorates from New England to Wisconsin. The *Kansas State Journal* glowingly reported her debate with an anti-suffrage judge, noting that when the audience was asked to stand if they agreed with her, "nearly every man and woman in the house rose simultaneously."

After this, the opposition never allowed another debate. They preferred to cast slurs on the women in the press—to the point that even supporters were misled. For example, when Susan B. Anthony and Elizabeth Cady Stanton arrived in September, a Kansas woman, Susan E. Wattles, was delighted to hear that Stanton would sleep at her home—but when she found that Anthony would be her guest instead, she was so thoroughly misled by Anthony's newspaper image that she went "to tell Governor Robinson…that I don't want Miss Anthony." As she got to her gate, she "met a dignified, quaker looking lady." Confused and embarrassed, Wattles reluctantly invited Anthony in for tea, and while she prepared it, "Aunt Susan" so charmed her family that she remained welcome for six weeks. The journey to Kansas was Stanton's first trip away from her seven children, the youngest of whom was now eight. She joined the others on the stump—where some rallies ran past midnight—but Anthony continued to hone her behind-the-scenes organizational skills. She stayed in Lawrence, where she planned and advertised meetings, distributed materials, and in Wattles's words, "attended to all the minutiae and drudgery of an extensive campaign."

Among these details was the matter of raising money to rent halls, print materials, and otherwise pay for the campaign. Anthony depended not only on $100 checks from ardent supporters, but also used her longtime tract-sales and lecture-admission techniques. "Our collections," she wrote, "fully equal those at the East. I have been delightfully disappointed, for everybody said I couldn't raise money in Kansas." In fact, sales were easier than in the cities, because "reading matter is so very scarce that everybody clutches at a book of any kind." By the end, as Anthony said, "there was scarcely a log cabin in the State that could not boast one or more of these documents."

Rev. Olympia Brown, a bastion of the suffrage movement at the time this photo was taken in the 1910s. (Library of Congress)

Busy though they were and hard though they worked, the suffragists began to feel victory slipping away before election day. The fact that no one ever responded to Lucy Stone's request back in May that black lecturer Frances Watkins Harper be invited to Kansas was one ominous sign. No one organized the black women of Kansas and that omission—although not noted in the *History of Woman Suffrage*—doubtless hurt the cause. The election came to be defined as a battle between white women and black men, as defenders of the status quo cleverly pitted these two natural allies against each other.

In the tangled web of partisan politics surrounding the election, women could barely gain a foothold. The minority Democrats were supported by Irish and German immigrants, men who usually brought from Europe a conservative view of women's place. At the same time, the Republican Party that suffragists had supported also deserted them. Not only was the party proclaiming this the "negro's hour," but also, they expected to manage these new votes, political-machine style, in a way they felt could not be predicted with women. At the last minute, suffragists reached out to the Irish and actually won more Democratic votes than expected, but, as Stanton summarized, "Kansas being Republican by a large majority, there was no chance of victory."

Still, she refused to count it a loss: with "both parties, the press, the pulpit, and faithless liberals as opponents," the women, at 9,070 votes, did nearly as well as the black men, who polled 10,843, despite all of this support. The sad fact, however, which the women understandably chose not to emphasize, was that these 9,000 or 10,000 votes were out of a total of some 30,000. Fewer than one in every three men had supported women, even in this liberal place.

Susan B. Anthony had moved in with a stranger in Lawrence because, as a university town, it was expected to be most supportive—but she would have been better off to have stayed with her brother's family in Leavenworth. Daniel Anthony was the former mayor, and published a newspaper there, and in the end, Leavenworth—a Democratic Party stronghold—gave the highest margin of votes to women. When Anthony and Stanton left the state on November 14, the *Leavenworth Commercial* paid a long editorial tribute to them, and its analysis of the failed election portrayed their views exactly:

> While negro suffrage was specially championed and made the principal plank in the Republican party...female suffrage stood, not simply as an ignored proposition, but as one against which was arrayed all party organizations, whether Republican, Democratic or German. And yet, notwithstanding this the combined and active opposition of these powerful and controlling organizations, nearly as many votes were cast for female suffrage as for negro suffrage.

More than a decade later, Stanton and Anthony were still hurt and angry when they wrote of their male colleagues: "With arms folded, Greeley, Tilton, Beecher, Higginson, Phillips, Garrison, Frederick Douglass, all calmly watched the struggle from afar.... Of the old abolitionists who stood true to woman's cause in this crisis, Robert Purvis, Parker Pillsbury, and Rev. Samuel J. May were the only Eastern men." Anthony and Stanton would never forget nor completely forgive. A Kansas woman, "Mrs. R. S. Tenney, MD," was more generous and optimistic when she wrote her recollections in 1881. "While the opponents of woman suffrage in 1867 thought they had achieved a great victory," she said, "it was only an overwhelming defeat for a future day, a day when...[men] will be ashamed of the position which they occupied and the doctrines they advocated." That day, however, was much longer in coming than it appeared. Most Kansas women would lie long under its prairies before the victory finally came in 1912.

It never seemed to occur to the Eastern suffragists that one of the reasons why Kansas went down to such dramatic defeat might have been that their effort was not sufficiently home grown. The term "carpetbaggers" was just beginning to be used in the South: it was a disparagement of political influence by people who packed their clothes in a carpetbag (the era's suitcase) and descended on an area to tell long-term residents how to vote. Doubtless many Kansans saw the Easterners who dashed in and out of their state exactly this way. Their votes against suffrage might not have been intended so much against their own wives and daughters as against these outsiders.

That may be the best explanation of why women's first suffrage victory was not in Kansas, but instead came two years later and a few hundred miles northwest, in the territory of Wyoming. So little notice did the Easterners take of this precedent, however, that they completely omitted it from the second volume of the *History of Woman Suffrage* and did not tell the story until the third one came out in 1886—17 years after Wyoming women won the vote in 1869. Even then, the authors were still so oblivious of Western women that their sole source was a Wyoming man, Justice J. W. Kingman, whose report mentioned virtually no female names.

It is axiomatic that the American frontier was always more liberal than so-called civilization. People who went to frontiers were adventurous and amenable to new ideas; they rarely had any stake in the status quo. Women there endured the same hardships as men and the notion of a separate "woman's sphere" was less plausible. Moreover, because there were always fewer women in newly settled areas, men were more eager to please them. Frontier people tended to be more egalitarian, less tied to formal social codes, and certainly less afraid of change. All of that made men more apt to see women as like themselves and equally capable of casting a ballot.

These factors made it relatively easy for the handful of white Wyoming women to ask for and receive the vote when the territory was officially organized. As in Kansas, it was wives of elected officials who were the behind-the-scenes powers: Julia Bright persuaded her husband, the president of the territorial council, to introduce a suffrage bill to the council, which functioned as the upper house of territorial legislative bodies. William Bright was candid about the fact that he "had never been to school a day" in his life, but, according to Kingman, he "venerated" his "well-informed" wife "and submitted to her judgment and influence…willingly." He worked at persuading his colleagues, using as his best argument that making Wyoming unique in this respect would "attract attention to the…territory more effectually than anything else."

His second argument was not based so much on principle as on partisanship: because the governor said he would veto a suffrage bill, Bright encouraged Democrats to vote for it "to show that they were in favor of liberal measures while the Republican governor and the Republican party were opposed." Then, after the bill passed, he led its supporters in lobbying Governor Campbell to reverse himself on the promised veto. Many letters, "particularly from women," landed on his desk, while other women lobbied him in person. He finally decided that "he did not want the responsibility of offending women… or of placing the Republican party in open hostility to a measure he saw might become a political force." He signed the bill, and thereby "drew down upon himself the bitter curses" of legislators who, hypocritically, had voted for it but actually were opposed.

William Bright, president of the Wyoming Territorial Council. (Photograph Archives, Wyoming Historical Society)

Political gamesmanship won for women what decades of principle and reason had failed to do, and on December 10, 1869, Wyoming women became the first in the nation to have an unrestricted right to vote. A repeal attempt two years later was foiled, and the Wyoming legislature also passed other model legislation. Its property rights law allowed women to sue, enter into contracts, and otherwise conduct business on the same terms as men. Amazingly enough, as an inducement for women to come west, the legislature even assured equal pay for equal work in public employment. Esther Morris, one of the women who lobbied the governor, became the nation's first female government official on February 14, 1870. At the suggestion of her neighbors, who "manfully sustained her," the governor appointed Morris as justice of the peace for South Pass City. The pass was a key point between the Rockies on the Oregon Trail, and, at the time, the town was the largest in the territory. The miners and mountaineers who visited its saloons were so wild that law enforcement was daunting to anyone, but Morris, who was almost six feet tall, proved highly successful. She handled at least 70 cases in less than a year without any higher court reversal, and her example encouraged Laramie's sheriff to appoint a female bailiff, Martha Boies.

It was jury service, however, that brought the attention William Bright believed so desirable. When two circuit-riding judges, J. W. Kingman and J. H. Howe, came to Laramie to hold court in March, suffrage opponents included women on jury lists—confident that this would make "the whole subject odious and ridiculous, and [give] it a death-blow at the outset." Women interested in serving were subjected to "threats, ridicule, and abuse…and some husbands declared that they would never live with their wives again if they served on the jury." Howe and Kingman, however, turned the tables on these men who would have overthrown the law through intimidation. Although they personally had not favored women's suffrage, it was now the law; jury service was the duty of registered voters, and they intended to enforce the law. Judge Howe announced to a packed courtroom:

Esther Morris, the nation's first female government official. (Library of Congress)

> It is a great novelty to see…ladies summoned to serve as jurors. The extension of political rights…is a subject agitating the whole country. I have never taken an active part in these discussions, but I have long seen that woman is a victim to the vices, crimes, and immoralities of man, with no power to protect and defend herself from these evils…. The eyes of the whole world are today fixed upon this jury of Albany county. There is not the slightest impropriety in any lady occupying this position, and I wish to assure you that the fullest protection of the court shall be accorded to you.

Only one woman asked to be excused from the jury pool. The first grand jury included six—an unmarried teacher, a young widow, and four married women. "The lawyers," according to Judge Kingman, "soon found out that the usual tricks and subterfuges in criminal cases would not procure acquittal, and they began to challenge off all the women called. The court check-mated this move by directing the sheriff to call other women in their places, instead of men." The grand jury met for several weeks and in the end, the judges asserted, "there was never more fearless or efficient work performed."

That was not the impression given by the national press, however, whose cartoonists had a field day. So outrageous were their portrayal of mixed-gender juries, so insulting were their sexual innuendos on the theme of a jury locked up together, that Judge Howe took the unusual step of refuting the "malignant perversions of truth" in the *Chicago Legal News.* He wanted his name withheld, however, for he was weary of publicity that "I never anticipated or conceived of, and which has been far from agreeable to me." The judge acknowledged that he had been "prejudiced against" this innovation, but now was obliged to say that it had been a success. Women served with "dignity and intelligence" and were "careful, pains-taking, and conscientious," as well as "firm and resolute." Two days after the grand jury began, he said, "the dance-house keepers, gamblers, and *demi-monde* fled out of the city in dismay.... I have never, in twenty-five years of constant experience in the courts of the country, seen more faithful, intelligent, and resolutely honest grand and petit juries."

An 1869 *Harper's Weekly* cartoon ridicules the idea of Wyoming women participating in government "Sorosis" noted on the signs refers to the first women's professional organization established the previous year. (Library of Congress)

In September 1870, Wyoming held its first election since women were enfranchised, and their presence once again convinced the doubters. In Judge Kingman's words:

> The morning of the election came, but did not bring out the usual scenes around the polls. A few women came out early to vote, and the crowd kept entirely out of sight. There was plenty of drinking and noise at the saloons, but the men would not remain, after voting, around the polls. Even the negro men and women voted without objection or disturbance. The result was a great disappointment...to the whiskey shops.... Their favorite candidate for Congress, although he had spent several thousand dollars to secure the election, was left out in the cold.

A Baptist minister from Vermont who came to Wyoming two weeks before the election also felt that he had observed a miracle. He began by saying, "I had never sympathized with the extreme theories of the woman's rights platform to which...I had often listened in Boston." But the Wyoming experience transformed him. In an era when many men unabashedly exchanged their votes for drinks, election days were assumed to be mob scenes. In almost every state, canvassers stationed themselves immediately outside of polls, threatening voters and fighting with each other. Yet this election in a land of "cut-throats, gamblers and abandoned characters" was quieter than those of sleepy Vermont villages; the preacher marveled: "I saw the rough mountaineers maintaining the most respectful decorum whenever the women approached the polls." Judge Kingman added, "No one thought of trying to buy up the women, nor was it ever supposed that a woman's vote could be secured with whiskey and cigars!"

Wyoming's neighbor to the south, Utah, was the second territory to enfranchise women—but Utah women actually voted first because an election was held there sooner. Like Kansas, Utah had an extraordinary birth story. Members of the newly established Church of Jesus Christ of the Latter-Day Saints, more commonly called Mormons, went out to the remote deserts and mountains of the Great Salt Lake area in 1847. They were fleeing persecution in Illinois, where they had gone after their 1830 origin in the free-spirited part of western New York that produced the Seneca Falls phenomenon.

Mormons practiced the same sort of religious and economic communalism that characterized most utopian societies, but they were persecuted for their one great difference: especially after they established a theocracy in Utah, they openly practiced the polygamy sanctioned by the Old Testament. Not only were men free to marry more than one woman, but women's status in the church was lower than in any other religion. There never would be the slightest possibility that a woman would be ordained, for her very salvation depended on a man.

At the same time, Mormon women often considered themselves to be unusually independent. A husband with multiple wives might be away from home for weeks and months at a time, and women ran their own households and farms. Mormon women often earned their own income, becoming proficient in such unconventional industries as silkworm culture. More than most women in this era, they had a sense of sisterhood through organizations and communal businesses. Many adult women clearly chose this life deliberately, for they immigrated from northern Europe to marry strangers in Zion.

Some suffragists saw little reason to celebrate the granting of the vote to women in polygamist Utah. Founder of Mormonism, Joseph Smith, is pictured here, in the center with a beard, with his large family. (Photograph Archives, Utah State Historical Society)

As the nation moved West after the Civil War, however, more and more outsiders settled in Utah. Usually young, unmarried, fortune-seeking men, they had no intention of becoming Saints—but they did vote, and church authorities began to see the possibility that their theocracy might fall, and Utah be filled with the saloons and gambling halls that characterized the rest of the West. One easy solution was to emulate the Wyoming territory and allow women to vote. It was taken for granted that Mormon women would mark their ballots in the way that the church patriarchs commanded, and the nature of polygamy meant that already powerful men could more than double their votes. Thus, early in 1870, Utah women got the vote. They cast ballots in a municipal election, which observers noted was markedly solemn compared with the rowdy behavior of the previous all-male electorate.

Utah's suffrage precedent, however, was not particularly a matter of principle, and certainly not a statement of equality. Although the relationship between Mormon women and the national suffrage movement would improve later, the suffragists of this era did not telegraph their congratulations. Polygamist voters were a corruption of their deeply held convictions, and the official suffrage historians all but omitted this precedent from their second and third volumes. Those 1881 and 1886 tomes, with nearly a thousand pages each, devoted just one brief and largely irrelevant paragraph to Utah's initial enfranchisement. Polygamy, in the view of most suffragists, turned their noble goal into crass hypocrisy. These were not the women they wanted to see at the polls.

Because of the Mormon factor in Utah and because of the small number of Wyoming voters and because they were generally indifferent to the great unwashed of the West—for whatever reason—women back East only rarely pointed to these Western examples. Wyoming and Utah may as well have been on the moon, as most of the nation continued to debate the endless "what ifs" of suffrage as though there were no political laboratory experiment to evaluate.

In the last days before the Kansas referendum burned out in defeat, one of the speakers who attracted great crowds, especially among the targeted Irish men, was George Frances Train. A wealthy eccentric, he traveled back East with Anthony and Stanton. Conversation centered on their tattered ties to Horace Greeley and other media champions of the past. "The editors of the *New York Tribune* and the *Independent* can never know," said the women, "how wistfully…their papers were searched for some inspiring editorial."

Before they had gone out to Kansas, Stanton and Anthony had "an earnest conversation" with Greeley that doubtless was the reason they looked in vain for helpful press. He had asked them to "hold your claims…until the negro is safe, and your turn will come next." They, in turn, asked Greeley to imagine himself disenfranchised; betraying the ingrained prejudice shared by many of the day, they asked what he would think "if editorials pressed the claims of Sambo, Patrick, Hans and Yung Fung to the ballot," while he was asked to wait his turn. They pointed out that they had "stood with the black man for half a century" and should be rewarded at the same time. "Enfranchise him," they added, "and we are left outside with lunatics, idiots, and criminals for another twenty years." Greeley terminated the meeting by telling them that they could "depend on no further help from me or the *Tribune,*" and, the women concluded, "he kept his word."

They clearly needed a viable communication tool of their own, and George Train promised to provide financing. In January—after leaving Kansas in mid-November—Anthony and Stanton began publishing *The Revolution.* They set up an office at 37 Park Row in New York City, in the same building where the Loyal League had been housed. The paper's masthead featured their slogan: "Men, Their Rights, and Nothing More; Women, Their Rights, and Nothing Less." The first edition took editorial positions on a number of issues, many of which had no connection to women, but instead reflected Train's trendsetting notions. As their specialties had worked themselves out over the years, Stanton concentrated on writing and editorial work, while Anthony functioned as publisher and handled the business end. Augusta Lewis (later Troup), who was beginning a career as a labor activist, did the typographical work. With an annual subscription fee of two dollars for weekly delivery, however, *The Revolution's* price was too low to be profitable in this inflationary postwar period.

That was one ominous sign, and another was the name. Harriet Beecher Stowe offered to write for the paper if they would adopt a less inflammatory title, but Stanton and Anthony refused this opportunity from America's bestselling author. A third danger signal was Train's involvement, for his ideas were often so unconventional that sensible women did not wish to see their views on the same page as his. Finally, the paper's editorial support for "educated suffrage, irrespective of color or sex" was a red flag. "Educated" was the key word, for Anthony and Stanton were venting their anger at what they saw as an outrage, as jarring as it sounds to us in 2020: white men's decision to give the vote to illiterate black men who would be managed by machine politicians, while withholding it from women, many of whom knew their country's history and government inside out.

This long-simmering argument began to boil in 1868, as the Fourteenth Amendment was officially added to the Constitution in July. This lengthy amendment begins, "All persons born or naturalized in the United States…are citizens." It continues to speak of "citizens" and "persons" throughout, except for the four little letters "male" inserted into the second of its five parts. The federal government, in effect, was insisting that state governments could not deny the vote to "any of the male inhabitants," no matter if the election were federal, state, or local.

Six months later, a proposed Fifteenth Amendment was the prime topic at what the authors of the *History of Woman Suffrage* termed the first "National Woman Suffrage Convention," that is, the first dedicated completely to women's right to vote. It took place in January 1869, in what had previously been seen as the Southern city of Washington D.C. Lucretia Mott presided, but except for Anthony and Stanton, most of the participants were newcomers to the movement, with Clara Barton as the most notable celebrity. Immediately after the meeting, Stanton and Anthony took off on their first tour of the Midwest, speaking in Ohio, Illinois, Wisconsin, and Missouri.

Congress sent the Fifteenth Amendment to the states, which would officially ratify it in March of the following year. The Fifteenth Amendment was a greater insult to women than the Fourteenth, for its language did not even bother to exclude them—the exclusion was simply taken for granted. A very brief amendment in contrast to the Fourteenth, it reads: "The right of the citizens of the United States to vote shall not be denied or abridged…on account of race, color, or previous condition of servitude."

The amendment was not a legal necessity, as its sole purpose already had been addressed in the Fourteenth. While it was an additional assurance to black men, many of its Radical Republican supporters in Congress also wanted to rub salt in the wounds of their defeated enemy, the white men of the South. They wanted to reinforce the supremacy of the federal government, for Southern governments had to ratify the Thirteenth, Fourteenth, and Fifteenth Amendments as a condition of readmittance to the Union. Even Northern states such as New Jersey and Delaware rejected the Fifteenth Amendment as unnecessarily antagonistic.

The Revolution.

PRINCIPLE, NOT POLICY: JUSTICE, NOT FAVORS.

VOL. I.—NO. 1. NEW YORK, WEDNESDAY, JANUARY 8, 1868. $2.00 A YEAR.

The Revolution;

THE ORGAN OF THE

NATIONAL PARTY OF NEW AMERICA.

PRINCIPLE, NOT POLICY—INDIVIDUAL RIGHTS AND RESPONSIBILITIES.

THE REVOLUTION WILL ADVOCATE:

1. In Politics—Educated Suffrage, Irrespective of Sex or Color; Equal Pay to Women for Equal Work; Eight Hours Labor; Abolition of Standing Armies and Party Despotisms. Down with Politicians—Up with the People!

2. In Religion—Deeper Thought; Broader Idea; Science not Superstition; Personal Purity; Love to Man as well as God.

3. In Social Life.—Morality and Reform; Practical Education, not Theoretical; Facts not Fiction; Virtue not Vice; Cold Water not Alcoholic Drinks or Medicines. It will indulge in no Gross Personalities and insert no Quack or Immoral Advertisements, so common even in Religious Newspapers.

4. The Revolution proposes a new Commercial and Financial Policy. America no longer led by Europe. Gold like our Cotton and Corn for sale. Greenbacks for money. An American System of Finance. American Products and Labor Free. Foreign Manufactures Prohibited. Open doors to Artisans and Immigrants. Atlantic and Pacific Oceans for American Steamships and Shipping; or American goods in American bottoms. New York the Financial Centre of the World. Wall Street emancipated from Bank of England, or American Cash for American Bills. The Credit Foncier and Credit Mobilier System, or Capital Mobilized to Resuscitate the South and our Mining Interests, and to People the Country from Ocean to Ocean, from Omaha to San Francisco. More organized Labor, more Cotton, more Gold and Silver Bullion to sell foreigners at the highest prices. Ten millions of Naturalized Citizens Demand a Penny Ocean Postage, to Strengthen the Brotherhood of Labor; and if Congress Vote One Hundred and Twenty-five Millions for a Standing Army and Freedman's Bureau, cannot they spare One Million to Educate Europe and to keep bright the chain of acquaintance and friendship between those millions and their fatherland?

Send in your Subscription. The Revolution, published weekly, will be the Great Organ of the Age.

Terms.—Two dollars a year, in advance. Ten names ($20) entitle the sender to one copy free.

ELIZABETH CADY STANTON, PARKER PILLSBURY, } Eds.

SUSAN B. ANTHONY,
Proprietor and Manager.
37 Park Row (Room 17), New York City,
To whom address all business letters.

KANSAS.

The question of the enfranchisement of woman has already passed the court of moral discussion, and is now fairly ushered into the arena of politics, where it must remain a fixed element of debate, until party necessity shall compel its success.

With 9,000 votes in Kansas, one-third the entire vote, every politician must see that the friends of "woman's suffrage" hold the balance of power in that State to-day. And those 9,000 votes represent a principle deep in the hearts of the people, for this triumph was secured without money, without a press, without a party. With these instrumentalities now fast coming to us on all sides, the victory in Kansas is but the herald of greater victories in every State of the Union. Kansas already leads the world in her legislation for woman on questions of property, education, wages, marriage and divorce. Her best universities are open alike to boys and girls. In fact woman has a voice in the legislation of that State. She votes on all school questions and is eligible to the office of trustee. She has a voice in temperance too; no license is granted without the consent of a majority of the adult citizens, male and female, black and white. The consequence is, stone school houses are voted up in every part of the State, and rum voted down. Many of the ablest men in that State are champions of woman's cause. Governors, judges, lawyers and clergymen. Two-thirds of the press and pulpits advocate the idea, in spite of the opposition of politicians. The first Governor of Kansas, twice chosen to that office, Charles Robinson, went all through the State, speaking every day for two months in favor of woman's suffrage. In the organization of the State government, he proposed that the words "white male" should not be inserted in the Kansas constitution. All this shows that giving political rights to women is no new idea in that State. Who that has listened with tearful eyes to the deep experiences of those Kansas women, through the darkest hours of their history, does not feel that such bravery and self denial as they have shown alike in war and peace, have richly earned for them the crown of citizenship.

Opposed to this moral sentiment of the liberal minds of the State, many adverse influences were brought to bear through the entire campaign.

The action of the New York Constitutional Convention; the silence of eastern journals on the question; the opposition of abolitionists lest a demand for woman's suffrage should defeat negro suffrage; the hostility everywhere of black men themselves; some even stumping the State against woman's suffrage; the official action of both the leading parties in their conventions in Leavenworth against the proposition, with every organized Republican influence outside as well as inside the State, all combined might have made our vote comparatively a small one, had not George Francis Train gone into the State two weeks before the election and galvanized the Democrats into their duty, thus securing 9,000 votes for woman's suffrage. Some claim that we are indebted to the Republicans for this vote; but the fact that the most radical republican district, Douglass County, gave the largest vote against woman's suffrage, while Leavenworth, the Democratic district, gave the largest vote for it, fully settles that question.

In saying that Mr. Train helped to swell our vote takes nothing from the credit due all those who labored faithfully for months in that State. All praise to Olympia Brown, Lucy Stone, Susan B. Anthony, Henry B. Blackwell, and Judge Wood, who welcomed, for an idea, the hardships of travelling in a new State, fording streams, scaling rocky brinks, sleeping on the ground and eating hard tack, with the fatigue of constant speaking, in school-houses, barns, mills, depots and the open air; and especially, all praise to the glorious Hutchinson family—John, his son Henry and daughter, Viola—who, with their own horses and carriage, made the entire circuit of the state, singing Woman's Suffrage into souls that logic could never penetrate. Having shared with them the hardships, with them I rejoice in our success.

E. C. S.

THE BALLOT—BREAD, VIRTUE, POWER.

The Revolution will contain a series of articles, beginning next week, to prove the power of the ballot in elevating the character and condition of woman. We shall show that the ballot will secure for woman equal place and equal wages in the world of work; that it will open to her the schools, colleges, professions and all the opportunities and advantages of life; that in her hand it will be a moral power to stay the tide of vice and crime and misery on every side. In the words of Bishop Simpson—

> "We believe that the great vices in our large cities will never be conquered until the ballot is put in the hands of women. If the question of the danger of their sons being drawn away into drinking saloons was brought up, if the mothers had the power, they would close them; if the sisters had the power, and they saw their brothers going away to haunts of infamy, they would close those places. You may get men to trifle with purity, with virtue, with righteousness; but, thank God, the hearts of the women of our land—the mothers, wives and daughters—are too pure to make a compromise either with intemperance or licentiousness."

Thus, too, shall we purge our constitutions and statute laws from all invidious distinctions among the citizens of the States, and secure the same civil and moral code for man and woman. We will show the hundred thousand female teachers, and the millions of laboring women, that their complaints, petitions, strikes and protective unions are of no avail until they hold the ballot in their own hands; for it is the first step toward social, religious and political equality.

Anthony and Stanton's newspaper, *The Revolution*. (Library of Congress)

Many of the veteran women's rights workers also saw it as an affront, but for a different reason. They had all been abolitionists, and in the words of Stanton and Anthony, voicing stereotypes offensive to today's readers, they "had labored untiringly for the emancipation of the slaves; but they were opposed to the enfranchisement of another class of ignorant men... to be their law-makers and Governors." In *The Revolution* for October 21, 1869, Stanton went so far as to ask her readers to work against the proposed constitutional amendment:

> All wise women should oppose the Fifteenth Amendment for two reasons: 1st. Because it is invidious to their sex...it reflects the old idea of woman's inferiority.... 2d. We should oppose the measure because men have no right to pass it without our consent.... If women understood this...there would be an overwhelming vote against the admission of another man to the ruling power.... It is mere sycophancy to man; it is licking the hand that forges a new chain.

Not everyone agreed. One might choose not to work for the amendment, many suffragists argued, but to actively oppose it was too much to ask. That was the feeling of Lucy Stone, Antoinette Brown Blackwell, and others who accepted the "half-loaf" argument. They could not bring themselves to work against black men and instead would rally around another amendment for women. In fact, just a month after Congress sent the Fifteenth Amendment to the states—while Stanton and Anthony did their Midwestern tour—Rep. George W. Julian of Indiana submitted a Sixteenth Amendment that would enfranchise women.

When Anthony and Stanton went to the Midwest and appeared to speak on behalf of the entire suffrage movement in opposing the Fifteenth Amendment, other suffragists grew understandably distressed, especially Lucy Stone. She had taken on jeering Ohio frontiersmen three decades ago, after all, and had let her household goods be impounded to protest taxation without representation, which neither Anthony nor Stanton had yet done. Now that these difficult precedents were set and public opinion increasingly seemed to accept women's rights, she saw Stanton and Anthony not only taking over the leadership, but also setting policy without involvement from others. Although versions of the events in the crucial year of 1869 differ, Stone and other Boston-based women also felt that they had been deliberately excluded from the vaguely announced January meeting in Washington.

The conflict came to a head in May, at the annual meeting of the American Equal Rights Association. Almost all of the movement's veterans were there in New York City's Steinway Hall; among the newcomers were Phoebe Couzins of St. Louis, the nation's first female law school student, and Mary Livermore, who headed the midwestern Sanitary Commission in the war. Because Lucretia Mott was absent, First Vice President Elizabeth Cady Stanton presided, which became an issue almost immediately. Stephen Foster, husband of pioneer abolitionist Abby Kelly Foster, rose to object to the nominating committee's report, and specifically to Stanton and her patron, George Francis Train. Foster spoke for the Massachusetts delegation, which included Lucy Stone, as he objected to *The Revolution*'s support for "educated" suffrage. "I can not shoulder the responsibility of electing officers who publicly repudiate the principles of the society," he said. "If you choose to put officers here that ridicule the negro, and pronounce the [Fifteenth] Amendment infamous, I must retire, I cannot work with you."

He couldn't have put it more candidly, and the lines were drawn between the Stanton/Anthony faction and Stone's Massachusetts friends. Perhaps if aging Lucretia Mott had been there, the meeting might have gone differently—it had been less than two years, after all, since Stone and Blackwell had written lovingly to Stanton from Kansas—but perhaps not. Like the Civil War itself, the question of racial or gender primacy was too bitter. Their old ally Frederick Douglass dismissed the women's concerns with: "Woman! why, she has 10,000 modes of grappling with her difficulties." Susan B. Anthony responded angrily, again expressing the racial biases of her times: "If you will not give the whole loaf of suffrage…give it to the most intelligent first." Lucy Stone still tried to conciliate:

Frederick Douglass's support of suffragists went back to the Seneca Falls meeting, but his relationship with Stanton and Anthony collapsed over the Fifteenth Amendment. (Library of Congress)

"Mrs. Stanton will of course advocate the precedence of her sex, and Mr. Douglass will strive for the first position for his.... We are lost if we turn away from the middle principle and argue for one class."

The morning after the two-day meeting adjourned, "the friends of woman's suffrage," in the words of the *History of Woman Suffrage,* met at Brooklyn's Academy of Music. On May 20, a week after what turned out to be the final convention of the American Equal Rights Association, there was a follow-up meeting of women at the 23rd Street home of popular novelist Elizabeth Stuart Phelps, and the National Woman Suffrage Association was born. Its president was Elizabeth Cady Stanton, who summarized, "There had been so much trouble with men in the Equal Rights Society, that it was thought best to keep the absolute control henceforth in the hands of women."

Lucy Stone, whose husband had worked harder for women in Kansas than anyone, did not agree. On August 5, she sent out a letter: "without depreciating the value of Associations already existing," she asked people to respond if they were interested in an organization that would be "more comprehensive and more widely representative." Within a few months, she had a stellar list of names on a call to create an American Woman Suffrage Association. The signers came from 20 states, ranging from Maine to Arizona. In alphabetical order, some of the most notable women were Antoinette Brown Blackwell, Amelia Bloomer, Myra Bradwell, Lydia Maria Child, Hannah Tracy Cutler, Abby Kelly Foster, Frances Dana Gage, Julia Ward Howe, Mary Livermore, Belle Mansfield, Lydia Mott, Clarina Howard Nichols, Caroline Severance, and Amanda Way. To underscore Stone's objection to Stanton's exclusion of men, many male names were on the list. Among the best known were William Lloyd Garrison, Rev. Henry Ward Beecher, Rev. Samuel J. May, and even Stanton's cousin, Gerrit Smith.

The fact that the American association's first meeting was in Cleveland was also telling, for it intended to reach a broader base in terms of geography as well as gender. During the next two decades, its leaders demonstrated their lack of parochialism by holding all of its meetings away from the Boston headquarters at 4 Park Street. It also intended to be more democratic in decision making. The problems of the old organizations could be read between the words of this call, for it included far more specific information on delegate selection and voting rights than ever before. Convention votes would be proportional to the population of the states represented; no votes would be counted except from credentialed delegates; and delegates were required to be "actual residents" of the states they claimed to represent.

On November 24 and 25, the American Woman Suffrage Association assembled in Ohio. It was a truly national group, including even people from the former Confederate states of Mississippi and Virginia—as well as Susan B. Anthony, who was invited to sit on the platform when she appeared in the audience. The constitution both restated the aims announced in the call and outlined the organization's internal structure far more completely than any previous document. Clearly, in the view of these suffragists, the seat-of-the-pants days were over; there was no longer any reason to operate without well-laid plans, open decision making, and other methods of democratic governance.

The same careful attention to detail and image characterized the *Woman's Journal*, which the American association began publishing in January 1870—on *The Revolution*'s second anniversary. As might be expected with the support of writers such as Harriet Beecher Stowe, Julia Ward Howe, and Louisa May Alcott, it was a quality literary magazine. The Boston-based women organized a stock company to provide the venture capital, and it was initially edited by Mary Livermore, whose Civil War memoirs would be a bestseller in the next decade. When her lucrative lecturing career pulled Livermore away, Lucy Stone, Henry Blackwell, and ultimately, their daughter, Alice Stone Blackwell, edited the *Woman's Journal* for almost a half-century.

It probably was not accidental that the year of the split in the suffragist movement also marked the first appearance of an organization devoted to opposing women's suffrage. Arguments on the Fifteenth Amendment, of course, centered in Washington, and it was there that two wives of popular Civil War military commanders, Mrs. William Sherman and Mrs. James Dahlgren, formed the Woman's Anti-Suffrage Association of Washington City. Perhaps their most accomplished member was Almira Lincoln Phelps,

Mary Livermore, the first editor of the *Woman's Journal*. (Library of Congress)

an author and educator who taught at Emma Willard's academy while young Elizabeth Cady was a student there.

Out in the countryside, however, many women seemed to be unaware of these splits between old friends. Susan Wattles, who had housed Susan B. Anthony during the Kansas campaign, was typical of those who were so hungry to keep in touch with other idealists that they joined any available communication network and sent their money off for reading material regardless of policy differences. Writing in 1886, she said:

> I took *The Una, The Lily, The Sybil [sic], The Pittsburgh Visiter [sic], The Revolution, Woman's Journal, Ballot Box,* and *National Citizen*; got all the subscriptions I could, and scattered them far and near. When I gave away *The Revolution,* my husband said, "Wife, that is a very talented paper; I should think you would preserve that." I replied: "They will continue to come until our cause is won, and I must make them do all the good they can."

She was wrong, however, about *The Revolution.* It could not possibly compete with the *Woman's Journal,* and three years after they began their paper, Anthony and Stanton had to declare it bankrupt. The National Woman Suffrage Association would never have anything comparable to the official publication of the American Woman Suffrage Association. For the next six years, Susan B. Anthony would go on the lecture trail, earning $10,000 to cover the debts that George Train had promised to pay.

Old-timer Paulina Wright Davis, who went with the National when the suffrage associations split, was one of the few who recognized a major reason why things had gone so wrong. The underlying problem, she said, was "leaving the negro woman wholly out of the question." Frances Watkins Harper was at some of the breakup meetings, but no one pushed her toward leadership. The suffragists—especially the women who formed the National association—allowed the argument to be framed as an either/or battle between white women and black men. Neither side looked to the obvious mediator: black women. Had someone sent a telegram to Michigan, Sojourner Truth might have come and saved all their souls.

Despite the intentions of its sponsors, the Fifteenth Amendment made a crystal-clear argument for women's right to vote. Its language had no gender restriction, and many women determined to test the word "citizen" by voting. The example had already been set by prescient women who tested the Fourteenth Amendment, despite the word "male." In November 1868 in Vineland, New Jersey, 172 women—four of whom were black—deposited their ballots, but in a separate box because officials assumed they would not be counted. The women—who should have been lawyers, given the acuity of their argument—pointed out that the part of the Fourteenth Amendment with "male" applied only to states that rebelled in the war. It was a brilliantly reasoned case: they were correct in that the second section of the Fourteenth Amendment dealt with readmittance to the Union, while the other sections spoke only of "citizens" and "persons."

This action should have been picked up and pursued by national suffragists, but instead, a brief item on it is buried deep in the *History of Woman Suffrage,* amid tedious pages on the semi-conspiratorial Washington meeting in January of 1869. Deborah Butler reported on her voting experience two months earlier, and her hometown of Vineland, New Jersey, was termed "the only bright spot in that benighted state"—presumably by Stanton, who nonetheless had moved to Tenafly the previous year. The American association's first meeting also had a brief report on the New Jersey innovation from Mrs. John Gage. Although neither suffrage association gave this action the attention it merited and although their votes were not counted, the New Jersey women were exceptionally creative and courageous. Moreover, theirs was the only state in which women could point out that they once had the vote, before losing it in 1807.

Far across the nation, a similar experiment—but with a different and stronger legal basis—also was ignored by nearly everyone, including the ostensible leaders of the suffrage movement. Mary Olney Brown, a pioneer in the Washington territory, told her story well when she wrote in 1881:

> At the [territorial legislative] session of 1867...an act was passed giving "all white American citizens above the age of 21 years" the right to vote. This law is still on our statute books; but like the fourteenth amendment, is interpreted to mean only male citizens.... I wrote to some prominent

> women, telling them of the law, and urging them to go out and vote at the coming election. But...I was looked upon as a fanatic, and the idea of women voting was regarded as an absurdity....
>
> Knowing that if anything was [to be] done someone must take the initiative, I determined to cast aside my timidity.... I [went to] the polling place, accompanied by my husband, my daughter, and her husband—a little band of four—looked upon with pity and contempt.... Many gentlemen tried to persuade me to stay home and save myself from insult. I thanked them...and told them that I had associated with men all my life, and had always been treated as a lady; that the men I would meet at the polls were the same.... Then they begged my husband not to let me go.... After watching the sovereign "white male citizen" perform the laborious task of depositing his vote, I thought if I braced myself up I might be equal to the task.

An election official greeted Brown with a copy of the dictionary, expecting her to "retreat before such an overwhelming array of sagacity." When she did not, and instead made it clear that the definition of "citizen" made her point exactly, virtually all of the men who had assembled to watch the show gave her their rapt attention. "They had heard of woman suffrage," Brown said, "but only in ridicule. Now it was being presented to them in a very different light." Most of them ended up supporting her, but the election judges refused to back down. By the next election, in 1870, she had educated both officials and other women on the law, and women successfully cast ballots in two parts of the territory. In her own area, however, local officials adamantly refused to carry out what legal authorities said was the law.

Because territorial law empowered women, Brown's argument was stronger than that of the New Jersey women, but even their case became unshakable when the Fifteenth Amendment was ratified on March 30, 1870. It was absolutely unambiguous: it spoke only to "citizens," and women were taxpaying citizens. The elections of 1870 marked an important turning point: enfranchised women in Wyoming and Utah went to the polls for the first time; black women in South Carolina, protected by federal troops, cast ballots under the Reconstruction government; and during the next four years, approximately 150 women in all parts of the country tested the new amendment.

Marilla Ricker was the first Northern white woman to test it. A young widow and substantial property owner, she cast a ballot in March at Dover, New Hampshire. Although she voted a straight Republican ticket, the local party, according to the *History of Woman Suffrage,* was "bitter in opposition" against her. She gave serious thought to suing the town government, "but being strongly opposed by her Republican friends, she silently submitted to the injustice."

Catherine A. F. Stebbins, who helped draft the Declaration of Sentiments for the very first convention at Seneca Falls, had moved to Detroit by 1871 and with her friend, Nanette Gardener, went to register to vote. City officials turned down Stebbins because she was married, but after lengthy discussion, decided that Gardener, as a widow, had a plausible case. She cast a ballot in the April election and went on voting for years before other Michigan women were enfranchised.

Perhaps the strongest case for the vote could be made by women in the District of Columbia: because no state government exists there, they could argue that the Fifteenth Amendment directly empowered them. Led by Sara Andrews Spencer and Sarah E. Webster, some 70 women attempted unsuccessfully to register to vote in April. Then, although unregistered, they marched together to polls—and again were rejected. They filed suit in October but lost both at the local level and on appeal to the Supreme Court. At the same time, however, women not only participated in the caucuses that were underway to select Washington's delegate to Congress, but Belva Lockwood—whose admission to local law schools was a current controversy—even received some votes as delegate. This was no personal precedent for Lockwood, though, for she had been elected school superintendent in her New York home of Lockport back in 1857.

Out in California, Ellen Rand Van Valkenburg of Santa Cruz was refused registration and filed suit against Brown County, but both her case and that of Carrie S. Burnham against Philadelphia were unsuccessful. Burnham, who was unmarried, had a particularly strong argument, for her name showed up on a list of taxpaying voters—but when she tried to cast a ballot, it was rejected. Finally, Catharine V. Waite of Hyde Park, Illinois, also filed suit in the fall of 1871, but despite the fact that her husband was a judge and argued her case, his judicial colleague found reason to turn down Judge Charles B. Waite's "exhaustive and unanswerable argument."

The election year of 1872 brought still more tests, including women in Nyack, New York, and Toledo, Ohio. Sarah M. T. Huntington of Norwalk, Connecticut, managed to register, but was not allowed to vote. More strikingly, Sojourner Truth again made it clear that for black women, sexism could be a more genuine legal barrier than racism. Explaining that she owned "a little house" in Battle Creek, Michigan, and that "taxes be taxes," she tried to vote. When an official addressed her as "auntie," she returned the favor by calling him "nephew," but her ballot was not counted.

Nor was that of Matilda Joslyn Gage, who was one of a number of New York women who tried to vote. As she had in Saratoga Springs long ago, Gage overcame her shyness on the platform and joined Susan B. Anthony in speaking almost every day for a month to draw attention to the issue. Once again, of course, it was Anthony who was the media celebrity when Rochester officials refused to accept votes from her and 15 other women and had them arrested. Unlike most other cases, that trial was reported in great detail. Without benefit of a jury, a U.S. district judge found Anthony guilty and fined her $100. She refused to pay and hoped that an appeal would bring both more publicity and a higher court reversal, but the authorities frustrated her by choosing to ignore the unpaid fine.

Anthony was not the only woman punished financially for having the audacity to ask for full citizenship. In 1873, two aging sisters, Julia and Abigail Smith, protested their lack of a vote by refusing to pay taxes in Glastonbury, Connecticut. They went to the annual town meeting and announced their intention, and the town proceeded with legal action against them. While the Smiths conducted well-publicized protests in their pasture, the town confiscated seven of their cows and a neighbor exploited the opportunity to grab 15 acres of their land for a fraction of the value. The latter point is rarely remembered, however, while the "Glastonbury cows" became a

Susan B. Anthony, with a reputation as a strident revolutionary, was so charming in person she came to be known as "Aunt Susan" to fellow suffragists. (Library of Congress)

long-running source of amusement, even among suffragists who should have taken the protest more seriously. At the same time, in a case also ignored by the media, Abby Kelly Foster and Stephen Symonds Foster allowed their Connecticut farm to be sold for taxes, but supporters bought it at auction and returned it to them.

Ironically, in the midst of this long effort to test the right of women to vote, there were two largely unnoticed victories on the right of women to hold office. In the off-year elections of 1873, the New England Woman's Club—perhaps the nation's most prestigious literary organization of women—successfully targeted the Boston school board. Although no Massachusetts women could vote, men were free to elect women to office, and they chose educator Lucretia Crocker and Civil War fundraiser Abby W. May for the city's school governance board. The incumbent men initially refused to accept these new colleagues, but the next legislative session passed an act clarifying that women were eligible, and by December of 1874, there were six on the board.

Philadelphia's action was equally significant: after the Pennsylvania legislature voted down full suffrage (75 to 25) in 1873, they passed a bill making women eligible to hold school offices. Philadelphia men elected two women, Harriet W. Paist and Mrs. George Woelpper, the following year.

Many men who were unwilling to see women involved in electoral politics felt differently about schools: not only did women have long experience in education, they also were thought to be less likely to give patronage jobs to friends or to join corrupt schemes to spend school funds for personal gain. Then, too, there was more than a little class bias involved in this; electing educated, affluent women to unpaid positions was a far different matter from giving the vote, according to contemporary biases, to every giddy girl and ignorant servant.

Nor did this minor victory change the debate on the Fifteenth Amendment, and the last election-year series of tests took place in 1874. Washington women, who had no contradicting state regulations, again had the strongest argument, and more than 60 attempted to register to vote in March. Black women had a particularly sound case that they, like their men, had been empowered by the Fifteenth Amendment, and Mary Ann Shadd Cary offered especially cogent reasoning for herself. She had published an abolitionist newspaper from Canada after the passage of the Fugitive Slave Law and then, when the war began, returned to the United States to recruit soldiers with official support from the governor of Indiana. Surely, Cary argued, this service should entitle her to vote as much as any male former slave who had done nothing for his freedom. Angelina and Sarah Grimké made a similar argument when they attempted to vote in 1870 in the village of Hyde Park, near Boston. They were, after all, the only white Southerners—male or female—to stand up against slavery decades ago. If anyone was to be rewarded with enfranchisement because of the war, it should be they. At nearly 80 years old, Sarah Grimké went to the polls, where some of the Massachusetts men who had burned an orphanage to express their pro-slavery views felt free to sneer at her.

It was a Missouri case that finally settled the issue of the Fifteenth Amendment. In October of 1874, the Supreme Court ruled in *Minor v. Happersett* that a St. Louis official named Happersett was free to refuse to register Virginia Minor to vote. A former president of the Missouri Woman Suffrage Association, she was married to an attorney who spent two years arguing her case all the way to the nation's highest court. Francis Minor was handicapped in that Missouri's constitution included "male" in its voter requirements, and a stronger case might have been made with a state that did not have this crucial word. Suffragists accepted the ruling as their final blow on the issue, however, for even if the court had taken up another case, the congressional intention to exclude women was indisputable.

Minor v. Happersett was heartbreaking. It meant that women had no choice except to conduct state-by-state campaigns—with the fearsome Kansas example to intimidate them—or to overrule the Supreme Court by passing an amendment to the U.S. Constitution, which requires two-thirds of both houses of Congress and ratification by three-quarters of the states. Achieving this daunting degree of legislative unanimity means that an issue is all but passé, and except for the postwar amendments that Southern states were forced to ratify, no controversial subject had yet overcome that tremendous hurdle. Now women, without benefit of the vote, had no choice but to try to climb a legislative mountain that men never had scaled.

To the inquiring minds of the public, perhaps the most attention-getting aspect of the women's movement in the 1870s was the emergence of Victoria Woodhull. Beautiful and absolutely free-spirited, she and her sister, Tennessee Clafin (sometimes spelled Tennie C.), grew up in their father's traveling medicine show, where they learned to wrap the gullible into their charming spells with seances, palm reading, and other spiritualistic techniques. By the postwar era, Victoria had married, divorced, remarried, and established liaisons outside of marriage; she bore two children, but kept only her daughter, Zulu Maude. Both she and Tennessee had been arrested several times for prostitution and various forms of fraud, and they even fled a manslaughter charge when the patient on whom they were practicing psychic medicine died. Their place in history might have been only that of petty criminals, except for the relationship they established with multimillionaire Cornelius Vanderbilt. His wife had died recently, he was lonely, and the women were happy to oblige with seances and companionship. He set them up in the investment world, where the sisters proved extraordinarily successful in stocks and real estate. When they opened a brokerage firm and obviously made money, they became New York City's hottest topic.

In April 1870—before women voted in any state (Utah being a territory then) and without any contact with the organized suffrage movement—Victoria Woodhull announced her candidacy for president of the United States. Most leaders of the American Woman Suffrage Association were scandalized, but those in the National association tended to admire her temerity. Woodhull, after all, was following the audacious example set by Elizabeth Cady Stanton in 1866, when she tested the right of women to run for Congress only shortly after moving to New York City—and won just 24 of some 12,000 votes. The sisters' newspaper, *Woodhull & Clafin's Weekly,* also bore a significant resemblance to *The Revolution.* Like the older paper, the new one covered the range of feminist ideas, as well as nonfeminist radicalism, including the first English translation of the *Communist Manifesto.* As George Train had written much of *The Revolution,* most of Woodhull's material was provided by two male gadflies, one of whom may or may not have been her husband.

Woodhull was politically astute enough to understand that her presidential candidacy was not an attempt to be elected, but rather an opportunity to raise issues. She lit oratorical flames, created an Equal Rights Party, and held a convention to nominate Frederick Douglass for vice president despite his flat refusal of this or any other honor. Douglass, of course, was a leader in the American Woman Suffrage Association, whose Boston-based leadership generally abhorred the Woodhull stories coming out of New York. Perhaps organizational rivalry was part of the reason that Stanton and Anthony initially encouraged this unconventional New Yorker; perhaps it was also that Woodhull was personally charming.

Victoria Woodhull addresses the Judiciary Committee, 1871. (Library of Congress)

When Woodhull went to Washington to testify against the Fifteenth Amendment in January 1871, there was not even standing room available in the chambers of the House Judiciary Committee. Almost everyone came prepared to be horrified, but instead they found a beautiful woman who made an intelligent argument in a melodious voice. National association leadership was so impressed that they invited Woodhull to address their next convention, but, within a year, they regretted the welcome they had extended, especially Susan B. Anthony. Her specialty as the movement's chief organizer, rather than its platform-writer or orator, made Anthony thoroughly aware of how difficult it was to create an image acceptable to enough mainstream members to sustain the organization financially and politically. Woodhull's Equal Rights Party not only subjected the movement to general ridicule; it also lured away some radicals who otherwise would be giving the National their money and energy.

Anthony was particularly outraged when, without permission, Woodhull printed Anthony's name on a call for the new party. She and Stanton had devoted decades of their personal lives and fortunes to building organizations, and, although they refrained from saying so, they held a tight rein on them. At the last meeting of the American Equal Rights Association, for example, Mary Livermore responded to Stanton's behavior as presiding officer: "It certainly takes a great amount of nerve to talk before you, for you have such a frankness in expressing yourself that I am afraid of you." Woodhull feared no one, nor did Anthony. Predictably, the two came into confrontation in May 1872 at the annual convention of the National association. Anthony gaveled Woodhull down, and, as the platform dissolved in uproar, Anthony arbitrarily adjourned the meeting and ordered the janitor to turn out the lights.

But this was not the worst of the fallout from Victoria Woodhull: just days before the November election in which she was ostensibly a candidate, *Woodhull & Clafin's Weekly* broke a story that would set the women's movement back by at least a decade. Despite the fracas at the national convention, Woodhull was especially annoyed by the American association and by what she saw as its excessively Christian sanctimony, so she struck out against it by telling a secret that suffragists in both organizations had tried to hide. She knew for a fact—because she had an intimate, quite possibly physical, relationship with Theodore Tilton—that Rev. Henry Ward Beecher, a former president of the American association, had conducted an affair with a member of his fashionable Brooklyn congregation, Theodore Tilton's wife, Elizabeth Tilton.

Woodhull wanted to strike a blow against hypocrisy and the sexual double standard, but the effect was to boomerang against her. Not that the public wasn't interested—her paper sold out within hours and some paid as much as $40 for a copy—but such scandalous news was not printed in that era, and certainly not by women. Postal censor Anthony Comstock, who would base his long and terrifying career on this case, quickly arrested Woodhull and Clafin for sending obscenity through the mail. The presidential candidate spent election day in jail. Finally released after seven months in the fearsome prison called the Tombs, the sisters went on to a second life in Europe, financed by Vanderbilt heirs who wanted them out of the country. Both again married well—Tennessee even obtained noble status as Lady Cook—and they continued to publish shocking ideas until their deaths in the twentieth century.

Susan B. Anthony and other National association leaders knew that *Woodhull & Clafin's Weekly* spoke the truth, for despite disagreements over the Fifteenth Amendment, they shared long years of friendship with the Tiltons. When Anthony spent a night there in 1870, years after Beecher broke off the affair, Lib Tilton had sobbed out her sorrows. The romance had taken place immediately after the Civil War, but Lib Tilton could not resist telling her husband about it in 1869. They both brooded and raged and told others. Orator Anna Dickinson, for example, wrote in 1872 of Lib Tilton's overwhelming need to confess: "She is very lovely and quiet and beautiful, but she is insane."

The trial lasted more than six months. The all-male jury, overwhelmed by the contradictory evidence, and probably by the knowledge that such male behavior was not uncommon, could not reach a decision. Henry Ward Beecher's reputation suffered no long-term damage, and Theodore Tilton went off to pout in Europe. Woodhull and Clafin, of course, went to jail for merely telling the story, but it was Lib Tilton who became a living example of the era's double standard: excommunicated from the church where Beecher retained his pastorate, she lived out the rest of her days in impoverished shame. Even her feminist friends tired of Lib Tilton, and her name never appears in the thousands of pages of the *History of Woman Suffrage.* All in all, the case proved Victoria Woodhull's point: when female sexuality was the issue, even progressives were hypocrites.

Literary celebrity Harriet Beecher Stowe supported her brother Henry at his 1875 trial. (Library of Congress)

While the trial led to some reform of adultery and divorce laws, it did inestimable damage to the effort for the vote. As Tilton's and Beecher's friends took sides, the animosities between the American and National associations were reinforced. The current president of the American was Mary Livermore; although her popular Civil War image, plus the fact that she was happily married to a pastor, did a good deal to save that organization from the embarrassment its former male president brought on it, it suffered nonetheless. The National cast more than one sneer at the problems of the American and supported Theodore Tilton. The trial obviously drained great amounts of money and energy, but, most importantly, it seriously damaged the public relations of both organizations. Tens of thousands of women who otherwise might have joined their local suffrage associations held back because they did not wish to be linked to such notorious characters as those they read about in the papers.

The presidential election of 1876 was arguably the nation's first genuine choice since the Civil War. Abraham Lincoln barely had been inaugurated for a second time when he was shot, and the rest of that unhappy term was filled by his vice president from Tennessee, Andrew Johnson, who barely survived impeachment by the "radical Republicans" of his own party. The 1868 election of Union commander Ulysses S. Grant was very nearly a coronation; a nation grateful for his military success chose to ignore his alcoholism and lack of credentials. He was reelected in 1872 as the Republican Party "waved the bloody shirt" to remind voters of the war. Therefore, 1876 was the first true contest for the presidency since Lincoln's near-accidental 1860 victory.

The Democratic candidate was Samuel Tilden, a moderately reformist governor of New York; the Republican was Rutherford B. Hayes, a very similar governor of Ohio. The election ultimately became one of the greatest political embarrassments of American democracy. Tilden clearly won the popular vote; he had more than 4,300,000 votes compared with barely 4,000,000 for Hayes. It initially appeared that he won the electoral vote, too, but congressional Republicans challenged the votes from Oregon and three Southern states. Without any precedent or constitutional basis, the Republican majority in Congress created a special commission that eventually, on strictly party lines, awarded every one of the disputed electoral votes to Hayes. With these additions, he became president of the United States by a margin of 185 to 184.

Tilden quietly bowed to this because to challenge it was, quite possibly, to restart the war. In exchange for Democratic acceptance, the Republicans agreed to remove the last of the troops from the occupied South—leaving blacks at the political mercies of their former masters. Twenty years after it began, the Republican Party sold what little remained of its old abolitionist soul to win an election it had lost. The Fourteenth and Fifteenth Amendments that were so heart-wrenching for women soon would mean nothing to anyone, and nearly a century would pass before black civil rights again would be enforced.

The leaders of the suffrage movement, of course, had long ties to the Republican Party; in fact, in 1868, it had reached out to the American Equal

Rights Association by inviting Susan B. Anthony and others to its national convention. Having women around worked wonders for male behavior, and, in the words of the *History of Woman Suffrage,* "seeing the improved tone and manner their presence had given, it was thought best to secure the same influence henceforth in Democratic conventions." A few weeks later, the women took it upon themselves to help "swell the immense audience assembled in Tammany Hall" for the dedication of the new Democratic headquarters. The women were astute enough to keep lines of communication open to both parties, and Stanton even asserted that "had the Democrats…put a woman suffrage plank in their platform, they would probably have carried the election."

From then on, the parties made regular gestures to women, although they never openly committed themselves to suffrage. The 1872 Republican platform acknowledged that the party was "mindful of its obligations to the loyal women" in the recent war; although it had offered little or no assistance, it added that women's "admission to wider fields of usefulness is received with satisfaction." More significantly, rival factions of the party paid significant fees to Anna Dickinson and Susan B. Anthony for speeches during the primary campaigns. In 1876, the movement's leadership generally supported Rutherford Hayes because Lucy Hayes was alleged to be a suffragist. Her presence in the White House, however, would prove another disappointment.

The other great event of 1876 was happier. One hundred years had passed since the American Revolution began, and Philadelphia, the home of the Declaration of Independence, hosted a great centennial. It was by far the most sophisticated extravaganza the nation had ever seen: almost 10 million people visited exhibits from some 50 nations that were housed in 180 buildings. Nonetheless, it was hard to find space for women. The authorities turned down requests from both suffrage associations, and no women of any political persuasion were invited to speak.

The American Woman Suffrage Association, more respectable to many, finally managed to get a small, obscure location in the fairgrounds, but the National association rented headquarters outside. In this, Pennsylvania showed how far behind it was in terms of property law: the women had to wait for Anthony's arrival because, as their only unmarried woman, only she could legally sign a rental contract. The headquarters proved to be a wonderful networking opportunity, as women from all across the nation and the world found each other there. Lucretia Mott, now 83 and just four years away from death, stopped by frequently, leaving five-dollar tips—when that was a week's wages for most women—for "the trouble" of serving her tea.

SUPPLEMENT TO FRANK LESLIE'S ILLUSTRATED NEWSPAPER

No. 1,086—Vol. XLII.] NEW YORK, JULY 22, 1876. [Supplement Gratis.

JULY 4th, 1876.—THE CENTENNIAL CELEBRATION IN PHILADELPHIA—THE SEVENTH REGIMENT, N. G. S. N. Y., PASSING UNDER THE ARCH IN CHESTNUT STREET.
See Page 327.

Cover of *Frank Leslie's Illustrated Newspaper* showing the nation's centennial celebrations in Philadelphia; the newspaper would be run by Meriam Leslie, wife of Frank Leslie and suffrage benefactor, after his death. (Library of Congress)

The fair officially offered a small display of women's achievements, including both the innovative and the mundane. Among them were exhibits by female pharmacy students, the work of a female taxidermist, and Rocky Mountain drawings done by a woman for the U.S. Geological Survey. Some household inventions by women were included, but much of the display simply presented books by female authors.

On the Fourth of July, women determined to do more. Susan B. Anthony and other National association women took over an empty bandstand and read a Declaration of Rights for Women to a receptive crowd. They also disrupted the official Independence Day ceremony by distributing hundreds of copies to the assembled men, many of whom stood on chairs and rushed past each other to get one of the unique publications.

The women expected to be arrested, but instead the day was one of hope—which was also indicated by the declaration itself. Many of the demands they had made in the 1848 Seneca Falls declaration were now coming to be true: they no longer had to plead that women be admitted to colleges, or that they be ordained, or be allowed to practice law and medicine. Instead of educational and employment opportunity, the new document placed its emphasis on political rights, especially the vote. As men eagerly reached out to the women that Fourth of July, there was reason to believe that the words of 1776 might finally come true: that women indeed were among those entitled to "life, liberty, and the pursuit of happiness."

Chapter Five

The Hour Not Yet, 1871 to 1888

At their Chestnut Street headquarters for the Philadelphia centennial, the National Woman Suffrage Association kept "an immense autograph book" for visitors. Greetings "from the old world and the new" in it showed that the women's movement increasingly was going global. Some international links had been part of the movement from the beginning: Scottish Frances Wright had set the example in the 1840s, while German Mathilde Anneke and French Jeanne (Jenny) d' Héricourt followed up by speaking to women's rights conventions in the 1850s and 1860s. After the Civil War, two feminist pioneers, Dr. Elizabeth Blackwell and Ernestine Rose, returned to Britain and helped to spread the equal rights gospel there. For different reasons, African American Sarah Remond returned to the United States only briefly after the Civil War; disappointed with the reality of black life in the United States, she lived out the rest of her life in Italy.

The first attempt at globalizing the women's movement came in 1871, when Julia Ward Howe and Caroline Severance, both officials of the American Woman Suffrage Association, called a women's conference on international understanding and peace. Although most people did not know it, Howe had a long list of literary credentials before she became famous for the Civil War's "Battle Hymn of the Republic." That militaristic song, however, clashed with her own liberal views, and this fame motivated Howe to work for peace. Along with Severance, she helped organize a Woman's Peace Conference in London, and she assumed the American presidency of the new Woman's International Peace Association. Some of the foreign women who signed the 1876 autograph book in Philadelphia probably had read Howe's *Appeal to Womanhood*

Throughout the World (1870) and were part of her loose network, but no one properly up on this in the 1870s.

Another organization that began in the 1870s also would become international, but the Women's Christian Temperance Union (WCTU) had its greatest effect in the United States. Its beginnings were less consciously planned than most organizations: in the winter of 1873–1874, women in small Midwestern towns began singing and praying outside of saloons, hoping to embarrass their men into spending less time and money there. The next year, Annie Wittenmyer, an Iowan who learned organizing skills in the Civil War's Sanitary Commission, linked these gentle protesters together into the WCTU. They met for the first time in Cleveland, and within a few years, the WCTU—which, unlike the women's rights movement, was endorsed by most ministers—would have 25,000 members, far exceeding the older suffrage associations.

Julia Ward Howe (Library of Congress)

The link between the temperance and suffrage movements, of course, was long and close. Although Amelia Bloomer's *The Lily* became known as the first feminist journal, she had founded it to advocate temperance (and her association with dress reform was accidental). Susan B. Anthony also initially worked as a temperance lecturer, and the refusal of men in the movement to allow her to speak at conventions was an important factor in her decision to prioritize women's rights. Countless other women who were involved in the temperance movement back in the 1830s and 1840s saw this goal coming to fruition in the post–Civil War years, and the move from temperance work to suffrage work was a natural evolution for tens of thousands.

The increase in the social and political activity of women meant an expansion of organizations. Until this time, the average woman belonged to virtually no groups; even church-based ones often were considered unacceptable if they were run by female officers. The endless round of meetings that seemed so commonplace for the women's rights leadership was still an unknown activity for most women—but finally, 30 or 40 years after the travel and speaking taboos had been broken by the exceptional, mainstream women began to emulate them. The 1870s and 1880s saw an explosion of organization-building, especially in the North, which came to be called the club movement.

This movement's best-known pioneers were the Boston-based New England Women's Club and New York City's Sorosis, both of which began in 1868. Loosely defined, these groups were either "study clubs" that aimed to give women educational and literary access or "civic clubs" that aimed to improve their communities with libraries, kindergartens, parks, and playgrounds. Most clubs were stepping-stones toward full emancipation and usually did not endorse suffrage, but suffragists almost invariably found them to be helpful campaign tools. Someone within, say, the Peoria Women's Club or the Portland Women's Club would step forward to assist Lucy Stone or Susan B. Anthony when they came to Illinois or Oregon.

An 1874 lithograph published by Currier and Ives; the original caption read, "Woman's Holy War. Grand Charge on the Enemy's Works." (Library of Congress)

Julia Ward Howe, the first president of the American Woman Suffrage Association, was particularly active in the club movement. This cross-fertilization of groups was more typical of the American association, which tended to meet women where they were intellectually and gently prod them into greater politicization. That was not the style of the National, whose leaders were more impatient with the temporizers. To a fairly large extent during the 1870s and 1880s, the American association reached out to mainstream women and men across the country through its *Woman's Journal* and its popular writers and lecturers—Howe, Stone, Livermore, Stowe, and others. Meanwhile, the National concentrated on political action, especially in Washington, where they became adept at lobbying the nation's most powerful men. Susan B. Anthony headquartered herself at the Riggs Hotel in Washington D.C. where the owners hosted her without charge partly because they believed in her cause and partly because she attracted other guests. In 1878, at the request of the National association, Senator A. A. Sargent of California introduced a slightly reworded version of the Sixteenth Amendment: "The right of citizens of the United States to vote shall not be denied or abridged by the United States or by any State on account of sex." This would be the lobbying target until its language finally was adopted by Congress in 1919. It came to be known as the "Susan B. Anthony Amendment," as other topics used up numbers 16, 17, and 18 before the "Sixteenth Amendment" finally passed. Senator Sargent became a hero to the women as year after year, he pushed for adoption, albeit unsuccessfully.

Literally millions of petitions would support the amendment—but at the same time, women also spoke against it from the beginning. In the same 1878 congressional session that Isabella Beecher Hooker and Dr. Clemence Lozier led the lobbying for the National Woman Suffrage Association, Madeleine Vinton Dahlgren, the well-pensioned recent widow of a Navy admiral and leader of the Anti-Suffrage Association, testified against the Sixteenth Amendment. Her objections, she said:

> ...are based upon that which in all Christian nations must be recognized as the higher law, the fundamental law upon which Christian society... must rest.... When women ask for a distinct political life, a separate vote, they forget or willingly ignore the higher law, whose logic may be condensed: Marriage is a sacred unity.... Each family is represented through its head.... The new doctrine...may be defined: Marriage is a mere compact, and means diversity. Each family, therefore, must have a separate individual representation, out of which arises...division and discord.

Dahlgren's supporters, although privileged enough that they were permitted unusual access to congressional chambers, remained few. Many more testified in favor of the Sixteenth Amendment, and they came year after year. This amendment and the city of Washington became the focus of the National association: its annual meetings were held there in January because, as Anthony said, "Congress is then in session, the Supreme Court sitting, and...

[it is] the season for official receptions, where one meets foreign diplomats…. Washington is the modern Rome to which all roads lead."

In 1880, however, the National emulated the American and took its show on the road. The suffragists held mass meetings in Indiana, Wisconsin, Michigan, and Illinois—where they met in Chicago during the Republican Party's convention. It offered excellent networking opportunities, and the women even had an unusual rallying point when the Arkansas delegation to the Republican convention came prepared with this resolution: "Resolved, that we pledge ourselves to secure to women the exercise of their right to vote." It was a happy surprise, for not only was this resolution proposed by Southern men, but also its wording assumed the applicability of the Fifteenth Amendment—women had a right to vote, and the party merely was asked to enforce it. Not surprisingly, however, the resolution was referred to a convention committee, where arguments by Belva Lockwood and Susan B. Anthony failed to move it forward.

The National also sent representation to the convention of the Greenback Party, a party aimed at improving the economy by ending the gold standard, which limited the circulation of paper dollars. Although a suffrage resolution was presented by a female delegate, it was not even spoken to in committee. "Women were better treated by the Democrats at Cincinnati," according to Anthony, "than by the Republicans at Chicago." The Democrats gave the suffragists seats "just to the back of the regular delegates" and even a room "was placed at their disposal." Although the final outcome was the same, Anthony was pleased that the resolution committee placed no time limit on the women's appeals, even though adjournment waited until two in the morning.

Not surprisingly, the new Prohibition Party, which was formed in 1872, was the most welcoming to women. Even if they did not grant women the sort of full participation that Rev. Antoinette Brown and others had desired so long ago, the party's founders had old and strong philosophical links to the suffrage movement. In adopting the word "prohibition," the new party exhibited greater candor about their old goal, for their objective actually was the same as the "temperance" of the Women's Christian Temperance Union and other, older groups. None of the so-called temperance organizations had ever truly promoted the temperate use of alcohol and other addictive substances; instead, they wanted to enact legal bans or "prohibition" of alcohol.

The fledgling party in Massachusetts reached out to women when it first began by inviting them to participate in the 1876 party caucuses and, most surprisingly, its primary. Although it proved to be a one-time experiment and made little long-term difference, this unusual opportunity to vote in a party election did give some women a taste of political action.

Like the official suffrage organizations, the Prohibition Party would never grow very large compared with other parties, but, unlike the suffragists, its men could vote—and they would provide a bloc just large enough to force the major parties to pay heed to them. In the presidential election of 1884, for instance, the Democratic nominee received approximately 4,875,000 votes, while the Republican won 4,852,000. Had even a portion of the 150,000 that went to the Prohibition candidate gone to the Republican instead, he would have won. The party demonstrated that although it was small, it could be crucial—and women were assumed to be a part of it, for the era's politicos took it as a given that if women could vote, they would vote for prohibitionist candidates.

An engraving from *Frank Leslie's Illustrated Newsletter*: "A fair voter besieged by canvassers in Boston." (Library of Congress)

The result was that some prohibitionist men encouraged female political participation—as in the Massachusetts experiment—but only tentatively, and for limited purposes. Most male prohibitionists were so fundamentally conservative that they could not bring themselves to wholeheartedly support this change in the status quo, even if it would mean at least a doubling of their political power. Generally unwilling to concede the injustice of excluding women from voting, they were more likely to push for the "half-loaf" (or more accurately, a slice or two), allowing women to vote in municipal elections on liquor questions only. Elizabeth Cady Stanton, better-traveled and more sophisticated than many suffragists, did not completely share the usual temperance views—but even she was so accustomed to this political alliance that she never straightforwardly challenged her sisters on it. Instead, she was scornful of male prohibitionists who opposed suffrage: "What people might drink," she said, seemed to them "a subject of greater importance than a fundamental principle of human rights." Ultimately, whatever slim support for suffrage that male prohibitionists offered was infinitely less important to women than was the opposition of the liquor industry and all of its powerful allies. Over and over again, women would lose suffrage elections because men were convinced that if women voted, the saloons would dry up. Especially in the West, this belief was devastating to the suffrage movement: already in the Kansas and Colorado referenda—long before the existence of a formal Prohibition Party—suffragists could see the negative effect when men went from the saloon to the polls and back again.

Even in the East, the prohibitionist views that many women held hurt the suffrage cause, and again the problem would grow worse instead of better with time. This was because the movement came of age at the same time that millions of immigrants began changing the national demographics. Prior to the 1840s, when the women's movement began, the United States had been almost wholly filled with Protestant descendants of British colonists. The Irish potato famine and revolutions in Europe began to change all that in the 1840s, as increasing numbers of foreigners began to arrive—many of them Catholic and most of them accustomed to the daily use of alcohol.

The Civil War and its aftermath slowed down immigration briefly, but by the 1880s and 1890s, millions were arriving every year. They came from southern and eastern Europe—from cultures very different from the British, Scandinavian, and German immigrants of the past. Few were Protestant; most were Catholic or Jewish. Virtually all considered a glass of wine to be a routine part of a meal. They were absolutely perplexed by prohibition, and as soon as they could obtain citizenship, their men would vote against it. Add to this the fact that most immigrant men were deeply conservative in their view of women, and a continual clash between these men and the suffragists became a foregone conclusion.

The clash was apparent long before the major wave of immigration and far from the cities usually associated with immigrants. Already in the 1867 Kansas campaign, the immigrant/prohibition factor hurt women. "The Germans in their Conventions," reported the *History of Woman Suffrage,* passed a resolution against liquor restrictions, which they linked directly to women: "In suffrage for women they saw rigid Sunday laws and the suppression of their 'beer gardens.' " The Irish to whom George Train had appealed in that campaign also were fearful that if American women could vote, they would force an end to their ancient pub habits, and so these men, too, voted against suffrage.

An 1869 lithograph by Currier and Ives depicts many men's fears of women's rights: "The Age of Iron. Man as he expects to be." (Library of Congress)

The innate conservatism of both Irish and German Catholics on women's roles was reinforced by church officials. During their 1877 campaign, for example, Colorado leaders Mary G. Campbell and Katherine G. Patterson wrote that the Denver bishop "preached a series of sermons…in which he fulminated all the thunders of apostolic and papal revelation against women who wanted to vote." Like other clergy, he predicted that female political participation would lead directly to the destruction of marriages and homes. Campbell and Patterson, who like most suffragists were happily married, took particular offense at this attack by an unmarried man whose understanding of women and of family relationships was clearly limited:

> The class of women wanting suffrage are battalions of old maids disappointed in love–women separated from their husbands or divorced by men from their sacred obligations.... Who will take charge

of those young children (if they consent to have any) while mothers as surgeons are operating.... No kind husband will refuse to nurse the baby on Sunday...in order to let his wife attend church; but even then, as it is not his natural duty, he will soon be tired of it and perhaps get impatient waiting for the mother, chiefly when the baby is crying.

Suffragists returned the antipathy they felt from most foreign-born men with language that would embarrass most Americans today. For instance, while presiding over meetings dedicated to civil rights, Elizabeth Cady Stanton used "ignorant" as an axiomatic adjective for "foreigner," and she unabashedly told a story denigrating Irishmen whose only consolation for their wretched lives was that they could vote while educated women could not. This kind of language was not limited to women of the National association: Julia Ward Howe, the first president of the American, had complained in an 1869 article on suffrage that "the Irish or German savage, after three years' cleansing, is admitted" to the voter rolls. Male liberals were capable of the same language and of even worse reasoning. The literary giant Oliver Wendell Holmes, for example, refused to support suffrage because enfranchising women would include the Irish women who invariably worked as servants in middle-class Boston homes—and Hannah, he said, already had enough power at the breakfast table.

Eastern urbanites were not the only xenophobes. In the 1870 debate on enfranchising women in the Colorado territory, women there had lamented, but nevertheless accepted, legislative objections that if "our intelligent women" were allowed to vote, then the government would be forced to extend the same right to "the poor, degraded Chinese women who might reach our shores—and what then would become of our proud, Caucasian civilization?" That most of these immigrants were men who might already vote seemed un-noteworthy—to say nothing of the fact that xenophobic American women could join their men to easily outvote foreigners of both genders. As in the case of black women and the Fifteenth Amendment, ethnic prejudice was apparently so great that Anglo-Saxon suffragists were unable even to consider an alliance with immigrant women. Instead of joining with these most oppressed groups, most suffragists preferred to blame their own delay on the public's association of them with these minorities. They allowed decades to pass while politicians used black women in the South and immigrant women in the North as their excuse for the disenfranchisement of all women.

A signed photographic portrait of Abigail Scott Duniway. (Library of Congress)

In 1871, two years after she formed the National Woman Suffrage Association, Susan B. Anthony traveled to the still-wild country of Oregon. Abigail Scott Duniway organized Anthony's West Coast lecture tour in return for "one-half the gross proceeds," which she needed to support her disabled husband and six children. Duniway, who also published the increasingly successful *New Northwest,* founded the Oregon Equal Rights Society in 1870—the same year in which her Wyoming and Utah neighbors first voted and the same year in which the first legislative effort for suffrage began in Colorado.

Mary G. Campbell and Katherine G. Patterson, sisters who wrote Colorado's 1886 report for the *History of Woman Suffrage,* did a beautiful job of describing their land's early history:

> In 1848, while those immortal women...[met] in Seneca Falls... Colorado, unnamed and unthought of, was still asleep with her head above the clouds.... In 1858, when the Ninth National Convention of Women...was in session in New York, there were only three white women in the now rich and beautiful city of Denver. Still another ten years of wild border life...and Colorado was organized into a territory with a population of 5,000 women and 25,000 men.

Campbell and Patterson astutely pointed out that women's best opportunity to obtain legal rights was in the territorial stage, for life during such a regency-type government gave men some experience with living in a woman's world. Men chafed at their loss of democratic rights in territories where governors were appointed instead of elected, and Washington second-guessed every action of the embryonic government. Men who felt they knew best what should be done in their home area instead had to wait for federal approval, and a taxpaying man "could no more enforce his opinion…by a vote than could the most intelligent woman." All of a sudden, these men understood what women were talking about.

Thus, at Colorado's fifth territorial legislative assembly in 1870, frontier men again showed more openness than those in the ossified East. Prompted by his "beautiful, accomplished, and gracefully aggressive wife," Gov. Edward McCook sent the assembly a message:

> It has been said that no great reform was ever made without passing through three stages–ridicule, argument, and adoption. It rests with you to say whether Colorado will accept this reform in its first stage, as our sister territory of Wyoming has done, or in the last; whether she will be a leader or a follower; for the logic of a progressive civilization leads to the inevitable result of universal suffrage.

Colorado's legislative majority that year was "unexpectedly Democratic, and almost as unexpected was the favor shown by the Democratic members." This partisan picture was so much the opposite of what had been expected that the vote for women came to be "characterized by the opposing Republicans as 'the great Democratic reform.' " But not quite enough Democrats fell into the column, and the proposal lost by one vote in the upper chamber. The House rushed to reinforce the loss with a two-thirds margin.

As they had elsewhere, women regrouped and carried on. Talk turned to achieving statehood during the centennial year of 1876, and that became the next target. On what turned out to be a bitterly cold January night in 1876, "a large and eager audience" filled Denver's spacious Unity Church long before the scheduled time. "The Rev. Mrs. Wilkes" of Colorado Springs, who opened the meeting, pointed out that women owned a third of the taxable property in that city, but had no voice in a recent election when men turned down a water system despite pollution that endangered public health. Lucy Stone sent an encouraging letter to the group, as did Wyoming's Gov. John M. Thayer, who declared "woman suffrage in that territory to have been beneficial."

The women once again gathered thousands of petitions, and the next month the constitutional convention for the new state took up the question. With a large number of women watching, "some of the gentlemen celebrated the occasion by an unusual spruceness of attire, and others by being sober enough to attend to business." After voting down both full suffrage and partial suffrage for school elections, the men put the question on the fall ballot and—ten years after the suffragists' defeat in Kansas—another referendum attracted national attention.

Apparently unaware of the strain between them, Dr. Alida C. Avery, who led the Colorado effort, invited both Lucy Stone and Susan B. Anthony; both came, along with Henry Blackwell. Colorado women, however, deemed two Pennsylvanians, Philadelphia's Leila Patridge and Pittsburgh's Matilda Hindman, as their most effective campaigners. None were good enough, however, and women were soundly rebuffed in the fall: about 10,000 of the male electorate voted for suffrage, while 20,000 opposed it. Mrs. H. S. Mendenhall wrote an excellent analysis of her experience canvassing at the polls:

> The day led me to several general conclusions.... Married men will vote for suffrage if their wives appreciate its importance. (2) Men without family ties, and especially if they have associated with a bad class of women, will vote against it. (3) Boys who have just reached [adulthood] will vote against it more uniformly than any other class of men. We were treated with the utmost respect by all except [young men]...destitute of experience, and big with their own importance.... I have been to-day tempted to believe that no one is fitted to exercise the American franchise under twenty-five years of age.... The main objection which I heard repeatedly...was women do not want to vote.... Men were continually saying that their wives told them not to vote for woman suffrage.

That no one would drag these conservative wives to the polls and force them to vote against their will, of course, was rarely pointed out. The movement might have met with greater success if it had stressed this point: that it was neither just nor logical to deprive all women of the vote because some professed not to want it. Instead, the leadership concentrated on convincing all women that they *should* want political rights—heedless of the fact that most women (like most men) were simply too absorbed with their personal lives and problems to care very much about remote issues or candidacies. Given the burdens of most women's lives, it was not surprising that they found it easier to say they did not want to vote.

In 1874, a referendum was held in Michigan, where it was again the governor's wife who inspired him and the legislature to place the question on the ballot. Once more, Susan B. Anthony and Elizabeth Cady Stanton went out to campaign. Michigan's report in the *History of Woman Suffrage* replicated the hopefulness of the Kansas referendum, with the same sad result:

> Everything that could be done…was done; meetings held and tracts…scattered in the most obscure settlements; inspiring songs sung, earnest prayers offered, the press vigilant in its appeals, and on election day women everywhere at the polls, persuading voters to cast their ballots for temperance, moral purity, and good order, to be secured by giving the right of suffrage to their mothers, wives, and daughters. But the sun went down, the polls were closed, and in the early dawn of the next morning the women of Michigan learned that their status…had not been advanced by one iota.

The next big state referendum was Colorado's disappointing 1877 campaign. Nebraska followed five years later. The American association held its 1882 convention in Omaha early in September; perhaps because the monthly *Woman's Journal* announced the American's plans, the National also held a convention there later in the month. According to Nebraska's report in the *History of Woman Suffrage,* Lucy Stone, Henry Blackwell, and Hannah Tracy Cutler "remained for some weeks…and were warmly received." Perhaps the most diligent worker of all was Margaret W. Campbell of Massachusetts: although she never developed the publicity-seeking personality that creates fame, by the time the third volume of the *History of Woman Suffrage* was published in 1886, Campbell had represented the American association in 20 different states and territories. Well-experienced in Midwestern statewide referenda by now, the women went through the same campaign trails and trials as before, and with the same result:

> As the canvass progressed, it was comical to note how shy the politicians [became] to those they had promised assistance.... Towards the close of the campaign, it became evident that the saloon element was determined to defeat the amendment. The Brewers Association sent out its orders to every saloon; bills posted in conspicuous places by friends of the amendment mysteriously disappeared; ...and the greatest pain was taken to excite the antagonism of foreigners by representing to them that woman suffrage meant prohibition. On the other hand, temperance advocates were by no means a unit for support.

They lost 50,693 to 25,756, although few believed that was the true count. Elections then were unlike modern ones in that voters—many of whom were illiterate or only semiliterate—did not actually mark their ballots, but instead deposited preprinted "tickets" with slates of party-endorsed candidates. In this election, the Nebraska women said, "many tickets were fraudulently printed...tickets that contained no mention of the [women's] amendment were counted against it" and even those that used "the abbreviated form, 'For the Amendment' were counted against it." Worse, this would be just one of many future elections controlled by the liquor industry.

Although Indiana had formed one of the first suffrage associations and although Amanda Way addressed its legislature back in 1860, it, too, defeated the suffragists in 1882. Women had lost a legislative vote (51 to 22) in 1877, and they decided to try a different approach in 1882: they worked to influence men to elect candidates to the legislature who were pledged to suffrage. They campaigned for a year; the leaders, who worked with both the National and the American associations, were May Wright Sewall and Helen M. Gougar.

"Large numbers of societies were organized, and many meetings held," according to Sewall. The women "sought every opportunity to reach the ears of the people," even including the campgrounds of religious revivalists. They went to "Sunday-school conventions, teacher associations, agricultural fairs, picnics and assemblies of every name." Even some politicians noticed their unusual ability and, "for the first time in the history of Indiana, women were employed by party managers to address political meetings and advocate the election of candidates." Meanwhile, however, "the animosity of the liquor league was aroused, and this powerful association threw itself against" the women's candidates. Another election—and another innovative political strategy—went down to defeat.

After so much disappointment, the next year brought hope. In the first victory since 1870, women in the Washington territory won full voting rights in 1883. Abigail Scott Duniway went up from Oregon on the big day and with "trembling hands," recorded each legislator's vote. When the victory was clear, she rushed to the telegraph office, "my feet seeming to tread the air," and notified her "jubilant and faithful" sons, who took the front page of her Portland-based *New Northwest* off the press to add the news. "A bloodless battle had been fought and won," she said, "and the enemy, asleep in carnal security, had surrendered unaware."

An 1885 lithograph honoring "the loyal subjects of liberty who paved the way to woman's enfranchisement in the Pacific Northwest." Suffragist leaders are pictured in the upper gallery. (Library of Congress)

When the "freed women of Washington" began to vote and serve on juries, "the lawbreaking elements," according to Duniway, "speedily escaped to Oregon." Although Oregon women "had carefully districted and organized the State, sparing neither labor nor money in providing 'Yes' tickets for all parties and all candidates," it was clear as soon as the polls opened that the opposition was equally well organized. "Multitudes of legal voters who are rarely seen in daylight" turned up at the polls, while "railroad gangs were driven to the polls like sheep and voted against us in battalions." Not surprisingly, the women lost 28,176 to 11,223.

Even the Washington victory turned out to be a heartbreaker. Just four years later, the Supreme Court struck down the territorial law that enfranchised them, and from 1887 to 1910, Washington women, too, would languish without the vote. The case once again demonstrated that the era's courts were much harsher to women than was its average man. While the Supreme Court ruled against women on the Fifteenth Amendment and again in this Washington case, ordinary men in several Western states voted to fully enfranchise women. Even in certain Eastern elections, women were winning some limited voting rights, but the nation's highest court repeatedly ruled against half of its citizens.

Nor would Washington women be the only ones to have the vote and then lose it. Utah's enfranchisement of women continued to be controversial, even with suffragists, because of polygamy. Despite the favorable attitudes of many in the Women's Christian Temperance Union toward suffrage, and despite the Mormon ban on alcohol, the WCTU nonetheless gathered 250,000 petition signatures requesting Congress to rescind the voting rights of Utah women. Their object was to help non-Mormons outvote Mormons by eliminating the women's votes. The petitions had their effect and, in 1887, at the same time that Utah outlawed polygamy, Congress rescinded the right of its women to vote. At about the same time, urged by WCTU lobbyist Angela F. Newman of Nebraska, Congress appropriated funds for women who wished to leave polygamous marriages.

Emmeline B. Wells, a Utah lobbyist who had successfully defended both polygamy and suffrage, was not present when Congress nullified the state's voter law, and she immediately organized a suffrage association to regain the vote. Through their mutual lobbying, Wells had become good friends with Susan B. Anthony and other leaders; in 1874, she was already a vice president of the National Woman Suffrage Association. It was another case in which the National and American associations differed: although the American would not go so far as to oppose Utah women the way the WCTU did, their leaders did not maintain friendships with Mormons either. Even the National did not rally in Wells's absence, for most suffragists feared that public association of polygamy with their cause would be harmful. Thus, when Congress rescinded Utah women's votes, no one spoke in opposition.

The WCTU also displayed its political muscle in Kansas that year: in addition to the school suffrage they had enjoyed since 1861, Kansas women also won the right to vote in municipal elections in 1887. This was much more significant than it may appear, for a community's decision to be "wet" or "dry"—to allow alcohol sales or ban them—usually is made in a municipal election. The WCTU even was active in municipal elections in the South, where suffrage organizations remained unwelcome. In this same year, a Tampa election on alcohol sales was strongly influenced by WCTU women. They served free food and lemonade at the polls and of more than a thousand ballots cast, the nonvoting women lost by just 25 votes. Foreigners were a factor in this election, too, for the alcohol issue was raised after large numbers of Spanish, Italian, and Cuban immigrants were recruited to work in the city's cigar factories. These men were not about to forego their daily wine and beer, and many Anglo men voted with them out of fear of losing their labor.

Emmeline B. Wells (Library of Congress)

So many campaigns of such diverse natures—from municipal and state elections to efforts targeting Congress, the courts, the parties, constitutional conventions, and state legislatures—were taking place in so many areas of the country, with so many people involved, that simply keeping track of them began to be nearly impossible. In 1884, women were defeated in the first of several referenda in Oregon; this election also marked the first national visibility of anti-suffrage women. About 20 wealthy Massachusetts women, not satisfied with sending "remonstrances" against suffrage to their own legislature, also sent money to oppose their Oregon sisters.

Just south of Oregon, women in California were akin to Eastern women in that they supported national organizations while dawdling at home. Although they had the West's oldest suffrage association, formed in 1869, and although Susan B. Anthony and Elizabeth Cady Stanton visited in 1871, progress there was exceptionally slow in comparison with other Western states. Ellen Clarke Sargent, who was married to U.S. Senator A. A. Sargent, saw that her husband remained the chief sponsor of the Sixteenth Amendment, but the Sargents' leadership was in their Washington context, not in California. In 1873, women became eligible to hold school offices, but not to vote for them, and unlike other Midwestern and Western states, California had little to report in the 1886 volume of the *History of Woman Suffrage.*

The only exception was something that most suffragists did not want to acknowledge, for few supported the 1884 presidential campaign of attorney Belva Lockwood. Although she was an Easterner, most of Lockwood's support for her National Equal Rights Party came from the West, and its vice presidential nominee was Marietta L. B. Stowe of San Francisco. Like Victoria Woodhull in 1872, Lockwood did not expect to be a viable candidate, but she had a method to her madness: her Equal Rights Party hoped to elect one member of the electoral college that formally chooses the president and thereby "become the entering wedge." Even that modest goal was not achieved, however, as she won some 4,000 votes in five states—out of 10 million cast. Not deterred, Lockwood repeated her campaign in 1888. This time, the Equal Rights Party met in Iowa, but the Midwestern attention made no difference in the fall, when the results were even more disappointing than those previously. As they had with Woodhull, the leadership of both national associations lamented Lockwood's ambition and audacity, but her response was reasonable enough. She pointed out that Queen Victoria was successfully reigning over a vast empire and responded to critics: "We shall never have equal rights until we take them, nor respect until we command it."

Belva Lockwood photographed in 1915. (Library of Congress)

The American association celebrated the thirtieth anniversary of the first National Woman's Rights Convention with great fanfare, meeting again in Worcester as they had in 1850. They featured speeches by women who had spoken then, among them 70-year-old Abby Kelly Foster. She refused to spend her time reminiscing, but instead used the occasion to denounce the concept of partial suffrage. New Hampshire, New York, and other states recently had granted women the vote for school elections, and in Foster's own state of Massachusetts, "school suffrage" was also a hot issue. She deemed "half a vote" worse than none, but most women disagreed: indeed, according to the *History of Woman Suffrage,* Massachusetts's enactment of school suffrage was plotted "in the parlors of the New England Women's Club." It was motivated by the male electorate's failure to reelect Abby May and other women to the Boston school committee, and its legislative sponsors seemed to believe that women would prevent future losses of such public-spirited officeholders.

For whatever reason, Massachusetts women gained school suffrage in 1880—sort of. Partial suffrage, as Abby Kelly Foster foresaw, made the potential voter subject to the whim of local officials who empowered themselves to decide whether or not to grant ballots in these special cases. "The law," according to state suffrage official Harriet H. Robinson, "was very elastic and capable of many interpretations." Six years after the act passed, she counted at least 20 variants, as tax collectors and voter registrars "interpreted the law according to their individual opinion on the woman suffrage question." Some officials required that women pay the state and local poll taxes. Massachusetts's poll tax at this time was two dollars, or more than a day's wages for most women. Further, the poll tax did not allow women to vote in any races beyond school elections. "In some towns," Robinson reported, women who tried to cast their legitimate school election ballots were "treated with great indignity, as if they were doing an unlawful act."

Incidentally, while American versions of partial suffrage were defined by the type of election—school or municipal or, very rarely, party primary—partial suffrage overseas was more likely to vary by the type of voter. Defining voters by property ownership or by age or (in the case of women) by marital status was an effective way of keeping the vote securely in the hands of the upper class. In America, however, such blatant class distinction was not a political possibility. After politicians had allowed all men over 21 to vote regardless of taxpaying status or literacy, they could not expect to define women this way. Partial suffrage in America, therefore, was determined not by the status of the voter but by the type of election.

A cartoon parodying the supporters of Belva Lockwood, depicted here as men dressed as women. (Library of Congress)

School suffrage continued to be the measure of American progress through the next years. In 1874, Illinois gave a slight boost to women by allowing them to be elected without becoming electors: Illinois followed Boston's example and granted women the right to hold school offices—but not to vote for themselves. Michigan was more enlightened: although it had turned down full suffrage in 1874, it adopted the school version in 1875. Minnesota did the same that year—and, significantly, the new law was passed as a constitutional amendment voted on by the entire male electorate, rather than merely the legislature. Moreover, Minnesota men proved more enlightened than its women expected, for the measure passed by a wide margin: 24,340 to 19,468. The state suffrage association's carefully planned and successful strategy was to appear indifferent. Except for contacting the editor of St. Paul's *Pioneer Press*—who "had quite forgotten such an amendment had been proposed"—to write a few favorable pieces at the last minute, the women made "no effort to agitate the question, lest arousing opposition."

Suffragists were becoming astute politicians, but not quite astute enough for the Dakota Territory. In 1872 in another heartbreaker, the territorial legislature failed to enfranchise women by one vote—that of a man, W. W. Moody, who later changed his mind and became one of the suffragists' best supporters. The territory's position on school suffrage showed a similar change of mind: granted in 1879, it was repealed in 1883—except in 15 of the oldest and largest counties, which demonstrated once again the complex and whimsical nature of partial suffrage. But full suffrage was the object, so in this same year, Matilda Joslyn Gage went out to Dakota to work for inclusion of women in the new constitutions when the territory was divided into North Dakota and South Dakota.

Marietta Bones, the leader of the small movement in the sparsely populated area that would become South Dakota addressed a constitutional convention in Sioux Falls, and initially was successful. She went to every meeting of the elections committee, and at the last, the men peppered her with questions, most of which revealed their fear of prohibition, for three hours. When the committee turned out to be tied on the suffrage question, the chairman voted yes. "After weeks of hard work I had reached the goal!" Bones wrote. "With eyes brim full of tears," she thanked the committee and left to spread the good news. The next morning, to her "utter surprise," the committee recommended to the full convention only that "women may vote at school elections." Bones was both humiliated and angry. "After all our work and pleading," she summarized, "they turned a deaf ear—worse they were dishonest!" Two years later, the legislature did better: both houses voted for full suffrage by healthy margins, but the governor vetoed the bill. Like so many others, Dakota women were discovering that their hour was not yet.

The hour would be even longer in coming to the South. Not surprisingly, its most western state, Texas, was the most activist. In an 1868 constitutional convention there, a committee of five men proposed granting the vote to "every person, without distinction of sex." Although the full convention did not go along with the committee on suffrage, Texas law was far more liberal than that of most other states. Sarah W. Hiatt, reporting to the National association in 1886, said that she had "never lived in a community where the women are more nearly abreast of men in all the activities of life." The 1885 legislature even passed a law "making it compulsory on the heads of all departments to give at least one-half of the clerical positions in their respective offices to women," something that was considered "a victory for the woman's rights party."

All states in the former Confederacy had to adopt new constitutions for readmission to the Union, and Texas's neighbor to the east, Arkansas, also considered enfranchising women during its 1868 rewrite. The proposal caused so much tumult, however, that the meeting adjourned; the next day, the sponsor of the suffrage clause insisted on speaking. Miles L. Langley was from the state's delta country where slavery had prevailed, and yet he declared: "I have been robbed, shot, and imprisoned for advocating the rights of the slaves, and I [will] speak for the rights of women if I have to fight!" His speech, of course, was met with only "ridicule, sarcasm, and insult," and he concluded sadly, "the Democrats are my enemies because I assisted in emancipating the slaves. The Republicans have now become my opponents because…[of] women. And even the women themselves fail to sympathize with me."

Arkansas's neighbor to the south, Louisiana, also addressed the subject in a later constitutional convention. In 1879, over 400 "influential" people signed a petition to allow taxpaying women to vote. They pointed to the favorable influence of women on male behavior at Wyoming's polls, and carefully presented a conservative image. A woman testifying before the convention was quick to "assure you we are not cherishing any ambitious ideas of political honors or emoluments for women." The petition's language was similarly couched: "Surely the convention would not ask these quiet house-mothers, who are not even remotely akin to professional agitators, to do such violence to their old-time precedents if the prospect of some reward were not encouraging and immediate." The only reward, however, was very limited: the convention allowed Louisiana women to hold school offices, but not to vote in these or any other elections.

In Florida, Georgia, Mississippi, North Carolina, and Virginia, the era saw no legislative action at all. South Carolina was more successful: members of the American association managed to get a favorable committee report in 1872 for a constitutional amendment enfranchising "every person, male or female," but it never went beyond the committee. Kentucky women, led by women of the state's prominent Clay family, actually held their suffrage meetings "in the legislative hall" at Frankfort. Although members of the legislature were in the audience along with "the best classes of people," they took no genuine political action. Women in the border states of Tennessee and Maryland were even less active, while an 1881 constitutional amendment proposed to a legislative committee in Delaware was shot down with just two favorable votes. Susan B. Anthony, Elizabeth Cady Stanton, Phoebe Couzins, and Belva Lockwood all had appeared before the Delaware legislature, and the two supportive votes they received made it clear that conservatism and prejudice were not traits confined to the Deep South.

Because partial suffrage was a question of state jurisdiction, and because the National association was dedicated to full suffrage, no half-measure for school or municipal suffrage was ever proposed to Congress. Instead, women concentrated on an amendment to the federal Constitution that would overturn the Supreme Court's 1874 *Minor v. Happersett* ruling on the Fifteenth Amendment. They met their first successes in the winter of 1881–1882, when Congress created a special joint committee "to look after the interests of women." It was not without debate, for some congressmen objected to creating any committee beyond the standing ones, while others objected to doing anything at all, but the measure passed 115 to 84 in the House and 35 to 23 in the Senate.

Lithograph depicting a meeting of the National Woman Suffrage Association. (Library of Congress)

The National association, meeting as usual in Washington in January, went to testify to the new committee, but this time with an updated strategy:

"Miss Anthony…in making the selection for the first hearing…[chose] some who were young, and all attractive…in order to disprove the allegation that 'it was always the same old set.' " Despite their inexperience, these women acquitted themselves well. One unnamed woman made a particular point of responding to Southern congressmen who said their women did not wish to vote, and perhaps because of Anthony's "attractive" strategy, she succeeded well enough that "the member from Mississippi showed a great deal of interest and really became quite waked up." Senator Morgan from Alabama alleged that no woman from his state had "ever sent a petition…or letter to either house of Congress on this question"—but after the hearing, three wives of Southern congressmen thanked the suffragists for saying what their husbands simply failed to hear when they said it.

This committee marked the movement's greatest congressional success thus far. A House committee had reported favorably on suffrage in 1871 and a Senate committee in 1879, but 1882 was the first time that the women received a favorable majority report in both houses. On June 5, Senator Elbridge Gerry Lapham of New York proposed to the full Senate "an amendment to the Constitution of the United States to secure the right of suffrage to all citizens without regard to sex." The Senate ordered a thousand extra copies of the bill because of the unusual interest, but summer drifted on and no floor vote was taken. In the fall, both congressmen and suffragists again hit the campaign trail for state elections, and the precedent was set adrift. Although committees continued to issue favorable reports, never in the nineteenth century did the full House cast a vote on the proposal to amend the Constitution.

The Senate did so just once. On January 25, 1887, for the first and only time, senators cast a roll call vote on amending the Constitution to enfranchise all American women. After "a long and earnest discussion," the women got just 16 affirmative votes; there were 34 votes against and 25 senators who effectively voted against suffrage by failing to vote at all. They hypocritically abstained, hoping that because they had not voted against either side, they could appeal to both.

America, at the time, led the world in questions of women's rights, but the European continent looked north to Britain as its model. English Harriet Hardy Taylor, publishing under the name of her companion, philosopher John Stuart Mill, had explicated the ideas of the United States's first National Woman's

Rights Convention in 1850, and the British suffrage movement thus predated that of other European countries. When Mill was elected to Parliament in 1865, English suffragists began to make their first political moves. The very next year, they experienced a quick victory: the great prime minister Benjamin Disraeli said in Parliament: "In a country governed by [Queen Victoria]…I do not see…on what reasons she [woman] has not a right to vote."

Disraeli stuck with his quirkily announced position and, according to English suffragist Caroline Ashurst Biggs, "backed it up with his vote and personal influence for many succeeding years." Two petitions with more than 3,000 names on each followed up this encouraging news, and the next year, suffrage associations were formed in London, Manchester, and the Scottish center of Edinburgh. In 1870, the *Woman's Suffrage Journal* was established in Manchester, the industrial city where the very first suffrage meeting had been held in 1868.

Things began to move much faster in the relatively homogeneous climate of Britain than they did in America, for it had none of the complexities—prohibition, immigrants, former slaves, or tensions between territories and states—that American women faced. British Parliament first voted on suffrage two decades before the American Congress. Mills's 1867 proposal to substitute "person" for "man" in British voting law lost by 81 to 194, but he did not view this as a defeat: "We are all delighted," he wrote, for the vote was "far greater than anybody expected the first time."

After Mills was no longer in Parliament, the women's champion became Jacob Bright. He refused to let the issue die, bringing it up for a vote an amazing four times before 1874, when famous women such as Florence Nightingale and writer Harriet Martineau were among the 18,000 petitioners. Each new Parliament brought another test vote, and each time the margin was closer. Meanwhile, women won various forms of partial suffrage, including the right to vote in school elections and to hold school offices in 1870. Suffragists then targeted municipal elections: every time a town or village went to the polls, they held a meeting and explained to women the local issues and candidates on which they had no voice. That this clever strategy was never emulated in the United States probably is explained by its quick, and therefore unnoticed, success: British women won the vote in municipal elections in 1882. Scottish women voted for the first time, since the earlier partial suffrage victories had applied only to English women.

Partial suffrage in its many complexities was clearly inadequate, and in the 1880s, women began holding rallies and demonstrations for full enfranchisement. The first was in a Manchester union hall, as British suffragists—unlike their U.S. sisters—understood that working-class women were key to political success. This hall held 5,000 and, according to Biggs, on February 3, 1880, it was packed with "factory women, shop-keepers and hard toilers of every station [who] sat on the steps of the platform and stood in dense masses in every aisle and corner." The strategy was repeated in London and elsewhere, and by 1886, the British electorate had been expanded from three million men to five million men and women.

Although women's rights languished on the Continent, even there hope began to spring. The French female writer known as George Sand had a tremendously liberating mid-century influence on France and the world, and the first international meeting on women's rights took place just two years after her 1876 death. Just as people flocked to Philadelphia for the American centennial fair in 1876, they came to Paris for a trade exposition in 1878, and the first International Woman's Rights Congress met there during July and August. It included representatives from Switzerland, Italy, Holland, Russia, and the United States; the French delegation included two senators and several other officeholders. Sixteen organizations sent delegations; from the United States, Julia Ward Howe and Mary Livermore represented the American suffrage association, while Chicago's Jane Graham Jones and Theodore Stanton spoke for the National association.

Like its Seneca Falls progenitor, the new "organization" did not bother with bylaws and similar formality, but instead plunged straight into the motivating issues. Those present divided their workload into the five categories of women's history, education, economics, moral issues, and legislative interests. The loose structure called for two permanent presidents, one of each gender; Frenchman Antide Martin, a Paris city council member, and Julia Ward Howe were chosen. By the last session of the Congress, more representatives had come: the permanent committee that would carry on between meetings included not only the six countries listed above, but also Alsace-Lorraine, England, Germany, Holland, Poland, Romania, and Sweden. Importantly for internal unity back home, the National association's Elizabeth Cady Stanton and Susan B. Anthony joined the American's Julia Ward Howe and Lucy Stone for the final banquet, and 200 people from at least 12 nations sat down together.

Five years later, on November 16, 1883, the women's movement made its first permanent move toward globalization. Women from France, Ireland, Scotland, and England met in Liverpool and honored Elizabeth Cady Stanton and Susan B. Anthony, who came to share their organizing experience. Like every other good meeting, they began by adopting a resolution: "Recognizing that union is strength and that the time has come when women all over the world should unite." They created committees and decided to follow up five years later, in 1888, when women would be celebrating the fortieth anniversary of the Seneca Falls convention.

Group portrait of the Executive Committee of Women, which arranged the First International Council of Women in 1888. Susan B. Anthony is in the front row, second from the left, and Matilda Joslyn Gage and Elizabeth Cady Stanton are second and third from the right. (Ohio Historical Society)

They did as planned, and five years later, their efforts paid off better than anyone could have ever expected: the women who gathered in Washington in 1888 came from as far away as Finland. Many were recruited by the Women's Christian Temperance Union and its amazingly successful feminist president, Frances Willard. The previous year, a call had gone out from a committee of seven headed by Susan B. Anthony and Elizabeth Cady Stanton, advocating the formation of an International Council of Women. "It is impossible to overestimate the far-reaching influence of such a Council," they said. "An interchange of opinions on the great questions now agitating the world will rouse women to new thought...and give them a realizing sense of the power of combination." They sent 4,000 notices and spent $12,000 on planning for the council, much of it on printing. The 16-page program for the event was duplicated so often that a "low estimate" was 672,000 pages of printing.

The eight-day meeting, which involved far more speeches and resolutions than can be detailed, was an impressive beginning for a permanent body poised to deal with the widely varied status of women around the world. President and Mrs. Grover Cleveland visited the conference, and the speakers included women of color. The women decided that each nation would hold a national assembly every three years, and they would join together for international follow-up every five years. The platform that was adopted spoke to the range of educational and economic barriers women faced, as well as to the burdens of marital and family law. Unlike Seneca Falls, however, this platform stopped short of demanding the vote. Such an encompassing idea of equality was still too radical for most of the delegates.

They came from countries in which the very idea of democracy was still new: after all, only a little more than a century had passed since the United States created a model for governing without a monarch or other supreme authority. That model grew out of the ideas of the Enlightenment, and the words of two of its French philosophers helped prepare for feminist theory as an expansion of democratic theory. Montesquieu, on whose ideas much of the American Constitution was based, presumably would not have approved of the exclusion of women from that constitution. "The powers of the sexes," he said in 1748, "would be equal if their education were too. Test women in the talents that have not been enfeebled by the way they have been educated, and we will then see if we are so strong." Voltaire, whose 1778 death occurred just after the American Revolution began, had even stronger words for his fellow men: "Women are capable of doing everything we do, with this single difference between them and us, that they are more amiable than we are."

Chapter Six

The Century Turns; The Movement Turns, 1881 to 1912

When Elizabeth Cady Stanton and Susan B. Anthony joined Julia Ward Howe in Europe for the initial meeting of the International Council of Women in 1883, they began to perceive more than a need for world unity. The gathering also demonstrated, on a very personal level, a glimmering of recognition that it was time to heal old wounds at home. Stanton's son Theodore, who lived in France, had worked with Howe on peace and progressive causes in Europe, and her daughter, Harriot Stanton Blatch, also urged their mother to look at the wider world and to bury the rivalries and resentments between the National and American associations.

Blatch, who had been living in Europe, returned home in 1881 just in time to review the manuscript for the second volume of the *History of Woman Suffrage*. When she pointed out how unfair it was that the coeditors—all of whom were National association leaders—omitted any recognition of the American association, they allowed her to append a chapter correcting this bias. She returned to England, married an Englishman, and, like her mother, stayed intellectually active while living as a village housewife. Blatch earned a master's degree from Vassar College by correspondence, read the *Woman's Journal*, and urged her mother to move beyond the old animosities.

Alice Stone Blackwell, who grew up helping her parents edit the *Woman's Journal*, did the same. In the year that Blatch was rewriting her mother's second volume, Blackwell graduated Phi Beta Kappa from Boston University—in an all-male class that elected her president. She never married and instead—

like Susan B. Anthony—made the women's movement the singular goal of her life. Together, these two young women urged their pioneer mothers toward reconciliation.

Thus, in 1890, after two decades of rivalry, the National American Woman Suffrage Association was born. Like a household expecting guests, the suffragists began cleaning up their unhappy past before the first international gathering held in the United States. Buried deep in the minutiae of the American Woman Suffrage Association was this item: "Resolved, that Mrs. Lucy Stone be appointed a committee of one from the American W.S.A. to confer with Miss Susan Anthony, of the National W.S.A., and if on conference it seems desirable, that she be authorized…to consider a satisfactory basis of union."

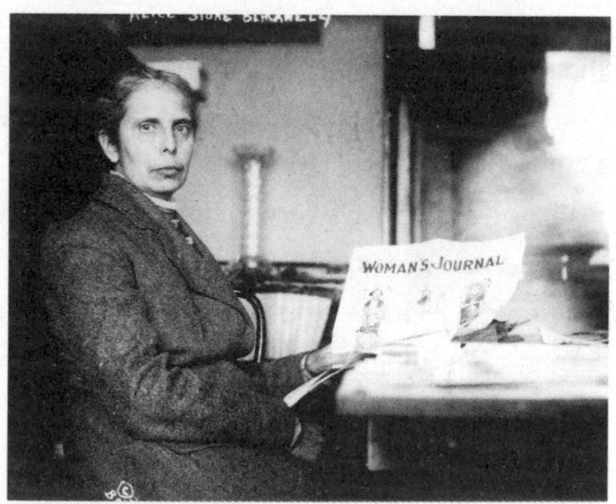

Alice Stone Blackwell and the *Woman's Journal.* (Library of Congress)

An objective analyst must conclude that the American "lost" these negotiations, for the National won on all major points: Anthony successfully insisted that the word "National" be placed first in the new organization's name and Stanton became the first president, with Anthony following two years later. Although they had no publication to offer in this organizational exchange, Stanton and Anthony, as the first presidents of the merged group, also inherited the prestigious *Woman's Journal.* (The National had no publication at the time; Matilda Joslyn Gage, an excellent writer, had issued the *National Citizen and the Ballot Box* from 1878 to 1881, but it was a four-page newsletter and could not begin to compare with the American association's *Women's Journal.*)

Anthony even won on her insistence that annual conventions of the merged association be held in Washington, while Stone chalked up no particular points.

Moreover, it was women of the National who compiled the *History of Woman Suffrage,* and its fourth volume, which covers this era, came very close to not even acknowledging that there had been a merger. Just one paragraph spoke to the change, and it was hidden in the pages on the 1890 National American convention, which followed the 1889 National's report as though nothing differed. Future conventions would be referred to as the "twenty-fifth" or "twenty-sixth," for example, with no indication that the National American was a new organization, not one that dated to 1869.

Perhaps because Lucy Stone was closer to death's door or perhaps because—as the division over the Fifteenth Amendment showed—the American association was composed of women who valued tolerance, Stone allowed the National to be the clear "winner" in the merger. Her husband and daughter both spoke at the first National American convention—and she would speak again in 1891 and 1892—but she stayed in the background at the first crucial meeting of the merged rivals. She let Stanton and Anthony retain center stage and allowed the National to view itself as the negotiation's "winner."

Most women agreed that all were winners when they presented a united front, but a few did not. Matilda Joslyn Gage was perhaps the National association's most stereotypically demure woman, with her stylish wardrobe and her timidity about public speaking, but she became more ideologically radical as she aged, and she did not agree to the merger. Gage feared that the new organization would be too social and insufficiently political, and indeed, her trepidations would prove prescient. Although 66 years old, she did not resign herself to complaining from the sidelines, but instead formed an alternative organization, the Women's National Liberal Union. Always more historically astute than others, Gage had moved far beyond her old friends in matters of feminist theory, and they no longer understood each other. The fourth volume of the *History of Woman Suffrage* would be written and compiled without her input.

Rev. Olympia Brown also believed that her former heroes were too comfortable with the status quo, too willing to spend their Washington winters reminiscing at the Riggs and preaching to the choir instead of lobbying the strangers they needed to educate. In 1892, she formed the Federal Suffrage Association, which aimed at creating coalitions with other, non-suffrage organizations. Although neither Gage's nor Brown's associations would grow very large, they showed that from the beginning there were thoughtful people who viewed the National American Woman Suffrage Association as inadequate to the task that lay before it.

Brown was correct in seeing the need for coalitions with groups that did not specialize in suffrage. In the same year that the National American Woman Suffrage Association began, the club movement that Julia Ward Howe had pushed during the last two decades also coalesced into a huge body: the General Federation of Women's Clubs (GFWC) soon would grow to two million members. It was led by journalist Jane Cunningham Croly, an outstanding writer and organizer who knew that once women got involved in local civic clubs, they would come to understand the need for female enfranchisement from a practical point of view. She worked to help them take this first step.

The Women's Christian Temperance Union (WCTU) also showed suffragists a remarkable model for numerical success. The WCTU appended "World" to its name in 1891, and its first international meeting produced an astonishing seven million petition signatures appealing to governments around the world to control addictive substances. Frances Willard continued as its energetic president and like Croly, she gently pushed her members toward further feminist goals. Perhaps the most striking example of needs beyond the vote was reform of state laws on "the age of consent." This was the age at which a man could argue in court that he was not guilty of rape because the "woman" had consented. A turn-of-the-century WCTU study reported that in many states, the age was ten; in Delaware, it was seven. (See Chapter 10 for more.)

Willard was a particularly important mentor to Anna Howard Shaw, a WCTU employee who later became the National American's president. Licensed in Michigan as a Methodist minister in 1871, Shaw also earned an 1886 medical degree from Boston University, but never practiced either profession. She lectured instead, and her oratorical skill and conservative image appealed to mainstream women. The millions of WCTU and GFWC members lay between suffragists on the left and anti-suffragists on the right—and the latter also grew in this era. Massachusetts women had issued their first "remonstrance" against suffrage back in 1868, when some 200 Lancaster women asked the legislature not to give them the vote, lest it "diminish the purity, the dignity, and the moral influence of women." More than two decades later, the anti-suffragists began their first publication, which, like the *Woman's*

Journal, would be based in Boston. Initially edited by a man, *The Remonstrance* was taken over by a woman who attracted a national audience for the quarterly publication. Funded by some of New England's oldest families, *The Remonstrance* would scold against suffrage until its last losing battle in 1920.

Bostonians in this era unabashedly referred to their city as "the Hub of the Universe," but it was the West that continued to establish the progressive milestones for an indifferent, even hostile, East. Congress demonstrated some of that hostility in 1890, when Wyoming came up for statehood. Although even suffrage opponents had to concede that women had a favorable influence at polling places in the Wild West, many congressmen objected to the fact that Wyoming women had voted for two decades. The territorial government was loyal to its women, however, and insisted on including them as full voters under statehood. The congressional tally was close in both houses, but the state's women won.

Reverend Doctor Anna Howard Shaw (Library of Congress)

Thus, when the National American association began in 1890, Wyoming was the only state in which women had full voting rights. Congress had denied the vote to Utah women with a special legislative act in 1887 and, in the same year, the Supreme Court had struck women's suffrage down in Washington. More than two decades after the suffrage associations began in 1869, they were going backward on this fundamental issue, not forward. Olympia Brown and Matilda Joslyn Gage had good reason to believe that women were losing their cutting edge, but the suffrage associations instead counted their victories in the half-loaf of partial suffrage. By 1890, 19 states had some version of partial rights. By far the most common was school suffrage; Kansas was the most liberal, allowing women to vote in both school and municipal elections—but not for congressman, governor, president, or any office of a very powerful nature.

The suffragists had not come close to achieving the goals they had set for themselves when they campaigned in Kansas just after the Civil War, and so, in 1890, the new organization tried again. They went out to South Dakota, which along with North Dakota, had achieved statehood the previous year. But the lesson that Wyoming women had tried to teach—that the time for action was during the territorial stage—had been ignored, and the campaign could not have gone worse. Farmer and labor organizations that had promised to help—if women would just kindly wait until after their first goal of statehood was won—now had no reason to fulfill those promises. Even though the National American spent $5,000 on this campaign, the women lost by a wide margin.

The language of the South Dakota report in the *History of Woman Suffrage* shows how, instead of joining with the women of oppressed groups, suffrage leadership continued to decry political participation by immigrant and other minority men. At the 1891 convention, Rev. Dr. Anna Howard Shaw spoke of the "much greater consideration the Indians received from the men of that State than did women." While women won only 37 percent of the vote in the South Dakota election, 45 percent of the voters cast ballots for "male Indian suffrage." Shaw lamented that "Indians in blankets and moccasins were received…with the greatest courtesy, and Susan B. Anthony and other eminent women were barely tolerated." At the 1893 convention, Carrie Chapman Catt continued the disparaging theme: she spelled out "the contrast between the Government's treatment of the Sioux Indians, [who are] exempted from taxation and allowed to vote, and law-abiding, intelligent women in the same section of the country, compelled to pay taxes and not allowed to vote."

But women in the Far West inched further forward. In 1892, Wyoming Republicans elected Theresa A. Jenkins as the first fully credentialed delegate to a major party's national convention. Democrats in Utah followed in the next presidential year and elected Dr. Martha Hughes Cannon, who demonstrated her independence from other Mormons by voting for a candidate who had been excommunicated from the church. From then on, both political parties would include women as delegates to national conventions, decades before most women could vote for the candidates that they nominated.

Carrie Chapman Catt (Library of Congress)

It was Colorado, however, that provided the only real ray of hope in the 1890s. In November 1893, Colorado men made their state the second in the nation in which women had full voting rights. Newcomer Carrie Chapman Catt managed the campaign. When Catt joined the Iowa Woman Suffrage Association in 1887, she had life experience far beyond her 28 years. Within three years of graduating first in her class at Iowa State Agriculture College, Carrie Lane was so recognized by her community that she was promoted to superintendent of the schools in Mason City, Iowa. This early career success contrasted greatly with the experience of Eastern suffragists, and the relative lack of discrimination against women on the frontier was a political point that Catt never forgot.

She married journalist Leo Chapman in 1885 and followed him to California—only to discover that he had just died. She worked as a San Francisco journalist before returning to Iowa to marry George Catt in 1890; he signed a prenuptial agreement promising that she could travel for the women's movement four months of every year. Having grown up on virgin Iowa land, Catt understood the pioneer mentality; she related far better to Western men than did the Easterners who had dominated previous campaigns. The key to her victory in Colorado was that she did not allow the damaging prohibition link to develop.

At the very next opportunity, Colorado elected three women to its House of Representatives. In November 1894, Clara Clessingham, Carrie Holly, and Frances Klock became the nation's first women in a state legislature—more than 25 years before most American women voted. The three were liberal Republicans, and both that party and the new Populist Party organized women's divisions for this election. Even the state's Democrats, although they had "no chance of electing their ticket," organized 12 women's clubs in Colorado. Once women had the vote, men took them seriously on issues and as candidates.

In the same year, Wyoming set still another precedent. Esther Reel not only won her race for state superintendent of public instruction, she was the first woman anywhere to win a statewide race for an executive position, and she collected more votes than any candidate in the state's history. Later she would be the first woman confirmed by the U.S. Senate for a national position, the superintendent of schools for American Indians. Wyoming voters continued to elect women to head the state's educational system for years into the future.

A Midwestern victory, albeit a minor one, made 1894 indisputably the best electoral year yet. Because 17 percent of the students at the University of Illinois were female, both political parties nominated a woman for its board of trustees. Illinois women were allowed to vote in this one race, and Republican Lucy L. Flowers was elected over Democrat Julia Holmes Smith, making Flowers the first woman to win a large statewide race. Perhaps overly excited about this breakthrough, 11 women filed as candidates for this position in the next election. Most won only a small number of votes, but they demonstrated how eager women were to participate in the democratic process.

As early as 1889, Susan B. Anthony began to plan ahead to October 1892, when the nation would celebrate the 400th anniversary of Christopher Columbus's voyage to the western hemisphere. Her exclusion from the festivities at the Philadelphia centennial in 1876 had taught Anthony to involve women's issues in national events at the planning stage. Congress was already appropriating funds for a great Columbian Exposition, and Anthony was determined that women be part of the action. She was both astute and humble enough to recognize that such an effort would meet with easier success if known feminists were not visible, and so she quietly gathered petition signatures from, as she described them, 111 "wives and daughters of Judges of the Supreme Court, the Cabinet, Senators, Representatives, Army and Navy officers—as influential a list as the national capital could offer."

Men in Congress dared not refuse the women of their own households, so they created a 115-member Board of Lady Managers, with representation from each state, to oversee women's activities at this huge international event. Its chair, Chicago's Bertha Honore Palmer, was a beautiful socialite who reigned over Chicago's most prestigious hotel, the Palmer House. She also was a shrewd businesswoman who doubled the millions she inherited with sharp real estate investments. Despite her wealth, Palmer was a liberal Democrat who supported suffrage and labor reform. She immediately set about making the fair an exploration of women's status worldwide.

Like male task forces, the board's women had personality conflicts as well as geographical and organizational rivalries, but Palmer held down their clashing egos. Her problems were exacerbated by the women's relative inexperience in such work, as well as by a hostile press and auditors who were excessively suspicious of women's ability to manage money. She even successfully defended herself when Phoebe Couzins sued the board after they fired her as their paid secretary because her inefficiency and self-importance were slowing down their work.

Despite such distractions, Palmer's committee sent out a huge number of letters to involve women from all around the globe. Although several Middle Eastern nations were not embarrassed to respond to the committee's invitation by saying that their women would not be allowed to participate, the general response was terrific. When the exposition opened on Columbus Day 1892, women were in complete control of their area: some 80,000 exhibits from 47 nations portrayed the diversity of women's lives. They were housed in a building designed by 22-year-old Sophia Hayden, who had just become the first female architect to graduate from MIT. The artwork and sculpture were all by women: the most famous contributors were painter Mary Cassatt, who shipped a giant commissioned mural from Paris, and sculptor Anne Whitney, who had won an anonymous commission from the state of Massachusetts in 1875 that was withdrawn when the judges discovered they had chosen a woman. The opening music, Festival Jubilate, was composed by 25-year-old Amy Beach; as Mrs. H. H. A. Beach, she went on to a long career in Europe as a composer and concert pianist.

The only group that had to fight to participate in the expo was black Americans. Chicagoan Ida B. Wells-Barnett, who was developing a national reputation as an anti-lynching activist, received far less of a welcome from suffragists in the 1890s than that which some of the same women had offered to blacks decades earlier. She finally managed to obtain a small space for "Evidences of the Advancement of the Colored Women of the United States" and got a few black women on the agenda as speakers, but she herself was not allowed to speak.

An orator widely recognized by men and women at the fair was the Populist Party's Mary Ellen Lease of Kansas. Known for urging farmers to "raise less corn and more hell," she drew large audiences with her fiery speeches. She also followed the examples of Woodhull, Lockwood, and others this year and made a daring run for the U.S. Senate, even though she could not vote for herself.

The Isabella Association, a group of Chicago women who focused on the role that the Spanish queen had played in Columbus's voyage, triumphed in getting the U.S. Post Office (now more than a century old) to issue its first stamp honoring a woman—albeit a foreigner who never set foot on American shores. The honor also was limited in that the stamp was designed solely as a collector's item. Only seven of the $4 stamps were printed, and they clearly were not intended to be used in the mail; at the time, $4 was a week's wages for many women.

The expo continued until Columbus Day of 1893. In May, the International Council of Women met there, for, conveniently enough, five years had passed since its 1888 convention. Indiana's May Wright Sewall presided over a World's Congress of Representative Women, which drew 150,000 women from 27 countries who heard 330 scheduled speakers. Sewall had traveled two years recruiting speakers, and a 10,000-seat auditorium quickly proved too small. So many women spoke to so many subjects that the printed proceedings made six fat volumes, which were distributed to those unable to come to Chicago. This benchmark collection of information on the status of women in many areas of life and many parts of the world provided both an excellent analysis of the current situation and a motivation for the future. Beyond that, the expo was the best networking opportunity yet. The National Council of Jewish Women, for example, was a direct result, as was the American Nurses Association.

Mary Ellen Lease (Kansas State Historical Society)

Nor were the pioneer feminists neglected. Thousands of women crowded into the reception for Susan B. Anthony during the International Council of Women's May meeting, and Lucy Stone was honored with the unveiling of a statue by Anne Whitney. Stone's speech turned out to be the last of her life. In it, she made a point that at first may seem banal, but on reflection, is crucial to understanding the nature of progress: "These things," she said while recounting decades of women's achievements, "did not come about by themselves." Nothing is preordained, she spelled out; nothing happens unless people make it happen. The great exhibit showcasing women's progress would not have come about without countless hours of work by Palmer, Sewall, and others; women's tremendous achievements in the five decades since Seneca Falls would not have come about without women such as Mott, Stanton, Anthony, and Stone herself. Although much remained to be done, much progress had been made in educational and occupational opportunity, in inheritance and other law, and in enfranchisement itself—and these things did not come about on their own.

The last decade of the nineteenth century was called the "Gay Nineties," and the Columbian Exposition's celebratory spirit was characteristic. The era, however, was not gay—in the older meaning of the word—for everyone, for 1893 brought the greatest economic depression yet. With a huge disparity between rich and poor, it was the "Gilded Age" for one class and the "Age of the Robber Barons" for the other. For women, it was especially the "Victorian Age": as the British queen worshiped at the shrine of her dead husband, the era turned toward social and political conservatism. Its clothing reflected this, with bustles and wasp waists introducing even more confinement and artificiality. Women and men who had been free-spirited abolitionists and utopians at mid-century now turned away from these values. The lawbreakers of the Fugitive Slave Act, for example, protested little as Southern governments effectively overturned the Fourteenth and Fifteenth Amendments—even though idealists had paid a heavy price for these principles in their younger, more morally committed days.

Matilda Joslyn Gage was one in whom the old fires did not die. In 1893, she was not a featured star of the Columbian Expo, but instead was publishing the most daring of her innovative books: *Woman, Church and State* was an attack on Christianity as a primary cause of women's secondary place. Gage moved historically from matriarchal societies to Western civilization, in which permanent subordination of half of the population was viewed as divinely ordained because Eve ate a forbidden fruit. Not surprisingly, members of the Woman's Christian Temperance Union and others were appalled at the book, and most suffragists rushed to distance themselves from it.

Two years later, Elizabeth Cady Stanton—who had been saying much the same thing for decades—echoed Gage's ideas in her *Woman's Bible.* Both her book and Gage's were widely read, but Gage's was not as upsetting to suffragists, perhaps because she had already broken from the National American association. Stanton, on the other hand, was one of its two most visible leaders. At the 1896 annual convention, National American vice president Rev. Anna Howard Shaw introduced a resolution condemning Stanton's book and disassociating the organization from its former president. The "long and animated" debate replayed the arguments between Ernestine Rose and Rev. Antoinette Brown Blackwell decades earlier, and most of the longtime members spoke against Stanton. Susan B. Anthony was virtually alone in arguing against the resolution; she made an eloquent plea to her membership on behalf of her old friend's right to free speech, but the condemning motion passed 53–41.

The old warhorses were being pushed out, both because of their ideas and the natural effects of wearied lifetimes. Lucy Stone died in October 1893, just months after she spoke at the Columbian Exposition. Matilda Joslyn Gage, whose son-in-law wrote *The Wizard of Oz*, died in 1898 while she was writing a speech for the fiftieth anniversary of the Seneca Falls convention. While suffragists were celebrating that anniversary, they received news of Frances Willard's death. Memorial services became a standard part of the National American's meetings. Among those eulogized at its first convention were Amy Post, a Seneca Falls founder; Prudence Crandall Philleo, who had withstood assault in the 1830s when she opened a Connecticut school for black girls; and the famed astronomer Maria Mitchell. Pioneer suffragist Ernestine Rose was remembered in 1893, along with Abby Hopper Gibbons, who sheltered the runaway wife of a Massachusetts senator. In 1896, Frederick Douglass's grandson played the violin in his memory, and the 1897 convention records say sadly, "There never had been so many deaths in the ranks as during the past year." More than 45 names were called, including Hannah Tracy Cutler of Illinois, a former president of the American association; Elizabeth M'Clintock Phillips, a signer of the Seneca Falls declaration; and the immortal Harriet Beecher Stowe.

In contrast to these dedicated lives, the young women with commissions at the Columbian Expo did not involve themselves with the suffrage movement. A sense of futility seemed to grip many of its aging leaders. They had given their time and money to the cause since forever; they were tired, and their efforts appeared more and more mechanical, a repetition of past practices that seemed to expect—and got—the same negative results. Congress signaled this negativity in 1893, when they issued the last favorable committee report on suffrage for two decades.

Every year, between 1893 and 1913, suffragists went through the motions of introducing the constitutional amendment and watching it die. Even in 1898, when they put extra effort into the House Judiciary Committee hearings because the year marked the fiftieth anniversary of the Seneca Falls convention, the women did not seem to expect a positive result. The fourth volume of the *History of Woman Suffrage* details the speeches—including some by female elected officials in Western states—but the long section ends with: "The chairman said that in all the years there had never been so dignified, logical, and perfectly managed a hearing." No one demanded that the congressmen take a vote, no one expressed outrage that the committee planned no report to the full House. The second generation of suffragists simply was not as fiery as the first had been in their youth, and this is particularly clear in the official history. Without input from Stanton and Gage, its fourth volume devotes an excessive amount of attention to pageantry, pomp, and even floral decorations.

The volume is organized by annual conventions, and four years after the merger, the National American association changed its policy on holding all of them in Washington. Anthony had been obdurate on this point, even in 1893, when most wanted the meeting to be in Chicago because they would be going there for the expo and the International Council. At Anthony's insistence, it was held as usual in Washington in January, but leaders from the old American association moved to have future meetings outside of the capital in alternate years. Anthony made a self-described "forcible speech" against this: "Our younger women," she said, "naturally cannot appreciate the vast amount of work done here in Washington in the last twenty-five years." Not surprisingly, her tone alienated enough delegates that she lost the vote, and future conventions would be held in Washington only every other year.

Thus, in 1895, the National American not only held its first major convention outside of Washington, but also—marking a first for any suffrage association—went to the Deep South, to Atlanta. For years, convention minutes had said that the organization would prioritize the South; the following year, instead of a follow-up report, there would be another note of intention. When the suffragists finally did make the move, some delegates made a particular point of attending, with some, such as Oregon's Abigail Scott Duniway, coming thousands of miles. At the meeting, 28 states were represented. Southern states took the opportunity to send an extraordinary number of delegates, including a

New Orleans cousin of former Confederate President Jefferson Davis, who sat on the platform and shocked the audience with her short haircut.

The object of holding a convention in the South, of course, was to organize women there, but much like the National American itself, Southern suffrage associations tended to be excessively dominated by a few strong women and insufficiently broad-based to garner genuine political support. Florida was a perfect example: just after the Civil War, one of the National association's vice presidents was physician Esther Hill Hawk, who ostensibly represented Florida. In fact, she was from Massachusetts, and, after her Reconstruction work was over, Dr. Hawk spent only winters in Florida. Tampa's Eleanor Chamberlain represented some 100 members of the state suffrage association—but when she moved to the Midwest, the state association again evaporated. Even Anthony sometimes reinforced such personalization: when she introduced Chamberlain to the Atlanta audience, she did not speak of political action in Florida, but instead thanked her for oranges that Chamberlain sent from Tampa to Rochester. A few years later, Anthony would visit Anna Howard Shaw's winter home in Florida, but neither took the organizing opportunity.

While Anthony was in Atlanta, women back in her home state were organizing the New York Association Opposed to Woman Suffrage. Linked to the previously existing groups in Boston and Washington, the anti-suffragists began to build a network that eventually included women in 19 states. They were happy to publicize the 1897 conversion of erstwhile feminist Phoebe Couzins to their side; it did not matter to them when suffragists pointed out that the United Brewers Association had bought Couzins by offering her a job as their lobbyist. Most anti-suffragists continued to be women married to wealthy men, and some did not hesitate to openly state that the reason they opposed the vote was that they wanted to keep their servants and other working-class and black women in their secondary place. They were also effective at inculcating these conservative views in their daughters: an 1898 survey of students at Radcliffe College—which, until 1894, was commonly called "Harvard Annex"—found just 2 of 72 young women who were willing to say that they wanted the vote.

Opposition to suffrage was strongest in Eastern urban areas. This headquarters was in New York City. (Library of Congress)

It appeared that the National American and its great leader, Susan B. Anthony, were indeed losing their political edge, but they continued to work hard—especially given their age. At 75, Anthony spent much of 1895 in California, where women finally were holding the first suffrage referendum in this oldest Western state. The National American poured more resources into California than any campaign thus far—about $19,000. Anthony hired California journalist Ida Husted Harper as the campaign's publicist. As in Kansas and so many other places, the women thought they were winning—and they probably were ahead—until the liquor industry poured big dollars into a last-minute campaign against them. California went down by 26,744 votes out of 247,454 cast; a change of just slightly more than 13,000 votes would have carried it. The women had editorial support from some 250 newspapers, but most were small compared with the opposing *San Francisco Chronicle* and *Los Angeles Times.* Instead of following up on this near victory, however, Harper moved to Rochester with Anthony, where she worked on her biography and on the fourth volume of the *History of Woman Suffrage.*

A quieter campaign with less outside influence, on the other hand, proved successful in the same year in Idaho. Oregon's Abigail Scott Duniway had prepared the way in the decades prior to statehood in 1890, for many Idahoans subscribed to her *New Northwest.* The National American sent Carrie Chapman Catt to run her second statewide campaign here in 1896, and she won by an amazing margin: 122,126 for, 5,844 against. It gave Catt a 2–0 record, for she also had won the Colorado victory, and she was demonstrably the movement's best political organizer. However, the leaders who lost California did not seem to grasp the point that Catt's work effectively made: Western men would never vote for suffrage as long as Eastern women dominated campaigns and linked them to prohibition.

The Idaho referendum was also significant because, for the first time ever, a court sustained the women's victory instead of snatching it away. Anti-suffragists sued to overturn the election: they argued that instead of a majority on this issue (which women won), a constitutional amendment required a majority of all who voted in any aspect of the election (which they would have lost). Idaho's Supreme Court ruled unanimously that this legalism had not applied in other elections and would not in this one.

It was also a good year in Colorado, which elected three more women—all from minor parties—to its legislature. Moreover, Utah women finally regained the vote in 1896, when the Mormon Church renounced polygamy in exchange for statehood. Utah set another precedent this year when Dr. Martha Hughes Cannon became the first woman in the nation elected to a state senate. A physician, she was also the fourth wife of a Mormon official and had once exiled herself in England to protect him from arrest on polygamy charges. No dependent harem member, however, she ran against him for this senate seat: she was a Democrat and he a Republican, and she won.

Martha Hughes Cannon (Utah State Historical Society)

With enfranchisement in four Western states—Wyoming, Utah, Colorado, and Idaho—1896 marked the high point of the century. All of them were small states in terms of population, however, with little influence in Washington, and none of their victories had involved significant help from feminism's pioneers. Perhaps because they saw that local women were better off without an intense national presence or (more likely) because they were so dispirited by the California loss, the National American association cut back on state organizing, as well as on congressional lobbying. During the next 14 years, just six referenda would be held; with the exception of New Hampshire, all were in the West, and all lost. Even in the more open-minded West, the turn of the century was an age of conservatism.

In January 1898, suffragists celebrated the fiftieth anniversary of the Seneca Falls convention in Washington, even displaying the table on which the 1848 declaration had been written. The convention's attendance was the best ever: all but four of the states and territories were represented and many international groups sent congratulatory letters. Among those present from the second generation of leaders were Utah Sen. Martha Hughes Cannon, Colorado Rep. Martha A. B. Conine, and Wyoming's state superintendent of public instruction Esther Reel. Abigail Bush, the first woman to preside at a women's rights convention, was unable to travel from her new home in California, but she sent a letter: "You will bear me witness," Bush said, "that the state of society is very different from what it was fifty years ago."

Bush was right, of course—even if full enfranchisement was slow in coming, many other barriers had fallen. The 1848 Declaration of Rights, for instance, had said that man denied to woman "the facilities for obtaining a thorough education, all colleges being closed against her" and that "as a teacher of theology, medicine, or law, she is unknown," but 50 years later, thousands of women were establishing themselves in all professional fields. Even if Radcliffe students were too timorous to stand up for the vote, at least they viewed college as routine for women. Although the states of Washington and South Dakota again voted suffrage down in 1898, the margin of loss was much narrower. The territories of Arizona and Oklahoma also stopped suffrage in their upper chambers, but the margins in lower chambers had been excellent. Progress, the women understood after five decades, is typically piecemeal.

In the last year of the century, the National American held its convention in Michigan, where Sojourner Truth had been buried in 1883. Unfortunately, in at least one way, the convention seemed to be heading backward. Where Truth had been a beloved attraction at suffrage meetings decades earlier, her intellectual heirs at this meeting were barely tolerated. Unlike most states, Michigan's chapter of the National American association was integrated, but when "light-skinned" African American Lottie Wilson Jackson offered a resolution "that colored women ought not be compelled to ride in the smoking cars" of the era's segregated trains, her point was not accepted. "We women are a helpless, disenfranchised class," Susan B. Anthony argued from the platform. "It is not for us to go passing resolutions against railroad corporations or anybody else," she said. After "a lively discussion," Jackson's motion was "tabled as being outside of the province of the convention."

Issues of color and culture sparked an unusual amount of discussion at this convention, but it was not African Americans in their own country that concerned the delegates: it was people in territories newly acquired after the Spanish-American War. In the same way they responded to the Fifteenth Amendment, suffrage leadership was insulted that men in Puerto Rico, Cuba, and the Philippines might be enfranchised while they were not. Even Henry Blackwell—who had risked his life to end slavery and who had supported the Fifteenth Amendment at the cost of friendships—did not argue for these males. If anyone should vote in the Philippines, he argued, it should be the women:

> Their social status ranges from barbarous promiscuity to Moslem polygamy.... But everywhere exist masculine domination and feminine subjection.... Let no one imagine that the so-called "matriarchate" of early ages was an ideal condition. It was based primarily upon the... irresponsibility of men.... Such women, even more than those of our own States, will need the ballot as a means of self-protection.

Susan B. Anthony responded that since these territories were acquired, she had been thinking of "how to save not them, but ourselves, from disgrace." Advocating her longtime position in favor of "educated suffrage," she followed up after the meeting by working for the vote for women, as well as men, in Hawaii—the one new territory she viewed as sufficiently educated. Its native culture granted women high status in government and religion, and for decades

Protestant missionaries had lived among the natives—an influence Anthony viewed as beneficial—and so the vote was appropriate. In the end, however, American men in the new territory overruled Hawaiian men and deprived women of the vote there.

The fundamental differences in the status of women around the world were also the focus of meetings of the International Council of Women. It ran a year behind schedule—its five-year meeting after 1893 should have been in 1898—but in 1899, the women met in London. The council, chaired by the countess of Aberdeen, became even more respectable when Susan B. Anthony was received by Queen Victoria. The queen was close to the end of her 63-year reign, just as Anthony was close to the end of a half-century leading the women's movement. Although their popular images symbolized very different things, the coming together of these two elderly women demonstrated to the world that women were capable of many things—and that a new time was coming.

Susan B. Anthony turned 80 with the turning of the century. At the Washington convention that took place during her birthday week, she and about 200 of her members were invited to the White House for a reception with President McKinley. The news that motivated the national press to send reporters, however, was that Anthony planned to step down from the presidency. The story turned out to have something of a surprise ending. Most assumed she would name Rev. Dr. Anna Howard Shaw as her successor: they had traveled together for years, bantered with each other at meetings, and Shaw clearly saw herself as Anthony's protégé. But Anthony was too politically astute to stray from the practical: while she enjoyed the flower-bedecked, sermon-and-music-filled gatherings that Shaw relished and that Ida Husted Harper recorded in happy detail, Anthony saw that it was Carrie Chapman Catt who won elections. Catt became the association's president in 1900—but, before she could accomplish much, she had to resign in 1904 because her husband fell fatally ill. Shaw then achieved her great desire and headed the organization until 1915.

As with the 1890 merger, there were dissidents from the 1900 presidential turnover. Shaw covered any resentment that she felt, but New Yorker Lillie Devereux Blake, who had been a faithful foot soldier in the National's army since 1869, also was a candidate and was angry to have received so little consideration. She joined with ousted former president Elizabeth Cady Stanton to form the National Legislative League. Both women were aging and unable to develop a strong organization before they died, but their league did predate the League of Women Voters in many ways, especially in its emphasis on issues other than feminist ones.

The era continued to be one of organizational expansion. African American women had brought many groups together under the umbrella of the National Association of Colored Women in 1895. With Margaret Murray Washington, the wife of Booker T. Washington, as its initial president, and with famed freedom fighter Harriet Tubman and Frances Watkins Harper among its founders, the association had delegates from 25 states at its first meeting in Washington D.C. Mary Church Terrell soon took over its leadership: with an 1888 master's degree from Oberlin, she was an extremely effective president. The association was only slightly to the left of mainstream; it did not endorse suffrage and worked instead toward such goals as "care for the children of absentee mothers."

It was not progressive enough for Ida B. Wells-Barnett, who continued to set her sights higher. She met with some success, for already in 1898, she had gone to the White House to lobby President McKinley for a federal anti-lynching law. Josephine St. Pierre Ruffin was another black woman of this era who resisted a secondary place. When she went to Milwaukee for the annual convention of the GFWC, officials refused to seat her in her role as president of an all-black Boston club, even though that club was a GFWC affiliate. They did offer to seat her with other integrated clubs of which she was a member, but she would not accept this insult to her race and left the convention.

Ida B. Wells-Barnett pictured in *The African-American Press and Its Editors*, 1891. (Library of Congress)

It was still another example of the failure of even progressive white women to work with African American activists, and the same generally was true of the suffrage movement's attitude toward white working-class women. To the extent that suffrage leaders attempted to work with labor unions, they sought out the male leadership, not the female members. It was not an unreasonable strategy, of course, given that men had the vote and women did not, and suffragists did garner some success with the men. As early as 1891, Lillie Devereux Blake, who chaired the National American's platform committee, reported on "cordial" meetings with Terrance Powderly of the Knights of Labor and Samuel Gompers of the American Federation of Labor. A decade later, at the 1899 convention of the American Federation of Labor, delegates listened to Susan B. Anthony speak and then unanimously adopted a resolution asking Congress to pass the Sixteenth Amendment. Still, when the Women's Trade Union League began in 1903, it was viewed as a stepchild by both men in the labor movement and by women in the suffrage movement. Not until two giant strikes took place in New York and Chicago did suffragists begin to see the potential power of working-class women.

Coalitions with prohibitionist women also became more complex with the emergence of Carry Nation in 1900. A poor Kansas woman whose life had been ruined by male alcoholism, she armed herself with rocks, bottles, and the hatchet that became her symbol, and began assaults on saloons. She did serious property damage, and arrest did not deter her. Her supporters sang and prayed outside of jails, and as soon as she was released, she repeated her crimes. WCTU women who initially applauded her soon had second thoughts, and in 1904, when she started selling hatchets in a Coney Island sideshow, they expelled her. But the issues she raised continued to be important, even if her family history of mental illness made her an easy target for ridicule.

Carry Nation with her trademark hatchet. (Kansas State Historical Society)

While most prohibitionists disassociated themselves from Nation's lawbreaking, a few pointed out that she was right not only morally, but also legally: many of the saloons she attacked were in areas that were supposed to be "dry," and the liquor sellers were violating the law. They, however, had the protection of politicians, and when she smashed the capital city's favorite bar, her Kansas career was effectively over. She roamed the country until finally, in 1910, a female bar owner in Montana beat Carry Nation so badly that she died six months later.

Although few saw past the caricatures to the legalities, Carry Nation's case raised a significant point: Kansas women (and men) voted in elections that determined alcohol sales, but even after the prohibitionists won, saloons continued to operate. Women's votes made no practical difference in their lives—and this became still another argument for apathy. Like Carry Nation, the era's famous labor leader "Mother Jones" (Mary Harris Jones) also did not consider suffrage to be worth the bother. An economic radical, she was a social conservative; a widow, she was a devout Catholic who believed that men should earn enough to support their wives, who in turn should limit their lives to motherhood. The only role Mother Jones saw for women was in auxiliaries that supported the men's goals, and suffrage, she said, was a distraction: "The plutocrats have organized their women. They keep them busy with suffrage and prohibition and charity.... You don't need a vote to raise hell." Anti-suffragists, of course, were delighted to have support from such unexpected quarters, and the true plutocrats continued to fall under their organizational umbrella.

In 1911, they came together as the National Association Opposed to Woman Suffrage, the organization that would be the conservatives' banner-carrier until they finally lost. With Mrs. Arthur M. Dodge as president for most of their existence, the association established a headquarters in New York. The officers were all from the Northeast, where full suffrage remained unknown. In 1912, they began publishing *Woman's Protest;* in 1918—at the peak of American involvement in World War I—the name was changed to the less rebellious-sounding *Woman Patriot.* Suffragists never took these women very seriously. Their membership remained small—as might be expected with a determinedly elitist group of women. Their anti-labor, anti-immigrant views ultimately became a boon to progressives, especially with independent-minded Jewish women in urban areas. That was not yet the case, however, and it never would be in rural New England, where the second Eastern suffrage referendum finally took place in 1902.

The first had been in Rhode Island in 1887 and this one also was in a very small state: New Hampshire. Although the women organized well and the

National American sent campaign workers, the opposition did the same, and New Hampshire's men rejected female suffrage 21,788 to 14,162. Meanwhile, Western women, especially Abigail Scott Duniway, could not help but notice that the large states of Massachusetts, New York, and Pennsylvania—where the women's movement was born—did not even hold elections. They grew understandably resentful of Eastern women who rushed to give them advice, while failing to do anything at all in their own backyards.

The National American did reach out beyond its eastern seaboard base with conventions in 1903 in New Orleans and in 1905 in Portland. New Orleans, however, only confirmed the organization's conservatism: Ida Husted Harper revealed more than she may have intended when she recorded, "notwithstanding the utmost care and tact on the part of those who had the convention in charge, the 'color question' kept cropping out." The president of the Mississippi Suffrage Association titled her speech "Restricted Suffrage from a Southern Point of View," and discussed possible mechanisms that would allow white women to vote while denying that right to blacks of either gender. "Educated suffrage" was again the favored solution, and the audience applauded a Louisiana man who reminded them of the Fifteenth Amendment: he "spoke of the crime of enfranchising 'a horde of ignorant negro men when…nearly 4,000,000 intelligent white women…[are] denied.' "

Knowing they were not welcome at the convention, New Orleans's black women held their own feminist assembly, which Harper covered in a small-print footnote in the fifth volume of the *History of Woman Suffrage.* Old abolitionists Susan B. Anthony and Elizabeth Smith Miller, along with Alice Stone Blackwell, the daughter of abolitionists, had the grace to respond to an invitation from the Phillis Wheatley Club, which ran a kindergarten, a night school, and a training school for nurses. The only Southern white woman who went with them made for a portrait in irony: Elizabeth M. Gilmer was nationally known as "Dorothy Dix," a

Sylvanie Williams, an African American suffragist leader in New Orleans.

New Orleans advice columnist who presaged Ann Landers and others. Club president Sylvanie Williams presented Anthony with a bouquet and said:

> Flowers in their beauty and sweetness may represent woman.... Some flowers are delicate and fragile, some strong and hardy, some are carefully guarded and cherished, others are roughly treated and trodden under foot. These last are the colored women. They have a crown of thorns continually pressed upon their brow, yet they are advancing.

The next non-Washington convention was held in Portland, Oregon. Abigail Scott Duniway convinced the others to come west for the first time because of the 1905 centennial of the Lewis and Clark expedition. The women used this opportunity to draw attention to the role of a woman, Sacajawea of the Shoshoni tribe, who helped lead Lewis and Clark and their all-male corps hundreds of miles across Dakota prairie and into the Rocky Mountains. National American leaders unveiled a statue of Sacajawea, done by Denver sculptor Alice Cooper, and the convention report ended by noting "a very significant...changing sentiment toward women."

Indeed, a changed sentiment was necessary, for Sacajawea was a very different role model from the Victorian image of women. Younger, more vital role models were bolstered by Republican Theodore Roosevelt, who assumed the presidency when McKinley was assassinated in 1901. Although Roosevelt was more progressive than any president since Lincoln, he did disappointingly little to truly advance women's agenda. When he met with Susan B. Anthony in November 1905, she presented seven specific items for his attention. They ranged from endorsing the Sixteenth Amendment to a timidly phrased request that he appoint "experienced women on boards and commissions relating to such matters as they would be competent to pass upon." All were ignored; instead, the White House placated National American leaders with invitations to social functions.

A few months later, Roosevelt was among those who sent greetings to Susan B. Anthony for her eighty-sixth birthday. This year's birthday was two days after the end of the National American's annual convention, which was held away from Washington—but only slightly away, in Baltimore. Ida Husted Harper called Baltimore "the very heart of conservatism," and it was true that Maryland's women had never done much for the vote. The association, however, was responding to hospitality from Mary E. Garrett, a wealthy woman who opened her mansion to Anthony, as well as to Bryn Mawr president Dr. M. Carey Thomas, who never used her first name, Martha. She and other academic women used this opportunity to begin the college-based Equal Suffrage League.

The convention's "College Evening" seemed to fit Baltimore's conservative image: all speakers were from the "Seven Sisters" colleges, to which the nation's wealthy sent their daughters. They were Smith, Vassar, and Wellesley professors; the presidents of Bryn Mawr and Mount Holyoke; a Vassar trustee, and a Radcliffe graduate. The meeting was presided over by the male president of Johns Hopkins.

Susan B. Anthony had caught a cold when she left Rochester and became ill at Garrett's home. Garrett brought in Baltimore's best physicians and nurses, and although "white and frail," Anthony rallied enough to make her final speech—which included the phrase that became the movement's battle cry, "Failure is impossible." While she lay in bed, Garrett and Thomas asked her what they could do for the cause, and the ever-practical Anthony replied that the movement needed better funding. They promised to "find a number of women like themselves who were unable to take an active part in working for suffrage but sincerely believed in it, and who would be willing to join together in contributing $12,000 a year for the next five years." This cheerful news may have helped Anthony make her return trip, but she was still ill. She died in the second-floor bedroom of her Rochester home the next month.

Anthony had outlived the giants of the early movement, for Elizabeth Cady Stanton had died in 1902. Even in death, however, Stanton breathed new life into the movement through her daughter, Harriot Stanton Blatch. Blatch, who moved back to America from England when her mother was dying, was appalled by the conservatism and apathy of the association that had become so timorous that it condemned her mother's writing. Blatch introduced the new organizational model of British suffragists, beginning by reaching out to working-class women with the New York-based Equality League of Self-Supporting Women. Within a decade, it had a membership of 20,000 women who had been overlooked by the longtime suffragists.

Elizabeth Cady Stanton with her daughter Harriot Stanton Blatch on the right and granddaughter Nora on the left, circa 1890. (Library of Congress)

The death of her old "Aunt Susan" left Blatch emotionally free to work independently of the National American, which was indeed spinning its wheels in reverse: after Anthony no longer spent winters in Washington, its headquarters moved to Warren, Ohio, in the home of its current treasurer, Harriet Taylor Upton.

Other suffragists continued to develop what they hoped would be more effective groups, some of them more or less under the aegis of their National American mother. Such was the case of the Equal Suffrage League, which was recognized by NAWSA in 1906 as the organization for feminists on college campuses. Led by Maud Wood Park, a Radcliffe graduate who was the youngest delegate at the 1900 National American convention, and by Bryn Mawr president M. Carey Thomas, the league attracted more professors and administrators than students. Although it never developed into a great political force, at least it was a beginning: it had taken 60 years for the academics who benefited from the Seneca Falls platform to join the women who had made their careers possible.

The 1907 National American convention was held in Chicago; coincidentally, 1907 was the high point of American immigration, with more than a million people arriving at Ellis Island. Chicago was far better organized than any other interior city to receive them, and its "settlement house" model was the creation of two women, Jane Addams and her friend Ellen Gates Starr. In 1887, they opened Hull House, a welcoming place where they offered assistance to Chicago's newly arrived. Addams soon attracted a coterie of progressive, well-educated women, many of whom also were associated with the University of Chicago; among the most notable were Edith and Grace Abbott, who were pioneer sociologists and economists, as well as Julia Lathrop, who later would head the federal Children's Bureau. These liberals supported suffrage—especially municipal suffrage on the issues that most affected their immigrant clients—and their leadership at the 1907 convention helped reduce the anti-immigrant bias of Eastern suffragists. They also understood how to work with coalitions, and this convention brought the news that National Grange, a farmers' union, and the American Federation of Labor had unanimously endorsed the vote for women. Another indication of Chicago's democratic attitude was the presence of black leader Fannie Barrier Williams on the dais.

State legislatures were meeting in February at the same time as the 1907 convention, and while the women were in Chicago, an amazing amount of news was developing elsewhere. In Nebraska, suffrage had lost on a tie vote in the Senate; in Oklahoma, the vote in a constitutional convention was so close that a change of seven hearts would have carried it; and it lost by exactly the same number in South Dakota's House. Just before the convention, suffrage went down in Vermont's Senate by a mere three votes; during the convention, the West Virginia House passed it 38–24, but its Senate had yet to vote.

Fannie Barrier Williams, a leading African American in Chicago's suffragist movement. (Wikimedia)

It hardly took a keen understanding of political science to recognize that these women should have been home lobbying their own legislatures at this crucial time of year, but many delegates truly seemed to prefer preaching to the choir at national conventions. Oblivious to the states' political calendar, they clung to their February national convention dates, even though they were no longer in Washington, and even though Susan B. Anthony was no longer alive for birthday celebrations. The unspoken coincidence, however, was that National American president Anna Howard Shaw also had a birthday in February, and suffragists observed her sixtieth during the Chicago convention.

The 1908 convention marked the sixtieth anniversary of Seneca Falls and was appropriately observed at nearby Buffalo. Again, the presence of a black speaker indicated a hopeful spirit of inclusion, as Mary Church Terrell reminded the audience of the historic links between black civil rights and those for women. Her own National Association of Colored Women also examined its internal color barriers in 1908, when a faction of its convention advocated electing darker-skinned women to office. "We prefer a woman who is altogether Negro," one delegate said, because the abilities of women who were as light skinned as Terrell were "attributed to their white blood. We want to demonstrate that the African is as talented." Although other women were elected on this platform, Terrell was so accomplished that she remained president.

The biggest news from the 1909 convention in Seattle was that the national headquarters was at last moving from Warren, Ohio, back to New York City. The change had not occurred because of aggressive internal leadership, however; the organization had accepted free office space from multimillionaire Alva Vanderbilt Belmont. Belmont expanded her leadership role in the fall of 1909, when the largest strike by women erupted in New York's garment district. More than 20,000 workers—most of them young, many of them Jewish—walked the picket lines through the garment industry's profitable winter season. More than 700 women were arrested in November and December, and the Women's Trade Union League averaged $1,000 a day on bail money. The league's president was Mary Dreier; she and her sister, Margaret Dreier Robins, were wealthy but devoted their lives to the poor. Supported by other affluent, college-educated women who volunteered in immigrant settlement houses, Dreier used the strike to develop links between these working women and those who bought the clothes that they sewed. Trend setters, including Alva Belmont and future ambassador Daisy Harriman, led a boycott on clothing purchases and donated money to the league. Faced with a united front of both their customers and their workers, the factory owners surrendered in February and gave in to most of the workers' demands.

For women on both ends of the class structure, it was a stellar example of what solidarity could do, and the strike—which had nothing to do with suffrage, an issue that some trade unionists argued was a distracting nuisance—

proved key to revitalizing the women's movement. The point was reinforced in Chicago in 1910, when 40,000 went on strike. Jane Addams helped settle that strike; the Women's Trade Union League president was Mary McDowell, an Addams protégé and head of the University of Chicago's settlement house. These strikes brought important new energy into the suffrage movement as working-class women, especially immigrants, connected with suffragists: strike leaders such as Polish Rose Schneiderman and Swedish Mary Anderson not only joined the suffrage movement, but also went on to careers in politics after the vote was won.

Signs of discontent with President Anna Howard Shaw became apparent at the 1910 convention. Her lack of political acumen had come into focus the year before: four elections were lost while suffragists were meeting in Chicago; Shaw did not aid the garment strikes; nor did she reach out to Blatch's innovative league. Her religiosity and prohibitionism offended some, especially Westerners, and her fondness for ceremony irritated others. Shaw's former vice president, Philadelphian Rachel Foster Avery, resigned at this convention. She had been Susan B. Anthony's confidante and financial benefactor for three decades, but she left to begin her own Pennsylvania group and work for state suffrage. From Baltimore to San Francisco, other women splintered off into organizations separate from the national, but Shaw failed to get the message.

As these women were leaving the National American in 1910, 25-year-old Alice Paul attended her first convention. Born a Quaker in New Jersey, she had a master's degree from the University of Pennsylvania and had just returned from graduate work in England. There, she joined the militant suffragists led by Emmeline Pankhurst: like the British women, Paul had been jailed, gone on a hunger strike, and endured the pain of being forcibly fed through a tube jammed down her throat. Her speech offered the convention a view of political activism very different from their own staid model:

> The essence of the campaign is...opposition to the Government. The country seems willing that the vote be extended to women. This last Parliament showed its willingness by passing their franchise bill through its second reading by a three-to-one majority, but the Government, that little group which controls legislation, would not let it become law.

It is not a war of women against men, but a war of men and women together against the politicians at the head.

Instead of considering this model of activism, the National American's minutes for this convention took up pages on whether or not some women in the audience had actually hissed when President William Howard Taft spoke. The leaders were so pleased with what they saw as evidence of progress—that a United States president welcomed the association to Washington for the very first time in all the years they had been meeting there—that they were mortified at the possibility that audience members may have been impolite. If the hissing could not be explained away as hushing, which some professed was the case, it had occurred when Taft said: "If I could be sure that women as a class, including all the intelligent women...would exercise the franchise, I should be in favor of it. At present there is considerable doubt." While never acknowledging that any hissing happened, the National American nevertheless sent an apologetic letter. Such deference to authority could not have been more different than what Alice Paul told the convention about England, and it reinforced the opinions of those who judged Shaw out of touch with the times.

Alice Paul (Library of Congress)

While attention focused on the women's strike in Chicago in 1910, suffragists in the Pacific Northwest were at work: with virtually no help from the National American, Washington women won a referendum. It was the first state added to the full-suffrage column in 14 years—and like Idaho in 1896, it was won by a grassroots campaign. The devoted leader was Emma Smith DeVoe, who did an astonishing job of effectively—but quietly—organizing.

As the opposition slept, she built a 2,000-member league, lined up legislative sponsors to put the question on the ballot, and won the election by a 2–1 margin. The strategy, according to the report in the sixth volume of the *History of Woman Suffrage,* was simply that "every woman personally solicited her neighbor, her doctor, her grocer, her laundry wagon driver, the postman and even the man who collected the garbage." With headquarters in Olympia and Seattle, they raised $17,000 for materials through such methods as selling a cookbook. DeVoe made a conscious decision not to hold rallies, but instead used other organizations' events to speak and distribute materials. Her campaign was brilliant, but the National association never invited her to share this expertise.

Western women were on the move again, though, and the following year, the giant prize of California was won. Unlike the losing 1896 campaign, this one had little influence from Eastern women. The methods used were highly sophisticated: it was the first to use advertising in a truly major way, including billboards and even electric signs. California women raised most of their own money, and although other out-of-state women made contributions, the National American sent only $1,800 for a campaign that cost at least ten times that. The association divided the campaign into Northern and Southern California, and no egos got in the way of thousands of grassroots workers. They printed some four million pieces of literature, including leaflets in Italian, German, and French, and were successful enough with newspaper publishers that one reporter estimated the women got $100,000 worth of free space.

A railroad car decorated with suffrage banners ran through the state, and during stops at small towns, women drew crowds by providing entertainment. Having learned from their 1896 experience, the women planned to guard ballot boxes, especially in San Francisco and Oakland. Precinct captains at each polling place were supplied with an automobile and money for telegrams, and hundreds of women watched the male voters from six in the morning until past midnight, when tallies had been "adjusted" before. Although they hired Pinkerton detectives to guard San Francisco ballots during the two-day count, as the hours and days went by, the women feared that their slim majorities in Los Angeles, Berkeley, and Sacramento would not be enough to overcome the huge San Francisco margin against them. Once more, however, the rural areas came through—it was California's farmers and ranchers who enfranchised the state's women.

California's big decision was made on October 11, 1911. Although for two decades the National American's conventions kept to a strict schedule of January or February conventions, in 1911, President Shaw allowed the meeting to wait until October 19—after the California vote, but not necessarily because of it, for the convention's minutes have little to say about the victory except to acknowledge it. The convention was in Louisville, but no thoughtful political strategy for border or Southern states was discussed either. Only two things distinguished the meeting. First was the report of the new corresponding secretary, Mary Ware Dennett, which showed increased activity at the New York headquarters with Dennett responding to inquiries from as far away as Japan; Dennett later would lead the birth control movement. The second noteworthy aspect of the Louisville convention was a speech by Emmeline Pankhurst, the fiery radical who regularly made the front pages of world newspapers as the leader of the Women's Social and Political Union in Britain. National American leadership under Anna Howard Shaw nonetheless was ambivalent about offering their rostrum to Pankhurst, who encouraged her followers to harass government officials, damage property, and go on hunger strikes in jail.

That sort of timorousness was the reason Abigail Scott Duniway left the National American soon after Susan B. Anthony's death. She had grown increasingly frustrated with sending dues money to the National American to see it pay for endless meetings in which women told each other the same things that they had for years. She resigned her National American vice presidency and pulled the Oregon Equal Rights Society out of the association in 1906. Referenda in 1908 and 1910 went down to defeat, but by increasingly smaller margins, and—after she threatened Shaw with arrest if the National American president came to Oregon to "assist"—Duniway conducted her last campaign in 1912 from a wheelchair. Oregon men finally were convinced that to enfranchise their women did not mean to enact prohibition, and after 40 years as an active suffragist, Duniway, at last, was victorious.

The year 1912 was an unprecedented success. In addition to Oregon, Kansas also fully enfranchised its women; it had held the first referendum on suffrage just after the Civil War. Arizona became a state in February, and in November, its women won a referendum for full voting rights. Yet in the same 1912 elections, Michigan, Ohio, and Wisconsin men said no, and thus Kansas was the eastern boundary of women's empowerment.

Some Eastern activists got the message: the way to win is to organize in one's own backyard. They joined Harriot Stanton Blatch, who led the grassroots effort that New York had lacked for so many decades. Her Equality League changed its name to Women's Political Union in 1910 and her members lobbied the state legislature, held outdoor rallies, and—most controversially—emulated the streetwise striking women by holding the country's first giant suffrage parade. The initial public reaction was hostile: marching in the streets was unladylike, and even many suffragists condemned it as likely to alienate their male supporters. But Blatch was the daughter of her courageous Stanton parents, and the parades continued; as they did, people saw that visibility meant power. At least once each spring until suffrage was achieved, New Yorkers marched.

Suffragists on a float in a New York City parade. (Library of Congress)

Blatch's "unladylike" behavior did not alienate supportive men. In fact, "Men's Leagues" began to spring up around the country, with Illinois first in 1909. These male auxiliaries to female political groups were unprecedented, and others followed. In some places, Men's Leagues were formed as quickly or even more quickly than women's suffrage associations. In Florida, for example, a Men's League began in Orlando—with the mayor as president—during a period when there was no viable women's association. With New York banker James Lee Laidlow as its longtime national president, the Men's League soon had chapters in 25 states, ranging from North Dakota to Texas and from California to Maine.

Finally, the bloc of states in which women could vote was becoming large enough to merit its own organization. The National Council of Women Voters that was formed in 1911 was an early model for the League of Women Voters that would begin in the next decade. The precursor, in fact, was in an odd way too much like the later league: its platform concentrated on such good-government issues as electoral reforms and protective labor laws—things that primarily concerned women in urban areas, who generally lacked the vote. The Western women who had the vote were not particularly interested in these ideas, and the issue-oriented organization proved ahead of its time. The concept of uniting women voters, however, would be key to success in the next decade.

The *Washington Post* had reported in 1902: "More than a thousand visitors were present at the first session…of the first International Woman Suffrage Conference. Perhaps no other meeting of its kind ever has occasioned as much interest." Women from ten countries came to discuss the formation of an international organization devoted to suffrage. They were growing discouraged with the timid International Council of Women and its failure to endorse the vote. Carrie Chapman Catt greeted the women and introduced international hero Clara Barton, while Susan B. Anthony reminded them of the international suffrage organization that she and Elizabeth Cady Stanton had proposed back in 1883.

The international meeting was held in conjunction with the National American's convention and evenings were devoted to seminars such as "the Australian Woman in Politics" and "Women in Egypt and Jerusalem." A Swedish woman amazed the delegates by telling them that women there had voted for local offices since 1736, longer than women anywhere in the world. When Catt introduced Russia's Sofja Levovna Friedland, she said: "Although I have been a taxpayer in four different States…I have never been permitted any suffrage whatever. I now have the privilege of introducing a Russian woman who has been a voter in her country since she was 21."

In 1904, the International Council of Women met in its first non-English-speaking location, Berlin. German hosts feted them with garden parties and receptions to the point that Katherine Anthony, Susan B. Anthony's niece, thought the social activity was intended to distract them from politics. It turned out to be the last international meeting for 84-year-old Anthony, and she was, of course, the object of much of the attention. The other star was Mary Church Terrell: she represented her National Association of Colored Women extremely well by delivering her speech in English, French, and German. Terrell's speech was quite possibly the first by a black person that many Europeans had heard, and moreover, she compared the status of blacks in the United States to that of Jews in Germany. She was well-received despite this candor, and decades before the first black woman was a guest at the White House, Mary Church Terrell sipped tea with the Empress of Germany.

Still, many women felt that the council was insufficiently political, and after the convention ended, these dissidents formally established the International Woman Suffrage Alliance, the outgrowth of their meeting in Washington in 1902. Their platform affirmed the equality of men and women and called for the ballot everywhere. The new group included women from Australia, Denmark, Germany, Great Britain, the Netherlands, Norway, Sweden, and the United States. Australia—a frontier like the American West—had granted women partial rights back in the 1860s and full rights in 1901, but Australian women joined the international organization to share their expertise. The group elected Carrie Chapman Catt as their president, and she retained this position when her husband fell ill, giving up only the National American presidency.

Mary Church Terrell, head of the National Association of Colored Women. (Library of Congress/Corbis)

Just months after Anthony's 1906 death, it was time for the International Woman Suffrage Alliance to assemble again, for one of the new group's 1904 decisions was a commitment to meet biennially. At the next meeting, held in Copenhagen, women came from all of the founding nations and were joined by others from Iceland, Canada, Hungary, and Italy. They celebrated success in northern Europe: Finland granted full rights to women this year, while women who qualified as taxpayers won the vote in Norway and Denmark. English women reported that 420 of the 670 members of Parliament had pledged themselves to support suffrage. The alliance also began a monthly English-language paper this year, *Jus Suffragii,* published in the Netherlands by Martina Kramers.

Suffrage protest outside the British Parliament, circa 1910. (Library of Congress)

By the 1908 convention in Amsterdam, Norwegian women had gone from partial to full rights as voters; taxpaying women in Iceland had won municipal rights; and the international alliance had grown to 20 nations. The militancy of English suffragists was the hot topic in Amsterdam. British leader Emmeline Pankhurst declined an invitation to the convention, saying she had "more important work," but the eight English delegates explained that British politics always had been more raucous than the U.S. and other European nations. Members of Parliament routinely booed and shouted at each other, and tumultuous campaigns were the norm. Suffragists decided that they would not succeed without adopting the same style. They not only crashed government meetings and heckled candidates, but also defaced public property with graffiti, refused to pay taxes, and sought attention-getting arrests—and, in fact, were hauled off to jail. The international meeting debated all this, and although most were unwilling to condone such tactics, neither were they willing to condemn the frustrated women who used them. They ended up with a well-reasoned resolution that objected to the imprisonment of such women as "common law breakers instead of political offenders."

The next convention was held early, in April 1909 in London, the hottest political place on the planet for women in politics. Hundreds attended, including white women from South Africa. Again, there was so much debate on the tactics of English suffragists that the meeting's minutes ran almost 60 pages. Again, Emmeline Pankhurst made her opinion clear on the alliance: even though it was in her own city, she declined the invitation of what she viewed as this excessively conservative group and instead ran her own show at Royal Albert Hall. Many delegates attended Pankhurst's rally as well, and they were impressed by what the alliance minutes called "a most impressive display of the earnestness of the British suffragists":

> A procession of women engaged in various trades and professions, carrying the emblems of their work, marched from Eaton Square to the hall. It was a wonderful inspiration to the brave bands of pioneers from other lands to see the...swinging lanterns along the darkening streets.... It would be impossible to give a list of the groups, but especially notable were the chain makers...and cotton operatives.... The group of women doctors...were loudly cheered, as were the nurses and midwives.... Women of all nations, classes, creeds, and occupations united for a common purpose.

In 1911, the alliance assembled in Stockholm, where a full-suffrage bill was being discussed in the Swedish Parliament. Swedish women currently voted only in municipal elections—and then only married women. The visitors watched "a stormy debate" in the lower house and rejoiced to see the bill pass, but the upper chamber, which Ida Husted Harper called a "stronghold of caste and conservatism," dealt it "the usual defeat." The alliance went on to its own agenda and made a point at this convention of showcasing women in nontraditional roles. Anna Howard Shaw preached in Sweden's ancient Gusta Vasa church, while a women's choir and organist performed music by a female composer. The 24 nations represented were proud to hear from Swedish Selma Lagerlöf, who recently was the first woman to receive the Nobel Prize for literature.

When the women assembled for their next meeting in 1913, they could not know that the following year, World War I would effectively end U.S. suffragists' involvement in the alliance. Unaware of the future, they traveled far into the heart of eastern Europe—all the way to Budapest. Many of the 240 delegates from 22 nations made a pilgrimage of the trip, stopping for mass meetings in Berlin, Dresden, Prague, and Vienna. Persian women also sent a cable of greetings, and peasants from Galicia, in the Carpathian Mountains of eastern Europe, walked 50 miles to the meeting, even though women there were not allowed "to form an association." The Chinese Woman Suffrage Society also joined, giving the alliance representation on five continents. Only three European nations—Greece, Luxembourg, and Spain—were not represented.

Presiding over the meeting, Carrie Chapman Catt kept the delegates focused on their task. During the past year, she reported, legislative bodies of 17 nations had considered suffrage bills; she announced that two million American women now could vote in all elections. The women again debated the tactics of British militants and unanimously adopted a resolution urging an investigation of "white slavery," the era's term for forced prostitution. There was also a "Young People's Meeting" and a meeting of the International Alliance of Men's Leagues, with Hungarian Georg de Lukács as president.

Carrie Chapman Catt (Library of Congress)

Catt detailed the trip around the world that she and Dutch Dr. Aletta Jacobs had just finished. Like May Wright Sewall, who spent two years traveling to recruit women for the Columbian Exposition, Catt globe-trotted for two years as alliance president. Decades before the United Nations undertook similar work, she reported:

> We held public meetings in many of the towns and cities of four continents, of four large islands, and on the ships of three oceans, and had representatives of all the great races and nationalities in our audiences. We are now in touch with the most advanced development of the women's movement in Egypt, Palestine, India, Burma, China, Japan, Java, and the Philippine and Hawaiian Islands....
>
> Behind the purdah in India, in the harems of Mohammedanism, behind veils and barred doors and closed sedan chairs, there has been rebellion in the hearts of women all down the centuries.... We spoke with many women all over the East who had never heard of a 'woman's movement,' yet isolated and alone, they had thought out the entire program of woman's emancipation....
>
> We must give aid to these sisters.... When I review the slow, tragic struggle upward of the women of the West, I am overwhelmed with the awfulness of the task these Eastern women have assumed.... I would that we could put a protecting arm around these heroic women and save them from the cruel blows they are certain to receive.... For every woman of every tribe and nation, every race and continent...we must demand deliverance.

Dr. Jacobs discussed the status of women in far places. She focused on China and tried to convey the reality of "feet-bound women" who played "an important part" in its 1911 revolution against the imperial dynasty. Catt and Jacobs brought back a banner from the brave delegation of Chinese women, who would disappear from the alliance into the murky waters of twentieth-century war and repression. But when this happy 1913 meeting drew to its close, the attendees firmly believed in a future in which failure was impossible. The U.S. delegation was looking forward to developing links with Central and South America and offered to host the 1915 meeting in conjunction with a planned Panama-Pacific Exposition in San Francisco. The alliance board opted instead for Berlin in 1915 and Paris in 1917; no oracle warned them that those cities soon would be enemy capitals, and that the women would be divided by one of the bloodiest wars the world had yet known.

Chapter Seven

The Longest Labor Ends, 1912 to 1920

Much like the election that Abraham Lincoln won in 1860, the 1912 presidential race marked a turning point for women and the country. There were four candidates in 1860 when the Civil War exploded with Lincoln's victory, and, in 1912, there were three candidates. A Republican split enabled Democrats to win in 1912: conservative Republicans went with incumbent President William Howard Taft, while former President Theodore Roosevelt pulled liberal Republicans into his Progressive Party. The result was a victory for Democrat Woodrow Wilson, a former president of Princeton University and governor of New Jersey.

It was the first national election in which women were an important factor. Four million women could vote in nine Western states by 1912, and they were too large a bloc to ignore. In addition, many women who could not vote campaigned on a national level. New York suffragists Mary Ware Dennett and Daisy Harriman, for example, were so helpful to Wilson that he rewarded them with significant appointments; the same was true for young Californian Annette Adams, who worked hard for Wilson and was appointed as the first female assistant attorney general. Roosevelt made a particularly strong effort to recruit women into his campaign, including Jane Addams and Mary Antin, an immigrant whose book, *The Promised Land,* was a bestseller.

As National American historian Ida Husted Harper summarized, the Progressive Party "made woman suffrage one of the principal planks of its platform, and…the Republican Party so long in power was defeated. Woman suffrage never had received any special assistance from this party during its long regime, but the entire situation now changed." For the first time in two decades,

Republicans lost the White House. Incumbent Taft did not reach out to women, and they were now powerful enough to demonstrate that this was a mistake.

The savvy women who studied at the British school of suffrage were determined to keep attention focused on the power of women. Instead of resting after the November election and enjoying the December holidays, young Rosalie Jones led Harriot Stanton Blatch's Equality League through bitter cold in a well-publicized walk from New York City to the state capital in Albany. The women marched for 13 days, stopping periodically to build fires, assemble outdoor audiences, and preach their suffrage message. Many men were moved by the devotion of these women and by the depth of the personal sacrifices they were willing to make merely to cast a ballot.

Other women also noticed and began making plans to join these leaders in Washington for Woodrow Wilson's inauguration, which under the Constitution of that time, was in March. Again, Blatch's young activists led the way: they walked the 250 miles from New York to Washington. Newspapers across the nation followed their route, and even anti-suffragists conceded a grudging respect for women so zealous for liberty. The *Cleveland Plain Dealer* published a famous drawing comparing their trip to that of George Washington crossing the icy Delaware.

About 8,000 marchers assembled in Washington for the capital's first giant parade of women. The city's police had no experience with thousands of marching women—or with the thousands of men who lined the parade route to jeer at them. Because of the long association between alcohol and political activity, more than a few of the men had imbibed more than a little, and some of them saw these liberated women as inviting physical contact. Police officers, who had no experience with such unladylike behavior, tended to agree, and they failed to protect the women from assault. A portion of the parade route turned into a mob scene so serious that it ultimately cost the police chief his job. Public sympathy swelled for women who were willing to take such risks for rights.

The parade was organized by Alice Paul, who quickly had risen to leadership since her first appearance at a National American convention three years earlier. The 1912 convention included hot debate on a resolution that the association's officers be nonpartisan, which clearly was aimed at Paul and her supporters, who had worked for Roosevelt. The resolution did not pass because the majority of suffragists understood that a political organization becomes impotent if its leaders are restrained from working in politics. However, the debate did indicate confusion over Paul's advocacy of the British model.

American women could not easily replicate British strategy because the two systems of government were too dissimilar. In Britain's parliamentary system, the chief executive (the prime minister) is himself an elected member of Parliament; he holds the prime ministership only as long as his party has a majority of the parliamentary seats. Moreover, elections are not necessarily held at fixed dates, but may be called whenever an issue or group brings enough power to bear to force one. In America, the chief executive (the president) not only holds office for a fixed term, but also is elected on his own, and Congress is a wholly independent branch of government. Most important, presidents have no direct role in constitutional amendments, which must be passed by two-thirds of both houses of Congress and ratified by three-quarters of state legislatures.

Suffragists march to the Capitol in Washington on April 7, 1913. (Library of Congress)

Alice Paul and others who wished to import the British style took no cognizance of these basic differences. They simply followed the British plan of opposing the party that held the prime ministership, and thus targeted the president and his Democratic Party. Thus, from the 1912 convention in Philadelphia to the end of the movement, Paul and her coterie would be a source of both inspiration and turmoil. She energetically followed up the 1913 parade by forming the Congressional Union (CU), which (like a number of other supportive groups) initially functioned under the National American's wide umbrella. The minutes of the 1913 National American convention, which was held in Washington in early December, referred to the group as "the new Congressional Committee."

With Alice Paul as chairman, it included Lucy Burns, Mary Beard, and Crystal Eastman. Like Paul, these women who made their homes in affluent areas of the East Coast were young, educated, and worldly. Burns was akin to Paul in having studied at several prestigious European universities, and Beard was a credentialed historian whose work should have been more recognized. Eastman's mother was famous enough as a clergywoman that she preached at Mark Twain's funeral. Suffrage historian Harper credited them with "excellent arrangements" for the convention, but she was less glowing about their genuine political successes. The ambivalence that the older leaders felt about these younger ones is clearly reflected in a sentence, typical of Harper, about 1913: "The association has cooperated as fully as was possible with the Congressional Committee in all its most creditable year's work."

The CU women opened a highly visible Washington office on F Street near the fashionable Willard Hotel; like everything else the CU did, they funded this themselves. After the March parade, they began "suffrage schools" to educate women on the issue and, according to Paul, they conducted "an uninterrupted series of indoor and outdoor meetings, numbering frequently from five to ten a day." Many of these were in the trendy form of "tableau," or silent skits; other dramatic forms included "theater meetings" and plays that drew attention from women who did not consider themselves interested in politics. During the spring and fall, they arranged parades in New York, Brooklyn, and Newark. In July, the CU greeted "hiking pilgrims" from "all parts of the country" with automobile processions through Washington, which culminated in the presentation of some 200,000 petition signatures to Congress. In November, they began a newspaper, *The Suffragist.* In December, they made the arrangements to lead National American members in an impressive march to the White House on the Monday after the convention ended, where for the first time, a president received an official suffrage delegation.

The "hiking pilgrims" on their way to Washington D.C. in 1913. (Library of Congress)

While the CU was branching off in one direction, another splinter group headed a different way. Louisiana's Kate Gordon, who had been a National American officer for many years, organized the Southern States Woman Suffrage Conference in 1913 with exactly the opposite aim of the Congressional Union: instead of working in Washington for a federal amendment, her group concentrated on state activity. Their strategy was to lobby Southern legislatures—which had abhorred the federal government since the Civil War—and to craft carefully worded legislation that would grant the vote to white women while keeping it from black women.

Meanwhile, activity continued in Western and Midwestern states. Just days after the 1912 election, Congress admitted Alaska as a territory, and one of the first acts of the territorial legislature was to enfranchise its women. In 1913, Colorado became the second state to elect a woman to its Senate, but the most significant activity of 1913 was a new model of partial suffrage adopted by Illinois, which enfranchised its women to vote for president, but in no other races. This idea had been long advocated by pioneer suffragist Henry Blackwell, who died three years before its Illinois adoption. He saw it as a mechanism for women to gain at least some voting rights, arguing that while the Supreme

Court had ruled that states could define their own voters, the president and vice president were national figures for whom women should be allowed to vote as citizens of the United States. Illinois legislators who voted for it, however, probably saw it as a mere sop to women because, under the Constitution, it is the electoral college that actually chose the president.

Yet these victories for women got the attention of politicians sensitive to any shift of the political winds, and the 1914 session of Congress looked at suffrage with new respect. The Congressional Union was successful in forcing the amendment out of committee and onto the floor for a vote. On March 19, 1914, for the first time since 1887, the Senate cast a roll call vote on what was now termed "the Susan B. Anthony amendment." It no longer could be called the Sixteenth Amendment, nor even the Seventeenth, because those numbers were used by the authorization of an income tax and the mandate that U.S. senators be elected by voters, not by legislatures—both ratified in 1913. Constitutional amendments require a two-thirds majority, however, and so the 34–35 Senate loss meant that the vote on the Susan B. Anthony Amendment was not as close as it appears. Nonetheless, it was closer than women had ever been before. Moreover, the Sixteenth and Seventeenth Amendments were important in breaking the long-held conservative belief that the Constitution should not be amended. To many activists, the Senate tally was evidence that the new visibility techniques were working.

At the same time, the National American's official lobbying head, Ruth Hanna McCormick, was pursuing a different path. She was the daughter of a powerful Republican, and although her idea was well intended, it was fittingly convoluted for a woman who grew up in the proverbial smoke-filled rooms. She got a complex bill known as the Shafroth-Palmer Amendment introduced into the Senate. It was designed to counter the arguments of congressmen—especially Southerners—who tried to placate women by saying that, although they supported suffrage, they had so much reverence for states' rights that they could not bring themselves to pass a federal amendment. The Shafroth-Palmer plan required that states hold a suffrage referendum if 8 percent of voters signed a petition calling for it, thus making it much easier for women to get suffrage on local ballots. Not surprisingly, this was too complex for most to be sufficiently excited about to do the necessary petition drives and the follow-up election campaigns. McCormick's excessive political sophistication served only to further alienate her and her National American from the straightforward style of the Congressional Union.

Although personally unfortunate, one event—the death of Miriam Leslie in September 1914—benefited the movement greatly. A brilliant publisher of newspapers and magazines, she managed the news empire of her late husband, Frank Leslie, even more successfully than he had. The women's movement had benefited from bequests since Charles Hovey's first, back in 1859, but never was there one as large as Leslie's: she left $2 million to be personally managed by Carrie Chapman Catt. Leslie's heirs sued, delaying and eventually reducing the amount by about one-half, but the knowledge that she could expect to spend at least a million dollars gave Catt the ability to plan for both the national suffrage campaign and for her International Woman Suffrage Alliance. Within a few years, Leslie's bequest would fund the salaries of some 200 full-time political organizers.

It was also another excellent reason to elect Catt again as head of the National American association. Discontentment with Rev. Anna Howard Shaw grew throughout 1913 and 1914, particularly as the more energetic CU women received so much media attention. Instead of welcoming this assistance, Shaw clearly saw the young women as a threat, and the November 1914 elections for Congress brought the conflicting styles to their inevitable breaking point. The Congressional Union, although still ostensibly a committee of the National American, set an independent course that Shaw—and other, more astute, observers—saw as little short of insane.

Following the British model of campaigning against the party that held the executive position, the CU worked against Democrats because President Wilson was a Democrat. Even though the National American strongly objected, CU members went west to the nine states in which women voted and campaigned against Democrats—even Democrats who supported suffrage. Their visibility techniques again were effective: they hired railroad cars, placarded them with banners, and traveled through the land. Reporters turned out to cover their whistle-stop speeches, and these young, attractive, attention-getting women succeeded in their highly questionable strategy. They defeated 20 Democrats who supported suffrage!

National American leaders were livid, but their own work in the traditional way had proved only slightly more successful. They conducted seven campaigns in Western and Midwestern states in 1914 and won just two. Nevada and

Montana brought the number of states in which women could vote to 11—all of them, like Wyoming way back in 1869, in the West.

At the 1913 National American convention, it was clear that much of the leadership feared the innovative ways of their Congressional Committee and its independent-minded leader, Alice Paul. Carrie Chapman Catt tried to moderate the division between Shaw and Alice Paul, but her motion "to cooperate…in such a way as to remove further causes of embarrassment" did not exactly reflect well on the energetic work of the newcomers. Millionaire Alva Belmont also had reached the end of her rope with Shaw, and Belmont withdrew the funding of the National American's New York office to galvanize a move to Washington, where Paul's faction clearly would be dominant. When Belmont made this motion in the convention, Shaw's allies quickly laid the motion on the table and "all discussion [was] cut off." Although Shaw was her dear friend, even Ida Husted Harper bluntly recorded that "the opposition of the national officers was so apparent that many delegates hesitated to express their convictions."

The 1914 convention was held in Nashville, and attention quickly turned to the West. Delegates applauded the president of the Nevada Suffrage Association, Anne Martin, as she pointed out that Nevada's recent victory made "a solid equal suffrage West." She also made an important observation in noting that her state was the "most male" in the nation and perhaps in the world, with more than two men for every woman. It was an excellent example of the harm done in the older states by conservative women who failed to support their own rights.

Rev. Dr. Anna Howard Shaw and Carrie Chapman Catt (Library of Congress)

Montana was not represented by the president of their suffrage association, for future congresswoman Jeannette Rankin stayed home from the convention to make sure that no ballots suddenly were "discovered" that would overturn Montana's victory, as had been the case in Michigan in 1912. Women from Missouri, Nebraska, Ohio, and the two Dakotas detailed their losses, some of which were attributed to "political tricks." The annual report of National American executive secretary Mary Ware Dennett was read—with almost no mention of the fact that Dennett had resigned a few months earlier. Knowing that President Shaw would never approve of her growing interest in the much more controversial birth control issue, Dennett "severed her connection with the association." (See Chapter Nine for more.)

Other divisions in the National American were reflected in the appointment of Ruth Hanna McCormick as the head of the Congressional Committee; she not only rented a Washington office separate from that opened by Alice Paul exactly a year earlier, but also introduced the complicated Shafroth-Palmer bill, which confused and divided the convention. Even Harper acknowledged that "more bitterness was shown than ever before at one of these annual meetings." Jane Addams resigned as vice president, and President Shaw received just 192 votes from the 315 eligible delegates; without any announced opponent, many cast blank ballots to demonstrate their lack of approval.

Not surprisingly, 1915 brought change, both within the suffrage movement and externally. As the year began in Washington, the House of Representatives cast the first vote it had ever taken on the proposed suffrage amendment. Although the vote seemed to be a victory for the Congressional Union, this historic tally had hidden ramifications, for it was cast on January 12, before the newly elected Congress was sworn in: the only reason to take a vote at that point was to provide defeated incumbents with an opportunity to vent their frustration with the CU's November strategy of working against all Democrats.

The House rejected the amendment by 204–174, a much greater loss than that in the Senate the previous March. Moreover, neither the new House nor successive Houses would replicate the historic vote for the next several years. Instead, congressmen were stating their disapproval of the CU's overly simplistic strategy—and yet, the CU women fairly could claim that their hard work was the reason that the House, after six decades of ignoring the movement, had finally taken women seriously enough to vote at all.

Undeterred, the CU carried on. In early May, they marched to the Capitol with 500,000 petition signatures for suffrage, some of them gathered during cross-country car rallies. The automobile was still an attraction for many rural people who had not seen one, and as international attention focused on the Panama-Pacific Exposition that took place in San Francisco in 1915, feminists created publicity by driving vote-placarded cars from coast to coast.

Alice Burke and Nell Richardson driving from New York to San Francisco in the "suffrage automobile," the Golden Flyer. (Library of Congress)

In the fall, major Eastern states finally held their first suffrage referenda. Massachusetts, New Jersey, New York, and Pennsylvania were the homes of heroes—Lucy Stone, Elizabeth Cady Stanton, Susan B. Anthony, and Lucretia Mott—and yet none of these states had grown politically along with these pioneer thinkers. All of the campaigns were hard-fought, but all went down to crashing defeats. Pennsylvania came closest, but only 46 percent of its men supported women. The favorable vote was just 42 percent in both New York and in New Jersey—even though President Wilson returned to his home state to cast a well-publicized affirmative ballot. The margin of loss was the worst in Massachusetts, where the earliest anti-suffragists also appeared. Despite a huge amount of work in a two-year campaign, Massachusetts suffragists won only an embarrassing 36 percent of the vote.

These losses in November of 1915 were so disastrous that even the most devoted friends of Anna Howard Shaw could no longer support her National American presidency when the convention met the next month in Washington.

With President Wilson's daughter Margaret as the honorary host, the membership returned to Susan B. Anthony's original choice as her successor, Carrie Chapman Catt. Shaw faced the inevitable and announced her retirement a few weeks before the convention, which enabled it to honor her in the way that her 11 years as president merited. Her farewell address displayed the oratory in which she shined, and the delegates literally crowned her with roses. More important, the presidential change infused a new spirit of energy into the National American. Pledges of money were more easily raised than ever before, and instead of the usual, tiresomely piled-on philosophical arguments in favor of suffrage, the convention's records were filled with practical reports on business plans.

None of this would be enough for Alice Paul's faction, however, for they considered Catt also to be hopelessly old-fashioned. At the same time, a majority of the convention was confused and angry that Paul's Congressional Union had not concentrated on the 1915 elections in the East where referenda were at last being conducted, but rather campaigned in the West, where they opposed Democrats, who supported suffrage. Worse, the House Judiciary Committee was holding hearings during the time that the convention met in Washington, and the differences between the two factions were forced into the open.

"There is a great deal of confusion among the members of the committee," Virginia Rep. Charles Creighton Carlin admitted, "as to the essential difference between…the National Woman Suffrage Association and the Congressional Union." After hearing of the CU's partisan strategy, the committee, not surprisingly, was "incredulous that suffragists would fight the reelection of their friends." The committee was chaired by Senator Charles S. Thomas of the longtime suffrage state of Colorado; although a faithful friend of the National American, he had been one of the CU's Democratic targets in the last election and was so angry that he refused to preside during the portion of the hearing when CU members spoke. Other politically sophisticated suffragists, including Mary Baird Bryan—the wife of three-time Democratic nominee William Jennings Bryan—thought that Paul's strategy was so antagonistic to Democrats that Bryan suspected the CU was funded by the Republican Party.

Back at the convention, Zona Gale, a future Pulitzer prize-winning dramatist, tried to unify the two factions with a motion that passed unanimously:

> Realizing that all suffragists have a common cause at heart and that difference of methods is inevitable, it is moved that an efficiency commission consisting of five members be appointed by the Chair to confer with representatives of the Congressional Union in order to bring about cooperation with the maximum of efficiency for the successful passage of the Susan B. Anthony Amendment at this session of Congress.

The group of five, headed by Catt herself, soon met with five representatives from the Congressional Union, led by Alice Paul, in the neutral territory of Washington's Willard Hotel, but no progress was made. The CU women stuck adamantly to their British model of opposing all candidates of the party that held the presidency, and neither Catt nor her members could accept this. The CU women did not believe Catt's quiet promise of a "Winning Plan," which she intended to keep secret so that the opposition would not be forewarned. They could not remember the Western elections that Catt won when they were children, and so thought of her as akin to Shaw in political ability—but within five years, the final victory indeed would be won.

Catt thus began her presidency in 1916, when Woodrow Wilson was up for reelection. He no longer could count on a Republican Party split, for it had reunited under Charles Evans Hughes, a formidable candidate who resigned from the Supreme Court to campaign. Wilson had held out a number of olive branches to women, including voting for suffrage in the New Jersey referendum and repeatedly receiving National American delegations at the White House. Although this was far more than any other president had done, it was not enough for the times, and Carrie Chapman Catt continued to lobby him for a full endorsement. This was a big move for a Virginia-born states'-rights believer who stressed that presidents had no legal role in constitutional amendments, but he took the political step: in June, he responded to Catt with a letter saying that he would see that the Democratic Party platform included a suffrage endorsement. In October, he and seven of his ten Cabinet members declared themselves in favor of the vote for women.

The same month that Wilson sent his promising letter to Catt, the Congressional Union formally broke its ties to the National American. It not only set itself up as an independent organization, it also called itself a political party: the National Woman's Party was founded in a Chicago meeting in June

1916, with Alice Paul as its head. Like the earlier parties of Victoria Woodhull and Belva Lockwood, the new party was small but behaved as though it were big. The Woman's Party held a convention, featuring keynote speaker Californian Maud Younger, a wealthy woman who nonetheless worked as a women's labor organizer; known as "the millionaire waitress," she had brought working-class women into California's winning 1911 campaign.

The party's first convention was noted for its timing: it was at the same place and time as the Republican convention, which some Democrats saw as more evidence that Paul's women were—consciously or unconsciously—merely Republican agents disguised in suffrage clothing. The Woman's Party reaffirmed its policy of working in the states where women could vote to demonstrate women's strength in the presidential election, which amounted to working against all Democrats as long as a Democrat held the White House. It did not matter to the Woman's Party that, as Catt pointed out, all of the 1915 rejections of suffrage in Eastern states had Republican majorities. The Woman's Party's strategy of demonstrating the power of voting women was excellent: had they not coupled this with a simultaneous strategy of working against the party that held the White House, their efforts would have inspired less criticism from other suffragists.

Headquarters of the National Woman's Party in Washington D.C. (Library of Congress)

There was in fact little difference between the two major political parties on the issue of suffrage, and National American women participated in both. As Ida Husted Harper put it, "the year 1916 marked a turning point.... Large delegations of women had attended the Republican and Democratic National conventions during the summer and for the first time each of them had put into its platform an unequivocal declaration in favor of suffrage." The National American continued on its nonpartisan course, but it also was keenly aware of the opportunity that the presidential campaign presented. Careful to be open to both parties, Catt interviewed Republican nominee Hughes in July and "had a long and satisfactory conversation." He announced his support in August, and later, would even defend suffragists in lawsuits.

Catt called an "emergency" convention of the National American—not in late November or December after elections were over, as had been the case with Shaw, but at the beginning of September. The women met in Atlantic City, where they took advantage of Labor Day crowds to hold "open air meetings on the Boardwalk" that attracted thousands of listeners to speeches. A "Dixie evening" marked increased representation from Southern states, and the treasurer's report alone showed revitalization: the budget had a comfortable surplus, and the women pledged to spend a million dollars between October 1916 and 1917. The publicity director, Charles T. Heaslip, reported on hundreds of newspapers that regularly used not only the National American association's press releases, but also its photographs and cartoons; Heaslip even had branched out into the new moving pictures. All this soon had its effect, and by the end of 1917, National American membership would soar to more than two million—more than any modern feminist organization.

The plan adopted at the convention's end also was impressive: it included monthly demonstrations "simultaneously conducted throughout the nation; at least four campaign directors and 200 organizers in the field, ...innumerable activities for agitation and publicity, ...[and] a national committee to extend suffrage propaganda among [the] non-English-speaking." Catt made it clear that there would be no more dissipation of effort on embarrassing losses as she tightened the reins on her less sophisticated members. State suffrage associations agreed to consult with national leaders before they committed resources, for Catt was tired of referenda that women had no chance of winning.

The convention's end was historic. Both presidential candidates had been invited to speak, but only President Wilson accepted. He arrived early but insisted on speaking last. He listened through the scheduled agenda, which included speeches by Margaret Dreier Robins, president of the Women's Trade Union League; Julia Lathrop, chief of the National Children's Bureau; and Dr. Katharine Bement Davis, who headed New York City's Parole Commission. All speakers aimed to make the point that women should vote on these important public welfare issues. Wilson, after saying that he "found it a real privilege to…listen," responded with a professor's insight:

Suffragists advertising the open-air meetings on Labor Day in Atlantic City. (Library of Congress)

> One of the striking facts about the history of the United States is that at the outset it was a lawyers' history. Almost all of the questions…were legal questions; were questions of methods, not questions of what you were going to do with your government but of how you were to constitute [it].… There was a time when nobody but a lawyer could run the government.…
>
> And then something happened. A great question arose.… That was the slavery question, and is it not significant that it was then, and then for the first time, that women became prominent in politics in America?
>
> The whole nature of our political questions has been altered. They have ceased to be legal questions. They have more and more become social questions, questions with regard to the relations of human beings to one another, not merely their legal relations but their moral and spiritual relations.…
>
> I get a little impatient sometimes about the discussion of the channels and methods by which it [suffrage] is going to prevail. *It is going to prevail* and that is a very superficial and ignorant view which attributes it

to mere social unrest. It is not merely because women are discontented, it is because they have seen visions of duty....

I have not come to ask you to be patient, because you have been, but I have come to congratulate you that there has been a force behind you that will...be triumphant.

Wilson's belief in the inevitability of the suffrage victory was good to hear, of course, but he was vague when Anna Howard Shaw expressed the hope that it would come in his administration. Although the women's vote was one of the main topics of the 1916 election, it was overwhelmed by the issue of American involvement in the European war that began in 1914. Indeed, this was still another factor dividing the National American from the National Woman's Party, for many of the latter were pacifists. Throughout 1916, however, Catt generally succeeded in her policy of insisting that the National American deal only with the vote for women, not with what would become World War I, or with any other issue or candidate.

One element of the 1916 election was unequivocally joyful: it marked the first female success in a federal election with Montana's election of Jeannette Rankin to the House of Representatives. A former employee of the National American, Rankin campaigned on a peace platform and thus appealed to both suffrage factions. All suffragists were eager to point out that well before most American women could even vote, progressive Westerners had so much faith in women that they elected an unabashed feminist to the nation's highest lawmaking body.

The National Woman's Party picketed Wilson throughout his 1916 campaign, but he was reelected in November. When he spoke to Congress in December, the Woman's Party was ready: they slipped into seats in the House gallery with a hidden banner and, in defiance of all rules of protocol, unfurled it as the president began to speak. Acutely aware of the workings of the media, they also were armed with press releases. Moreover, in emulation of the British style, members of the Woman's Party began actively seeking arrest. Some already had been arrested for disturbing the peace and other city code violations; Lucy Burns, in particular, was proud of the fact that her arrest record dated to

1913, and by the end of the campaign, she would be jailed more often than any other suffragist.

On January 10, they began picketing—not the Capitol, where congressmen controlled the amendment process—but instead the White House, where they continued to target Wilson. Picketing the president's home was a new thing in American politics, and women set this precedent. Through rain and snow, day and dark, summer and winter, sign-carrying women would encircle the White House until the suffrage amendment finally passed. Except on Sundays, as many as 1,000 women "of all races and religions," in the words of Alice Paul, demonstrated their ideas with their feet. Despite the radicalism of the idea, their right to free speech was initially respected, but after the United States entered the European war, administration security officials began to see these enemies at the White House gate as a potential threat to the president's life, and trouble soon would follow.

National Woman's Party picketers outside the White House, 1917. (Library of Congress)

Meanwhile, there was the first victory in the South. In March, Arkansas adopted still another form of partial suffrage. The legislature granted women the right to vote in primary—but not general—elections. This seemingly odd reasoning actually was very shrewd, for the result was exactly what was intended: in effect, white women got the vote while black women did not. The very few blacks who dared to register and vote in this era were almost invariably Republicans—"the party of Lincoln"—and in Arkansas, like most Southern states, the Republican Party was virtually nonexistent and almost never held primaries. Thus, there would be few or no elections in which blacks would vote, for the Democratic primaries were the only elections that mattered.

It was a cynical way to win the vote, but Carrie Chapman Catt quietly worked through the strategy with Arkansas leaders, and the next year, Texas replicated it, passing this form of suffrage 17–4. Women set up their headquarters in Austin, and when a legislator from Dallas thought that he had dismissed them by demanding 5,000 petition signatures, they returned four days later with 10,000. Although this form of suffrage was racist, Catt's view was that it was better that some women have the vote than none, and that any expansion would be helpful in passing the federal amendment—which would be applicable to black women as well as to white ones. The "Negro's Hour" argument had come full circle: instead of white women being asked to prioritize black voting rights, race was now secondary to gender.

A month after the Arkansas victory, Catt hosted a breakfast for Jeannette Rankin, who made a speech from the outdoor balcony of the National American's Washington headquarters, and on April 2, 1917, women had the privilege of escorting the first of their own to the House of Representatives. With Catt and Rankin at the head of a parade of automobiles, they went to the Capitol and proudly watched the young Montana suffragist sworn in. On the very same day, however, Rep. Rankin would be faced with the most crucial decision of her brief elective career. President Wilson asked Congress for a declaration of war against Germany, and she was one of about 50 representatives who voted against it. When Rankin's reelection

Jeannette Rankin (Library of Congress)

coincided with victory in what initially was called the Great War, her campaign promises for peace would be forgotten and Montana voters would vote against the woman who voted against the war.

In the meantime, however, she would become the ranking Republican on the House committee dealing with suffrage—but the House was the more recalcitrant body on the issue of the vote. In the Senate, years of lobbying had paid off so thoroughly that Ida Husted Harper wrote that the 1917 committee hearing was "largely a matter of routine, as the entire committee was ready to report favorably." Carrie Chapman Catt exhibited the same confidence when she began her speech by saying: "The Senate Committee of Woman Suffrage was established in 1883. Thirty-four years have passed since then. We confidently believe that we are appearing before the last of these committees."

Much of the rest of the hearing was given over to senators from the West, who tried to impress their Eastern colleagues with the good sense of equality. Wyoming's Senator John B. Kendrick, a former governor, reminded his colleagues that "no state that has adopted woman suffrage has ever even considered a plan to get along without it. It is soon realized that the votes of women are not for sale at any price, and, while they align themselves with different parties…they never fail to put principle above patronage." Senator Reed Smoot of Utah echoed these thoughts, adding that "nothing on earth will stop" the movement. "The country," he pointed out pragmatically, "will not much longer tolerate it that a woman shall have the privilege of voting in one State and upon moving into another be disenfranchised."

The Senate committee also heard from their new House colleague, Rep. Rankin, who, as an experienced National American field worker, was ideal for making clear the impossibility of amending the laws of each state in the absence of a federal amendment. Many state constitutions, she said, presented "almost insurmountable difficulties" and a federal amendment was clearly the only way that American women could move freely without losing rights. Other Western congressmen also spoke, and Catt closed the hearing by pointing out that recently "Great Britain and her colonies had recognized the political rights of women as the United States had never done." This, she said, had "dimmed" the view of women toward "American ideals and lowered their respect for our Government." If the Congress intended that women be enthusiastic supporters of the war they had declared a few days earlier, she said, then Congress must demonstrate its respect for women.

A week later, the Senate committee granted a separate hearing to the National Woman's Party. Vice Chairman Anne Martin presided, while the speakers included Mary Beard and Rheta Childe Dorr, a syndicated war correspondent and future feminist biographer. Rep. Rankin also testified at that hearing. On May 3, the committee heard from the National Association Opposed to Woman Suffrage. Its longtime president, Mrs. Arthur Dodge, and its New York president, the wife of U.S. Senator James W. Wadsworth, Jr., headed a list of women and men who spoke—and the westernmost of this group was from Ohio. Finally, the House Rules Committee held a hearing on May 18, which included speakers from all sides. On June 6, by a vote of 6–5, the committee adopted a motion by Rep. James Campbell Cantrill of Kentucky calling for the creation of a Committee on Woman Suffrage.

This was something for which "suffrage leaders were profoundly thankful," and Maud Wood Park of Massachusetts, the young head of the National American's Congressional Committee, hoped "never again to address a hostile" Rules or Judiciary Committee. After its summer recess, the full House cast something of a test vote on the amendment by accepting this new committee. With what Park called "cordial support" from House Speaker Champ Clark, the tally was 180–107—but 145 representatives dodged the issue by not voting.

During the springtime Washington action, Catt was also busy with state legislatures, which traditionally met at that time. She concentrated on this more manageable number of better-educated men, rather than trying to appeal to the masses in statewide referenda. As was the case with the Southern partial-suffrage primary rights, she also showed that she was willing to be pragmatic and to accept a half-loaf when a full one could not be had. Thus, in 1917, six other state legislatures joined Illinois in granting women the right to vote in presidential elections, but not in other races. Except for Rhode Island, which had held the first Eastern suffrage campaign back in 1887 when the governor vetoed the bill, and a temporary victory in Vermont, all of these presidential suffrage states were in the Midwest. Catt also managed to get longtime National American friend, Senator John E. Shafroth of Colorado, to sponsor a bill granting voting rights to women in the territory of Hawaii. Congress passed it, but Hawaii's legislature failed to implement it, and again, a potentially historic situation turned full circle. A few decades earlier, western territories had passed suffrage and Congress snatched it away; now the opposite was happening. It was still another demonstration of how difficult this political war was. Suffragists had to fight on many different fronts simultaneously, lest they go backward.

They in fact did go backward later in the year. The presidential suffrage that Indiana's legislature had granted was overturned as unconstitutional by its courts, while voters in Ohio cancelled out their legislature's grant in a fall referendum. In September 1917, Maine, too, defeated a suffrage referendum. Women there ignored Catt's disapproval and put the issue on the ballot, but Catt's predictions were right: despite a campaign that included motion picture advertisements and endorsements from President Wilson and former President Roosevelt, Maine's men voted it down by almost two to one.

And yet, these disappointments were slight in comparison with the biggest and best event of 1917—the first victory, at last, in a major Eastern state. The parades and other visibility techniques that Harriot Stanton Blatch had begun years earlier in New York finally paid off. Immediately after the 1915 defeat, all of New York's suffrage associations united. With hundreds of trained, full-time workers, the two-year campaign included publicity techniques that ranged from baseball games to advertisements in 728 newspapers—many of them in foreign languages. In late October, President Wilson met with a delegation of New York suffragists to focus public attention on the contributions that women were making to win the war.

A crowd assembled to hear suffragists speak in New York City. (Library of Congress)

Two days later, the last of the giant parades reinforced this point; it included a petition with 1,014,000 signatures. On November 6, 1917, New York men enfranchised their women by a narrow margin. For the first time, it was the urban vote that carried suffrage: Republican areas upstate voted against it by a slight majority, and it was the ads aimed at immigrants and the coalitions with labor that allowed New York City to barely carry the issue. Mary Garrett Hay, who chaired the National American's New York committee, reported:

> The campaign represented an immense amount of work in many fields. There were 11,085 meetings reported to the States' officers and many that were never reported. Women of all classes labored together.... The campaign cost $682,500. The largest gift...was $10,000.... Most of the money was given in small sums and represented innumerable sacrifices.

The year ended with what may have been the most physically miserable convention suffragists ever experienced. The war was in full swing, and many trains were given over to troop and supply movements, so travel was both difficult and expensive. Beyond that, the weather was terrible: Washington, where the convention met, had below-zero temperatures; snowstorms and railroad washouts from rain made some trains run more than a day late; delegates from Southern states were involved in two train wrecks. When they got to town, they were greeted with what National American historian Ida Husted Harper called a "coal famine." As fuel was going to the war effort, hotel rooms—when they could be found—were cold and damp. They were, according to Harper, "always cold," and because the war also involved a serious food shortage (resulting from America's attempt to feed much of Europe), many delegates went hungry.

Yet excitement about the genuine possibility that Congress would pass the amendment brought 600 delegates who represented over two million members—more than any previous convention. A feeling of confidence suffused the gathering, for as President Catt said in her opening address, "the New York campaign...carried the question forever out of the stage of argument and into the stage of final surrender." She followed through on this optimism by arranging meetings between delegates and their senators; all but Pennsylvania's senators cooperated. Missouri's meeting was particularly important, for its delegation included Speaker of the House Champ Clark; he promised the suffragists that he would cast an affirmative vote if it became necessary to break a tie. President Wilson also helped; both Cabinet members and another of his daughters, Eleanor Wilson McAdoo, spoke to this convention. More important, he honored Arkansas with an invitation to the White House because of its recent establishment of the first suffrage in the South—and this soon paid off, when Arkansas's congressional delegation was the only Southern one to cast all of its votes for the federal amendment.

Internally, the National American was growing at an exponential rate, spending over $800,000 this year. In addition to the Washington office, it continued to maintain its national headquarters in New York City, at 171 Madison Avenue. In 1917, its Leslie Bureau of Suffrage Education alone used the entire fifteenth floor, plus rooms on the fourteenth. The annual report of the Leslie inheritance fund director, Rose Young, filled 30 pages of fine print, with the most historic item being the merger of Alice Stone Blackwell's venerable old *Woman's Journal* with two smaller papers, the *Woman Voter* and the *National Suffrage News,* into the *Woman Citizen.*

Innumerable publicity items aided the cause, including almost a million copies of just one speech by suffragist-hero Senator John E. Shafroth of Colorado. An energized press department cultivated newspaper editors on a very personal level and was particularly effective at reinforcing positive relationships with the press; some 2,000 thank you letters were sent to the writers of editorials in 1917 alone. The result of such individual attention was that many editors "who were wavering have been persuaded to come out definitely in favor; this has been especially noticeable in the South." The headquarters also had a data department: it collected official records in the states where women could vote, which was used to counter misinformation.

The biggest problem for the National American's press department, ironically, was what it viewed as the negative press simultaneously generated by the Woman's Party. According to Ida Husted Harper:

> When the "picketing" began in Washington last January, almost every newspaper in the United States held the entire suffrage movement responsible for it. At once 250 letters were sent in answer to editorials, stating that the National American Association…had been always strictly non-partisan and non-militant; that it represented about 98 per cent of the enrolled suffragists of the United States…[and] strongly condemned the "picketing." The letter urged the newspaper…to make a clear distinction between the two organizations.

The women of the unified group that won New York's campaign also viewed the National Woman's Party as a burden, especially after Alice Paul and her supporters burned the president in effigy in the summer of 1917. Newspapers associated the New York group with the Washington one, and according to New York's report in the *History of Woman Suffrage,* "reproaches of disloyalty and pro-Germanism were hurled at suffragists in general." They called an emergency meeting in Saratoga, hoping to stop the source of the negative publicity. Upon learning that the leaders of the Woman's Party had refused "a direct appeal to suspend the 'picketing' until after the election," the New Yorkers adopted a resolution of disapproval and publicized it.

Suffrage activists picket in front of the White House, rain or shine. (Library of Congress)

The Woman's Party, in turn, was aghast that mainstream women went so far in distancing themselves from what the militants understandably viewed as the activity that was making the difference. Women had organized and lobbied for years, they argued; there was nothing terribly different about Catt's style of leadership, and they pointed out that while the National American had some victories in 1917, it also had some losses. The Woman's Party firmly believed it was their tactics, not the National American's, that were responsible for the changed tone of the debate and the new respect with which suffrage was treated.

Alice Paul and her members followed the tradition of Susan B. Anthony and Elizabeth Cady Stanton, while Catt and the National American were more nearly the intellectual heirs of Lucy Stone and the old American association. Catt, like Lucy Stone in the case of the Fifteenth Amendment, was willing to accept half-victories while working for the larger goal; she saw political action as a chess game with a long series of moves that she could win with cleverness and patience. Paul, like Anthony and Stanton before her, scorned this as mythology and believed in dramatic, uncompromising action. What Paul saw as principled, Catt saw as obdurate—but it is possible that the issue needed both political styles. The merger of the National and American associations arguably had sent suffrage into a long nap, and competition between groups with the same goal is not necessarily a negative.

There is no doubt that the National Woman's Party women reenergized the cause, and they believed they deserved credit for doing so. It was their women, after all, who showed such dedication that more than 200 of them had been arrested during White House demonstrations; almost half of these women were jailed, where they endured particularly harsh conditions, including rotten food and suffocating air. In October 1917, they began a campaign to draw attention to themselves as political prisoners, arguing that they were in jail because of their ideas, rather than for the petty crimes that were the ostensible reason for arrest. The war and Russia's Communist Revolution brought many jailings that were free-speech violations, as male and female pacifists and economic radicals also were jailed. Women, however, had made the point a decade earlier: at the International Woman Suffrage Alliance meeting in 1908, they adopted a resolution objecting to the imprisonment of English women as "common law breakers instead of political offenders."

Led by Lucy Burns, some began hunger strikes to protest a judicial system that refused to recognize their constitutional rights. Burns went without food for almost three weeks; only when she was too weak to resist did her guards finally manage to force-feed her. The newspapers were full of stories of the pain that these women endured when jailers shoved tubes down their throats, gagging and nauseating them. Their obvious devotion to the cause brought sympathy from many. More and more, the public responded with anger at those who continued to make the old authoritarian argument against the vote—the fundamental point of the democracy for which the nation allegedly was fighting abroad.

Lucy Burns (Library of Congress)

While she would never dream of condemning the antiwar vote of the first woman elected to Congress, National American president Carrie Chapman Catt did not see any reason to take the same pacifist position as Rep. Jeannette Rankin but did see many reasons to take the opposite one. Catt had more international experience than almost any of her contemporaries, for she had traveled the entire globe during her time as president of the International Woman Suffrage Alliance. She was keenly aware of world politics, and as early as the alliance's Berlin convention in 1904, she noted the growing animosity between German and British women. Like other suffragists, she made genuine efforts for peace, not only within the international alliance, but also by joining Jane Addams and 40 other women in a dangerous 1915 journey across the submarine-infested Atlantic to work for peace in Europe.

When the war continued nonetheless, and especially after the Germans sank neutral ships, Catt joined most Americans in siding with the more democratic British. But more important was her belief that American women could win the vote by supporting the war. To her, and to most National American members, the war offered a unique opportunity to demonstrate that no major governmental policy could be effective without women's support, and that women's participation in the war effort should entitle them to vote.

So, while carrying out her work as National American president, Catt cultivated President Wilson and congressional leaders by accepting an appointment to the Woman's Committee of the Council of National Defense. Many other suffrage leaders also used the war to demonstrate their desire for full participation in democracy; Daisy Harriman, for example, chaired the government's Committee on Women in Industry and helped create the Red Cross Motor Corps, which sponsored 500 female ambulance drivers in Europe. More than 1,000 women went to Europe as contract employees of the Army, where they worked as translators and telephone operators. More than 20,000 joined the Army Nurse Corps, 200 of whom died, while 36 members of the Navy Nurse Corps also gave their lives. Another 20,000 nurses served with the Red Cross, many under battlefield conditions, with 296 deaths. Late in the war, the Navy and the Marines enlisted some 13,000 women, 57 of whom died while in service.

Civilian women worked in dangerous munitions plants and replaced men in unconventional jobs such as driving streetcars. Millions donated their time and money to the Red Cross, Salvation Army, YWCA, and other relief agencies that attempted to abate the horrors of war for European civilians. The American Women's Hospitals Committee was just one organization that sent help; it financed hospitals that were staffed by some 350 female physicians from the United States. Virtually all women responded positively to major government programs that exhorted them to conserve food and fuel for the front.

It was therefore logical that President Wilson would begin arguing for women's right to vote as a war measure. On January 9, 1918, he issued a formal statement supporting the federal amendment, publicly moving beyond his former preference for state suffrage. The Congress had made it ideologically consistent for him to do so: less than a month earlier, it had passed on to the states a constitutional amendment prohibiting the "sale or transportation of intoxicating liquors." If the federal government could ask states to approve such an intrusion into citizens' personal lives, surely it also could recommend that female citizens be permitted to vote.

The day after Wilson's formal request, Jeannette Rankin opened debate in the House on a new suffrage amendment. Indiana's Rep. Merrill Moores and Ohio's Rep. Warren Gard offered damaging motions that the House fortunately struck down; Moores's was particularly offensive, for it would have mandated state conventions for ratification, something that had never been required for any other amendment in the history of the Constitution. At 5:00 p.m., the House passed the "Susan B. Anthony" amendment on a razor-thin margin that left no votes to spare: the 274–136 tally was exactly the requisite number for the constitutional requirement of two-thirds. Of the 48 state delegations, 23 voted for it unanimously; these solid supporters were Western, Midwestern, and rural New England states. Suffragists also were jubilant that 56 affirmative votes came from the South.

Speaker Clark had a terrible time keeping his members under control, and the House floor was so chaotic that the roll call was repeated three times to be sure of its accuracy. Suffragists sat in the gallery, holding their breath while marking and re-marking messy tally sheets. They found to their great relief that only one representative, Daniel J. Riordan of New York, betrayed his pledge to them. Several supporters made supreme efforts to be present. Rep. Sam Sells of Tennessee lived with the pain of a broken shoulder for two days, refusing to have it set lest he be needed on the floor. Rep. James R. Mann of Illinois came from a hospital bed in Baltimore, where he had been for months, just before the 5:00 p.m. deadline, and ailing Rep. Henry Barnhart of Indiana left a Washington hospital long enough to vote. An unnamed representative, whose wife Ida Husted Harper described as an "ardent suffragist," carried out her intention by casting his vote, and only then went home to New York for his wife's funeral.

There seemed, however, to be no end to heartbreaks for the women. The Senate, which had been the more supportive body for decades, now turned on them. Indeed, it almost seemed a divine trial of faith, for the winter brought an unprecedented number of senatorial deaths: ten men died, seven of whom had been pledged to suffrage. For months, Senate leaders refused to take a vote, even after suffragists presented them with a petition signed by 1,000 men with nationally prominent reputations, including leaders of both parties and of the American Federation of Labor.

Finally, in late August, the Senate took up the issue for a five-day debate that Ida Husted Harper predicted would "take its place with the debates on slavery before the Civil War." When the debate made it clear that equivocal senators, encouraged by Massachusetts's Sen. Henry Cabot Lodge, were coming down on the anti-suffrage side, the women again appealed to President

Wilson. On September 30, 1918, he took the unprecedented step of speaking to the Senate in person on the issue. In strong language, he said that a million women had entered the wartime labor force, and this contribution must not be repaid with congressional indifference. He urged senators to pass the federal amendment as "a necessary war measure." But, as is often the case in politics, it was as though the opponents heard a different speech than the supporters. According to Harper, to the women "it seemed impossible that a third of the Senate could refuse that never-to-be-forgotten plea." But "scarcely had the door closed on the President," when the opponents were on their feet.

Senator Oscar Underwood of Alabama offered a long diatribe on states' rights. Senator John Bell Williams of Mississippi received slight support—22 votes—for his attempt to change the amendment to read "the right of *white* citizens…." Senator Frelinghuysen of New Jersey, a state full of immigrants, seemingly was intent on political suicide with a motion to exclude "female persons who are not citizens otherwise than by marriage." Worn out by themselves, they delayed the vote until the next day, and on October 1, 1918—just a month short of the midterm elections—the Senate finally tallied its views. The vote was 62–34—two short of the two-thirds requirement.

A drawing from *The Brooklyn Magazine*, November 10, 1917. Uncle Sam embraces a nurse and says, "If you are good enough for war you are good enough to vote." (Library of Congress)

Although the president had been as helpful as he could be, and although the opposition leader was Henry Cabot Lodge, a prominent Republican who led his affluent anti-suffrage friends, the Woman's Party nevertheless continued to target Wilson and the Democrats. They not only believed that this tactic had gotten the issue to a vote, they also pointed out that their picketing had been justified in March, when the District of Columbia Court of Appeals dismissed their arrests and convictions, ruling that White House security was insufficient grounds for ignoring the women's constitutional right to free expression. But, from the National American's point of view, the confirmation of their rights did not turn picketing into smart political strategy for influencing the senators whose votes they needed.

Even after Wilson's appeal to the Senate, the National Woman's Party refused to reevaluate the effectiveness of its anti-Wilson stance, and it especially ignored the fact that 28 of the 34 opposing votes came from Eastern senators. Alice Paul excused these men by labeling the East "notoriously conservative," and in the November elections, her party continued to focus on Western states and to campaign against all Democrats, even those who voted for them.

They also worked for their officer, Anne Martin, in what was the first candidacy of a woman for the U.S. Senate. She ran as an independent in Nevada, where the overwhelmingly male population had responded to her 1914 plea for suffrage. Not enough of the men or the state's newly enfranchised women responded to her personally, however, and Martin won just 20 percent of the vote. The National American, not surprisingly, viewed this as a waste of resources, while the Woman's Party saw it as setting an important precedent.

The National American, in contrast, targeted the Eastern senators from whom women needed just one or two votes. It was a change from their usual policy of working only on the issue, not on candidates, but they made the move at their 1917 convention. They formally resolved: "If the 65th Congress fails to submit the Federal Amendment before the next Congressional election, the association shall select and enter into such a number of campaigns as will…insure its passage." Catt targeted four states—Delaware, Massachusetts, New Hampshire, and New Jersey—because they were geographically small, which made campaigning easier, but their Senate vote, of course, was equal to that of any other state.

A pro-suffrage tugboat in the waters off New Jersey. (Library of Congress)

Despite their size, New Hampshire and New Jersey were not particularly hopeful; according to campaign chairman Nettie Rogers Shuler, both states "were likely to poll Republican majorities" and in both cases, the Republican nominees were opposed to suffrage. The women ran tough campaigns and came closer than they expected, but they lost nevertheless. The hard work was rewarded in the other two states: in Massachusetts, they supported David I. Walsh, who defeated the incumbent anti-suffragist, Republican Senator John W. Weeks. In Delaware, they defeated Democratic Senator Willard Saulsbury, winning the seat for a pro-suffrage Republican, J. Heisler Ball. They won their two votes in the Senate, and House members noticed: 15 of the men who voted against them in 1918 would vote for them in 1919. The women also demonstrated their true nonpartisanship, for they defeated both a Democrat and a Republican who made the mistake of opposing female freedom.

In the meantime, state suffrage referenda also set a precedent this year, with women winning three of four, all in the Midwest: Michigan, Oklahoma, and South Dakota at last joined the full-suffrage states. A fourth referendum, in Louisiana, was conducted without National American approval; despite this and opposition from Southern conservatives and Catholics, women lost only narrowly. In Michigan, Catt visited the suffrage convention in March and promised national support only after they adopted a thorough campaign plan and raised $100,000. The state association did this, and with strong support from the Women's Christian Temperance Union and the General Federation of Women's Clubs, emphasized Michigan women's patriotism in war work. They ran creative advertising, especially the daily publication of 202,000 petition signers in state's newspapers, and they posted supporters' names in local store windows. Another helpful factor was that prohibition had become a moot issue in Michigan back in 1916, when male voters enacted a statewide ban. All of these combined to give women a comfortable win.

The national office sent more money to Oklahoma's state association than in any previous campaign because of a unique obstacle: any ballot on which the referendum box was not checked would be counted as a vote against it. National American field worker Marjorie Shuler did a superhuman job of educating the male voters on this esoteric fact, and she also overcame two other major hurdles: (1) there was a ban on meetings of over 12 people because of the great postwar influenza epidemic, which killed millions of people around the globe, and (2) thousands of ballots were distributed to soldiers without the amendment, all of which would be counted against it. Even after the election, there were more shenanigans until Governor Robert Williams stepped in. When the returns still had not been certified a month later, he took the ballot boxes from an election board which, in the words of Oklahoma leaders, "had always been counted on to defeat any measure that the party 'bosses' did not want." More than 95 percent of the ballots had the referendum box checked, and the women won by more than 25,000 votes.

In South Dakota—where campaigns had been lost in 1883, 1910, 1914, and 1916—the constitution was being amended to correct a problem created in pioneer days, when the territory was so eager for settlers that it allowed male immigrants to vote (and to obtain free land and other benefits) merely by stating their intention to become citizens. The war made it clear that many of these men never followed through on the citizenship process; most were of Germanic origin and thus, technically, enemy aliens. In amending the constitution to correct this, the women cleverly got supportive legislators to strike the word "male" in the relevant clause. By tying the two issues together into one vote, they won easily. The successful campaign was not an overtly feminist one, but instead quietly emphasized women's wartime patriotism and rightful citizenship.

Catt's judgment seemed right: it was the war that gave women these margins of victory. Just as in the Revolution and the Civil War, men saw that the part women played on the home front was vital. The seemingly interminable arguments for equality finally reached a critical mass with this crisis, and for most people, the good sense of democracy no longer was debatable. Under Catt's leadership, the National American did everything that it could during the 1918 congressional elections to tie the suffrage issue to the war, a strategy that the next congressional vote would prove successful. Because anti-suffragists were quick to associate the National American with the Woman's Party's pacifism and to label all suffragists as pro-German, the National American also developed a War Service Department under longtime officer Katharine Dexter McCormick. Every officer worked in some sort of war service, and at its end, Rev. Anna Howard Shaw received the Distinguished Service Medal, the highest of civilian honors.

The ironically liberating effect of war was clear in other nations: by the end of it, women had gained the vote in Austria, Canada, Ireland, Poland, and the United Kingdom. The next year, Germany, Luxembourg, and the Netherlands followed. These Europeans never faced anything like the fight that American women had: because their nations were smaller and more homogeneous and because they could follow a path carved out by others, their suffrage campaigns were much shorter, less expensive, and brought fewer heartbreaks. Catt reinforced this painful point when national suffrage finally passed, saying that her "rejoicing was sadly tempered by the humiliating knowledge that 26 other countries had outdistanced America in bestowing political liberty upon their women."

The guns of Europe fell silent on November 11, 1918, and in the first week in December, President Wilson sailed for France to work on a treaty—but first he included an appeal for suffrage in his departing speech to Congress. It would be the last Democratic Congress with which he would serve, for the Republicans won majorities in both houses of Congress in the November elections. Among the Democrats who would not return to Washington were many friends of suffrage, including Colorado's heroic John Shafroth.

After the Christmas holidays, the lame-duck Congress returned to Washington to cast its second historic vote on the proposed Nineteenth Amendment that would enfranchise women. As they had done the previous year, the House passed it, but the outgoing Senate was obdurate. Angry at the National Woman's Party, Democratic senators refused the pleas of their party colleagues in the House who argued that the incoming Republicans would pass it and get more credit than they deserved. President Wilson again tried to help; he sent cables from Paris and dispatched former Democratic presidential nominee William Jennings Bryan to Washington from his Florida retirement to exert his influence.

He was not successful, as some suffrage opponents of his own party sunk to great depths of deceit. At a Democratic caucus on February 5, the pro-suffrage senators won the vote 22–10—whereupon floor leader Thomas Martin of Virginia allowed the opponents to withdraw their votes, declared that the tally stood at 22–0, and that because 22 was not a quorum, there had been no vote.

In 1918, the Senate had defeated suffrage by two votes; this time, on February 10, 1919, they defeated it by one. The tally was 63–33—just a hair short of two-thirds. Nine senators who voted against it chose to ignore resolutions from their own state legislatures asking them to vote for it. There was nothing for suffragists to do but wait until March, when the newly elected congressmen—minus Republican Jeannette Rankin, who had been defeated because of her antiwar stance—would take their seats.

Meanwhile, state legislatures were meeting, and the National American focused on them—but with a smart new strategy. Instead of asking for full suffrage as they had done for decades, Catt led a push for presidential suffrage only. This apparent step backward actually was very clever, for many state legislators were quick to approve a change that did not affect their own reelection. Tennessee and Iowa started the trend in April; in Connecticut the next month, after what Nettie Rogers Shuler termed "a magnificent campaign," the measure failed by one vote. By the end of 1919, a total of 13 states offered presidential suffrage, some of them with municipal suffrage as well. Except for Maine and Vermont, all were in the nation's midlands. A 1919 map of women's rights thus showed 15 full-suffrage states. Except for New Mexico, the West was solidly enfranchised; the Midwest included Kansas, Oklahoma, and South Dakota; east of the Mississippi were just Michigan and New York. The National American also included Arkansas and Texas on its map of progress, even though suffrage there was not technically full.

The situation looked much better, however, when the presidential-voting states were added: from west to east, the list expanded to include North Dakota, Nebraska, Minnesota, Iowa, Missouri, Wisconsin, Illinois, Indiana, Ohio, Kentucky, Tennessee, Vermont, and Maine. The total then became 15 states with full suffrage and 13 with presidential rights: women in 28 of the 48 states would have a direct impact on the election of the next president. Catt planned to use this fact on congressmen of both parties, for when Wilson's two terms were over in 1920, the White House would be up for grabs.

In the midst of these legislative sessions, Catt took time to meet with her members. So much had happened so quickly in 1918, that, for the first time since its 1890 formation, the National American opted to forego its annual convention. Mostly, the leaders were simply too busy to plan a traditional convention, but skipping it also was another way to demonstrate patriotism by conserving resources. Moreover, no one was eager to repeat the miserable conditions of the last wartime convention.

The 1919 convention was held in St. Louis for five days in late March at the Statler Hotel and Odeon Theater. Termed the Jubilee Convention, it marked the 50 years that had passed since 1869, when the National Woman Suffrage Association began and when women won their first voting rights in the Wyoming territory. Many hard battles had been fought since then, and the character of conventions had changed along with them; this one, in Ida Husted Harper's words, was "almost transformed" from the early days:

> There were no longer eloquent pleas and arguments for the ballot.... Now there was business and political consideration of the best and quickest methods of bringing the movement to an end and the most effective use that could be made of the suffrage already so largely won. It was a little difficult for some of the older workers to accustom themselves to the change, which deprived the convention of its old-time crusading, consecrated spirit, but the younger ones were full of ardor and enthusiasm over the limitless opportunities that were within their grasp.

On the first day, Catt reached out to capture that ardor of the young with an appeal for her League of Women Voters, an idea that she first proposed at the 1917 convention. She intended the new organization to unite women from voting states to work for women in states without rights: "Shall the women voters go forward...as free women," she asked, "while the non-free women are left to struggle on alone?" The answer, obviously, was no. Beyond that, Catt wanted the new league to serve as a conduit for a smooth transition after the final win. She named nine "vital needs" in education and citizenship, the areas in which the league indeed would excel throughout the twentieth century.

The convention continued this forward-looking activity by dispensing with other routine reports and going straight to the Campaign Committee, which was chaired by Nettie Rogers Shuler. Her update reviewed the 1918 victories in senatorial campaigns and state referenda, and it spelled out that suffrage now had been endorsed in the platforms of 21 Democratic state conventions and 20 Republican ones, as well as by "all those of the minor parties." Much of the Campaign Committee's important work, however, was not mentioned in speeches, for unlike the oratorical days of Anna Howard Shaw, Catt's officers understood how important it was to keep their cards close to their chests.

Maud Wood Park, who chaired the Congressional Committee in 1919, alluded to this clandestine strategy when she thanked Helen H. Gardener, whose fifth vice presidency was the lowest ranked but perhaps the most vital. "Her work can rarely be reported because of its confidential nature," Park said, "but…whenever a miracle has appeared to happen in our behalf, if the facts could be told they would nearly always prove that Mrs. Gardener was the worker of wonders." Gardener was the untitled liaison to the Wilson administration; she and the president were old friends, and many of his statements on suffrage were drafted by her. Beyond that, she lived next door to House Speaker Champ Clark, and that brought the "miracles" Park referred to, for Clark indeed twice pushed the federal amendment through the House.

The convention closed with ceremonies honoring the pioneers of 50 years ago, especially Rachel Foster Avery and Alice Stone Blackwell. As usual, Anna Howard Shaw, who had held the title of "honorary president" ever since Catt took over, was the last speaker. "The suffragist who has not been mobbed," she quipped in the style that her listeners loved, "has nothing really interesting to look back upon."

While they looked back briefly on a half-century of progress, the convention's resolutions were aimed at the future. The National American already was transforming itself into the League of Women Voters, for only the first resolution focused on suffrage. Written with exceptional candor, it began: "Whereas…our eastern and southern States are now the only communities in the English-speaking world in which women are still debarred from self-government…." Other resolutions, however, addressed the good government, public welfare, and feminist issues that would characterize the league. The second called for a Cabinet-level education department because "one-fourth of the men examined for the army were unable to read English or to write letters home." Another called upon the census to "classify definitely the unpaid women housekeepers," while Congress was urged "to give military rank to army nurses."

National American leadership returned to Washington and, on May 21, 1919, the House took its final vote on the Nineteenth Amendment. The margin had increased steadily since the first tally, and the House approved it by an overwhelming 304–90—despite the fact that its new Speaker, Republican Frederick H. Gillette of Massachusetts, opposed suffrage. The Senate, of course, was the larger problem, and the election of a Republican majority had done nothing to improve its leadership situation: Senate President Thomas R. Marshall of Indiana, according to Ida Husted Harper, was an "unyielding opponent."

Although they thought they had the votes, suffragists nonetheless worked and worried ceaselessly until the Senate voted in June, when their efforts in the 1918 election finally prevailed. This time enough senators were aware that the die was cast; no minds would be changed, and so many did not attend the two days during which opponents railed to empty chairs. At 5:00 p.m. on June 4, 1919, the last congressional vote was tallied in an anti-climactic way: the floor count was 56–25, a total far less than the full membership, for many senators had not bothered to attend and instead paired themselves with a colleague of the opposing view. With these added, the tally was 66–30, two votes over the necessary two-thirds.

The Nineteenth Amendment goes to the states. Suffragists with Speaker of the House Gillette as he signs the resolution. (Library of Congress)

By careful political strategy and endless public persuasion, the National American women had turned their two-vote loss in 1918 into a two-vote victory in 1919. They had a giant party at their Washington headquarters, and, closing its doors forever at the end of June, hit the trail of the ratification campaign.

When the U.S. Constitution was written in 1789, its framers placed a huge hurdle in the path of those in the future who might want to amend what they saw as their good judgment. A change requires not only approval by two-thirds of both houses of Congress, but also by three-quarters of the states. In a nation with the regional diversity of the United States, that degree of unanimity was extremely difficult to obtain. In 2020, when it sometimes appears that Americans disagree on everything, passing and ratifying a constitutional amendment seems totally out-of-reach.

Suffrage opponents in the Senate were perfectly aware of this difficulty, and aware also that the longer they dallied, the more state legislatures would adjourn. Legislatures met in late winter and early spring, and by June, when the Senate finally voted, many had ended. It was the intention of some senators to thus slow down what they saw as the snowball of suffrage. They also could bet on both horses this way, getting themselves off the hook with liberals by voting for the amendment, while also pleasing conservatives by making it harder to get approval from three-quarters of the state legislatures.

They understood that inaction by just 13 legislatures would cancel the efforts of the others, and inertia is easy. Many legislatures at that time met only biennially, which meant no regularly scheduled sessions until 1921. Nearly anything could happen in almost two years, opponents told themselves, especially with a presidential election scheduled for 1920.

Catt, too, understood that ratification must come as quickly as possible for the wave of enthusiasm to cover three-quarters of the states—or 36 of the 48 at the time. She also was enough of a student of history to understand that a period of conservatism almost inevitably follows soon after any war, and that she must move quickly before the wartime spirit of cooperation began to be forgotten. It would not be easy to obtain the necessary states, for 18 Eastern and Southern ones had never adopted anything beyond school suffrage, and some not even that. Catt, however, refused to give the impression that this was as daunting a task as, indeed, it was. Her confident attitude, along with her undisclosed-but-working "winning plan," made even the movement's officers feel that if their general said victory was inevitable, then it would be.

On the same day that the Senate passed the Nineteenth Amendment, Florida Governor Sidney J. Catts, whose commitment to suffrage had seemed equivocal, quickly swung into action. He sent a message to the legislature:

> While this office has not received verification from…Washington, still The Associated Press would not dare publish something of so vast importance as this, if it were not true. The legislature…will adjourn tomorrow and it has an opportunity, while now in [session] to be the first state in the sisterhood of states to ratify this great movement.

His language was stirring, and most observers were surprised when women did not rush to support him. After years of heartbreaks, however, the leadership had become wary enough to see that extraordinary majority rules would trip them up again: while their head count showed that they could pass the measure, they could not get the two-thirds needed to waive the rules and introduce new business this late in the session. Women, especially May Mann Jennings (who was kin to nationally known William Jennings Bryan) showed their political sagacity once more, for they dismissed possible personal glory rather than risk the disaster of having the amendment lose its first state barely out of the starting gate.

Florida adjourned without voting early on Friday, and the following Tuesday, Illinois, Michigan, and Wisconsin all finalized their ratification on the same day. Their legislatures were still in regular session, as was Ohio's, which joined them on June 16. In New York and Kansas, the governors called special sessions to ratify. When Pennsylvania ratified on June 24, Nettie Rogers Shuler happily reported "its blackness wiped off the map," for the once-progressive Quaker state had never adopted any meaningful form of the vote. The same was true in Massachusetts, the home of the most active anti-suffragists, and Shuler reported: "the change of black Massachusetts to the ratified white on June 25 gave another big impetus to the campaign." Then she added, "Texas distinguished itself by ratifying on June 28. This made nine ratifications in nineteen days!"

Back on May 24, Catt had issued an emergency bulletin to her state leaders on how to proceed when the Senate ratified. She specified that state associations were to inform their legislators of the victory and secure their pledges to ratify, and they were to work the press to pressure governors in states where the session was over to call a special session. According to Shuler, however, the locals disappointed the national: "It soon became apparent that the States… were not carrying out these plans and instead of promises of special sessions, excuses came from the men with the endorsement of the women themselves. It was evident that the national office in New York must be in command." Catt followed up with direct letters to governors and legislators, and three Midwestern governors—in Indiana, Nebraska, and Minnesota—responded not only by scheduling their own sessions, but also by sending letters and telegrams to 22 of their gubernatorial colleagues asking them to do the same.

Texas's ratification on June 28 set the pattern for July. Three days later, Iowa ratified, followed by Missouri the next day. Arkansas followed on July 28, and finally on July 30 came the first Western state—Montana, the first to elect a woman to Congress. A few days later, on August 2, Nebraska ratified; it was the only state to call a session during the dog days of late summer. September brought votes from geographically disparate states: Minnesota, New Hampshire, and Utah.

Catt quite reasonably had assumed that the longtime full-suffrage states in the West would be the first to ratify, but they were disturbingly slow. As autumn fell, just two of the counted-upon Western states, Utah and Montana, had ratified. Shuler termed it an "ominous pause," and Catt implemented yet another plan. With a group of leaders on issues that appealed to women, she held 16 conferences in 12 states, 10 of them in the approval-expected equal-suffrage states.

Women such as Julia Lathrop of the Children's Bureau and Dr. Valeria Parker of the Committee on Social Hygiene joined Catt in her "Wake Up America" conferences, which Shuler called "an appeal to both men and women to use their votes for a better America." These were conducted in late October and November, and in December, their effect showed: North Dakota ratified on December 1, South Dakota on December 4, and Colorado on December 12. After a Christmas pause, Oregon ratified on January 12. Nevada, which ratified on February 7, was the last of the states that Shuler counted as a direct result of the conferences.

Meanwhile, California had ratified on November 1, and Maine followed on November 5. After New Year's Day, more Eastern states rolled in: both Rhode Island and Kentucky on January 6, followed by Indiana on January 16. Wyoming, which, as a territory in 1869 had been the first in the world to grant women full voting rights, ratified on January 26. On behalf of all women everywhere, Theresa Jenkins, who had been the first woman to serve as a delegate to a national party convention back in 1892, thanked the Wyoming legislature for its unanimous vote.

New Jersey was the first of the 1920 legislatures meeting in regular session to ratify; it did so on February 9, after a massive rally in which women presented 140,000 petition signatures. Because legislatures in many smaller states met only biennially, special sessions were necessary in four other states that ratified in February. They were Idaho on February 11, Arizona on February 12, and, on February 16, New Mexico, the only Western state that never granted the vote.

Governor Edwin Morrow of Kentucky signs the Nineteenth Amendment. (Library of Congress)

Moreover, an amazing 24 of these 32 legislatures had ratified in special sessions, a virtual political miracle. Governors, then and now, abhor calling special sessions not only because of the criticism they inevitably get when they call legislators to the capital at a cost of extra time and money, but also and especially because they present an opportunity for unplanned topics and other political mischief. However, in the strongest record ever established, women managed to pressure a huge majority of governors to accept this risk.

The steamroll clearly was on, and yet National American members arguably had been excessively optimistic when at their last convention, in March 1919, they moved to hold the next—and they assumed, the last—during the week of February 15, 1920. This would be the one hundredth anniversary of Susan B. Anthony's birth, and the always historically minded women hoped to celebrate it with the news that the federal amendment had passed out of Congress and been ratified by three-quarters of the states. It was an incredible amount of work to achieve in less than a year, and when they met as scheduled, the Anthony centennial instead became an inspiration for final ratification. As it turned out, Anna Howard Shaw—whose birthday was February 14—had died July 2, less than a month after Senate passage. Because many delegates were friends of Shaw and relatively few knew Anthony personally, they understandably ended up giving more attention to Shaw's memorial than to Anthony's birthday.

The call for the convention was ringingly historic:

> Suffragists, hear this last call to a suffrage convention!
>
> The officers of the National American Woman Suffrage Association hereby call the State auxiliaries...to meet in convention at Chicago. Rejoice that the struggle is over, the aim achieved and the women of the nation about to enter into the enjoyment of their hard-earned political liberty. Of all the conventions held within the past fifty-one years, this will prove the most momentous. Few people live to see the actual and final realization of hopes to which they have devoted their lives. That privilege is ours.

When she published the last volumes of *History of Woman Suffrage* two years later, Ida Husted Harper wrote: "It was almost unendurable that this commemoration of Miss Anthony's one hundredth birthday could not have been glorified by the proclamation that this amendment was forever a part of the National Constitution." Catt's attitude, however, was not that of "unendurable disappointment"; instead, she was her pragmatic self and went straight to the business of the convention: making plans for final ratification and for the transformation of the National American into the League of Women Voters.

The latter was essentially internal housekeeping, but it nevertheless involved many questions, ranging from the fundamental one of whether or not to dissolve the National American to the details of disposing of its funds, files, and other physical assets. Just one of its departments, for example, was a corporation set up for printing: Esther G. Ogden, who headed the National Woman Suffrage Company during the six years of its existence under Catt's presidency, reported that the company had printed and distributed over 50 million pieces of literature. Moreover, requests for their publications were ongoing, many of them from faraway places such as Argentina and Japan. Although seemingly trivial in the context of the national political scene, such complex internal matters deserved attention.

Yet this had to be accomplished in an atmosphere of almost unrestrained celebration. First Vice President Katharine Dexter McCormick said in part:

> We...[cannot] announce that our amendment has been ratified by the necessary thirty-six States, but thirty-one have done so and another [New Mexico] will ratify before we adjourn; three Governors have promised special sessions very soon and two more Legislatures will ratify when called together. There is no power on this earth that can do more than delay by a trifle the final enfranchisement of women.
>
> The enemies of progress and liberty never surrender and never die. Ever since the days of cave-men they have stood ready with their sledge hammers to strike any liberal idea.... It does not matter. Suffragists were never dismayed when they were a tiny group and all the world was against them. What care they now when all the world is with them? ...Let two ratification days, one a National and one a State day, make a happy ending of the denial of political freedom to women!

Although hopeful, Catt was not as ebullient as McCormick. Ever aware that the devil was in the details, she asked the convention to target Gov. Louis F. Hart of Washington with telegrams, as his was the only longtime suffrage state that had not ratified. She instructed her members at length on the necessity of calling for special sessions in the unratified states: "If the Governor is a Republican," she said candidly, "tell him that had it not been that two Republican senators, [William] Borah of Idaho and [James] Wadsworth of New York, refused to represent their States as indicated by votes at the polls...[and] resolutions by their Legislatures," the amendment would have passed in time for the regular sessions. The chief culprit in the Senate's delay, of course, was Majority Leader

Henry Cabot Lodge of Massachusetts, but the complexity of politics is shown by the fact that both Borah and Wadsworth were from states where women already had the vote.

These men were Republicans, but Catt did not let Democrats off the hook: "If the Governor is a Democrat," she explained, "say that had it not been for two Northern Democratic senators, Pomerene of Ohio and Hitchcock of Nebraska, who refused to represent their States…as indicated by their Legislatures and platforms, Congress would have sent the amendment to the 1919 Legislatures and it would have cost the States nothing."

From there she turned to a larger point, seldom mentioned in political annals but worth spelling out, for the history of these principles would form the basis of the League of Women Voters:

> We should be more than glad and grateful to-day, we should be proud—proud that our fifty-one years of organized endeavor have been clean, constructive, conscientious. Our association never resorted to lies, innuendoes, misrepresentation. It never accused its opponents of being free lovers, pro-Germans, and Bolsheviks [as we have been]…. It always met argument with argument, honest objection with proof of error….
>
> It sowed the seeds of justice and trusted to time to bring the harvest. It has aided boys in high school with debates and later heard their votes of "yes" in Legislatures. Reporters assigned to our Washington conventions long, long ago, took their places at the press table on the first day with contempt and ridicule in their hearts…but later became editors of newspapers and spoke to thousands in our behalf. Girls listened…and later…became intrepid leaders.
>
> In all the years this association has never paid a national lobbyist, and, so far as I know, no State has paid a legislative lobbyist. During the fifty years it has rarely had a salaried officer and even if so, she has been paid less than her earning capacity elsewhere. It has been an army of volunteers who have estimated no sacrifice too great, no service too difficult.

The convention also voted to send telegrams to pioneers too frail to come, but still living in hope of seeing their youthful dreams accomplished. One went to Rev. Antoinette Brown Blackwell, Lucy Stone's sister-in-law and long-ago Oberlin classmate, who in 1853, was the first woman ordained; nearly 95, she was living in New Jersey and would cast a well-earned ballot prior to her 1921 death. Charlotte Woodward Pierce of Philadelphia received an especially memorable telegram; at age 19, she had been the youngest signer of the 1848 Seneca Falls declaration.

Founders of the League of Women Voters with their advocacy platform. (Library of Congress)

It would have been easy to sigh happily and believe that the long labor was over, but that was not the case. On February 23, Oklahoma ratified, but only after much careful work by National American field organizer Marjorie Shuler. She led Oklahoma women in securing pledges from a majority of legislators that they would attend; they would serve without pay; they would consider no other legislation; and they would vote for ratification—but the governor still refused to call a session.

It took the intervention of President Wilson and of Oklahoma's Democratic senator—a presidential candidate—to move Governor J.B.A. Robertson. Attorney General S.P. Freeling was so strongly opposed that he took the unusual step of speaking to the legislature against ratification. They ignored him, however, and voted for it by healthy majorities. Doubtless they had their eye on the state's women voters, who had won full rights in the last election.

As difficult as Oklahoma was, it was nothing compared to West Virginia. Except for the final one, no state ratification was more dramatic than that in Charleston. It started quietly enough, when the Democratic governor called the Republican legislature into session on February 27. Anti-suffrage leaders from all over the United States appeared at the capital, along with a committee of conservative legislators from next-door Maryland. West Virginia's House ratified by seven votes, but the Senate tied 14–14, which meant defeat—but then a telegram arrived from Senator Jesse A. Bloch, who was in California: "Just received notice of special session. Am in favor of ratification." In the words of state leader Dr. Harriet B. Jones, "this was refused by the opponents with jeers," but Sen. Bloch "agreed to make a race across the continent."

The women struggled to hold the tie intact and to keep the House from moving to reconsider, as legislators fretted about the delay. When Bloch's train reached Chicago, the opposition played perhaps the most despicable card in their entire pack: it produced a former senator, A.R. Montgomery, who had resigned his seat eight months earlier and moved to Illinois. As Jones said,

> He demanded of Governor Cornwell to return his letter of resignation. The Governor refused and…President Sinsel promptly ruled that he was not a member. On appeal from this ruling he was sustained by a tie vote and the case was referred to the Committee on Privileges and Elections.

On March 10, after almost two weeks of holding their lines, Senator Bloch took his seat amid cheers. Then followed a dramatic debate over whether or not to seat Montgomery, but ultimately a majority of West Virginia senators could not bring themselves to be so deceitful. Bloch's vote made the tally 15–14, and another senator, after seeing that he would be on the losing side, switched to make the final tally 16–13. Thus, the thirty-fourth of the thirty-six necessary states was obtained.

Washington was the last of the worrisome Western states where ratification should have been routine. Presumably, its governor had been holding out for the drama of being the last state to ratify, for the Delaware legislature was considering the amendment at the same time, and state reporter Dr. Cora Smith King made it clear that Washington women hoped to be the ones to push the amendment over the top. Nonetheless, on March 22, the measure was introduced by a female legislator, the governor spoke in favor, and "not one vote was cast against it" in either house.

It was a good thing that Washington did not wait for Delaware, for the legislative fight there went on from March 22 to June 2. The legislature more or less stayed in session all through the spring, while national anti-suffragists made their last stand there. They were supported by conservative lobbyists, especially the Pennsylvania Railroad and, as usual, the never-say-die liquor industry, which was beginning its effort to repeal the Eighteenth Amendment on prohibition. Delaware's other powerful business interest, the DuPont family, supported suffrage, and the DuPonts all worked on the amendment's behalf—but without effect. Downstate men opposed it, and according to reporter Mary R. de Vou, "rushed every farmer and small politician they could secure" to Dover.

Speaker of the House Alexander P. Corbitt was strongly opposed, and on April Fool's Day, the House soundly defeated it, but, as de Vou said, "the lobbying went madly on." The previous day, suffragists had been cheered by a telegram reporting that the Mississippi Senate had voted 21–21 for ratification. A tie is a loss in political terms, and the Delaware lobbying went on. Both houses had strong Republican majorities, and the Republican state convention was scheduled in Dover on April 20. Suffragists met it with hundreds of marching women, a parade of decorated automobiles, and 20,000 petition signatures—a large number in such a small state.

The demonstration had its effect, and on May 5, Delaware's Senate ratified 11–6. Instead of forwarding its resolution to the House as is standard procedure, however, the Senate hung on to it. Literally placed "under lock and key," the resolution waited while the governor, U.S. senators, the president, the DuPonts, and others tried to change votes in the lower house. Weeks of effort made no difference, however, and Delaware's House formally delivered its deathblow on June 2; the last tally was 24–10.

Thus, as summer began, Catt had to go looking for her last vote in the New England states where abolitionism and women's rights first began, but which had grown increasingly conservative. Vermont, where Clarina Howard Nichols addressed the state legislature long before the Civil War, seemed a good prospect, but its Republican governor, Percival W. Clement, adamantly refused to call a session. He had vetoed a presidential suffrage bill that the legislature passed in the spring of 1919, and throughout the following year, he ignored pleas to allow the presumably willing legislature to vote.

Connecticut seemed more likely. It was the home of Harriet Beecher Stowe and other nineteenth-century liberals—but it, too, had a conservative government in the early twentieth century. As in Vermont, Republican Governor Marcus A. Holcomb refused to call a 1920 session, even after appeals from Connecticut Republicans. National American members visited him with a deputation from the National Woman's Party, which, unintentionally or not, had done so much to elect Republicans, but in the words of Annie G. Porritt of the Connecticut Woman Suffrage Association, he "remained obdurate."

During the first week of May, the women organized a tour of 36 Connecticut towns with Carrie Chapman Catt and other speakers. This ended with another meeting with the governor, who again was unmoved. State association president Katharine Ludington, who had chaired Connecticut's Woman's Division of the State Council of Defense during the war, especially felt betrayed, both by the governor and by the state's apathy:

> No women can vote in this election under the Federal Amendment until the 36th State has ratified. It is curious how slow the public–women as well as men–have been to realize this. They talk of our being "almost" voters. They do not seem to understand that although Massachusetts, Pennsylvania, New Jersey, etc., have ratified the amendment, the women of these States will not vote until the 36th State ratifies. Who is responsible for the delay which may keep over 10,000,000 women from the vote for President and about 20,000,000 from the vote for members of Congress...etc.? Both political parties, but the Republicans in greater degree.

Republican women responded to Ludington and pledged not to work or donate to the party as long as suffrage went unratified. Some even went to the national party convention, in Columbus, Ohio, during July, to pressure national officials to make good their platform words. But at the same time, male party officials from Connecticut met with their new presidential nominee, Warren Harding, who, in Porritt's words, "refused to attempt to persuade Governor Holcomb." Catt, who directed much of Connecticut's effort from her nearby New York City home, became convinced that the Yankee State looked hopeless and cast about for alternatives.

The National American's Katharine Dexter McCormick indeed used the right word at the February convention, when she called the opposition "hysterical." Anti-suffragists in several states were so upset by their losses that they filed suits in a number of states against the legislature's ratification. Inventing points of law that had never before been considered in the cases of the first eighteen amendments to the Constitution, they went to court. So stubborn were some about accepting women's new rights that they would pour money into legal fees on these cases until 1922, long after ratification.

The first case to reach the Supreme Court was from Ohio, and on June 1, 1920, the court ruled in *Hawke v. Smith* that the Constitution intended a majority vote in three-quarters of the state legislatures to be enough, and states could not impose additional burdens such as supermajorities or post-legislative referenda. The obstacle to ratification in Tennessee had been that the state constitution barred the legislature from acting until an election occurred, but its Democratic governor and attorney general interpreted the court's ruling to invalidate this. The Justice Department agreed, and on June 24, President Wilson added his voice, telegraphing Gov. Albert H. Roberts and requesting a special session.

Meanwhile, several special elections in Tennessee during the summer boded well for suffragists. T.K. Riddick ran and won explicitly "to lead the fight for ratification in the House," according to state association president Margaret Ervin Ford, and "an arch enemy" of women, incumbent senator J. Parks Worley, was replaced with a supporter. Carrie Chapman Catt arrived in mid-July to help, but she stayed in the background and put Tennessee women in the visible positions. She also worked the phone and telegraph wires to pressure the presidential nominees to announce their support. Republican Warren

Harding's reply was: "If any of the Republican members should ask my opinion as to their course, I would cordially recommend immediate favorable action." Democratic nominee James Cox expressed "confidence that the Legislature will act favorably, which will greatly please the national Democratic Party." Armed with this support, Tennessee Governor Roberts called the special session for August 9, and suffragists returned to the site of their 1914 convention.

It was hot in Nashville in August, and tempers would run hot, too, as the anti-suffragists put up what truly might be their last stand. So many supporters were there that the headquarters spilled over into two hotels, but the opponents were there in powerful numbers, too. "From the time the special session was called," said state president Ford, "anti-suffragists…from Maine to the Gulf of Mexico" arrived in Nashville, "many of them paid workers." Many women also went to Nashville to oppose their own enfranchisement, among them officers of the Southern Women's Rejection League, and of anti-suffrage associations from Delaware, Maine, Maryland, Massachusetts, and Ohio. Probably the saddest disappointment of all to longtime National American activists was the desertion of their former officers, Kate Gordon of Louisiana and Laura Clay of Kentucky, both of whom joined the opposition because their devotion to states' rights proved greater than their commitment to women's rights.

Despite his delay in calling the session, when the legislature convened, Governor Roberts made a strong speech. "Tennessee occupies a pivotal position and the eyes of all America are upon us," he said. "Millions of women are looking to this Legislature to give them a voice and share in shaping the destiny of the Republic." The next day, both houses moved through their committee structure, and on August 12, a joint hearing was held with long speeches from men and women, legislators and non-legislators, representing all points of view. The following day, the Senate voted overwhelmingly in favor, 25–4. And then the trouble began.

The opponents were down to one house of one legislature, and they were desperate. House Speaker Seth M. Walker had promised suffragists that, although personally opposed, he would be fair. He proved to be anything but. When he saw that his side was about to lose, he adjourned the session, and his members—presumably seeking more time to collect more favors—voted to support the adjournment. Carrie Chapman Catt, who was no stranger to political deception, said later:

Never in the history of politics has there been such a nefarious lobby as labored to block the ratification in Nashville.... Strange men and groups of men sprang up, men we had never met before in the battle. Who were they? We were told, this is the railroad lobby, this is the steel lobby, these are the manufacturers' lobbyists, this is the remnant of the old whiskey ring. Even tricksters from the U.S. Revenue Service were there operating against us, until the President of the United States called them off.... They appropriated our telegrams, tapped our telephones.... They attacked our private and public lives.

Representative Harry Burn of Tennessee. (McLung Historical Collection)

On August 18, the Tennessee House voted. As in Congress earlier, some supporters made superhuman efforts for women. Banks S. Turner literally threw off the Speaker's arm from around his shoulder, perhaps casting away his career as he cast his affirmative vote. R.L. Dowlen came from a hospital bed, and T.A. Dodson came back from a train that was leaving the station to vote, even though his baby was dying. The tally was 48–48—a defeat for women—when conscience struck 24-year-old Harry Burn. He remembered his mother's letter asking him to "help Mrs. Catt put the rat in ratification," and his promise to her that, in case of a tie, he would vote for suffrage.

After Burns switched his vote to the affirmative, anti-suffragists charged that he had been bribed. He demanded a point of personal privilege to record in the legislative journal this statement: "I changed my vote in favor of ratification because I believe in full suffrage as a right; I believe we had a moral and legal right to ratify; I know that a mother's advice is always safest for her boy to follow and my mother wanted me to vote for ratification." He did so, and by 49–47, American women gained their freedom.

No. 27,880. Entered as second-class matter post office Washington, D. C.

SUFFRAGE PROCLAIMED BY COLBY, WHO SIGNS AT HOME EARLY IN DAY

50-Year Struggle Ends in Victory for Women

NO CEREMONY IN FINAL ACTION

Secretary Felicitates Leaders; Hails New Era.

Ratification of the nineteenth amendment to the Constitution of the United States, granting suffrage to women, was proclaimed officially today by Secretary Colby of the State Department.

The proclamation was signed by Secretary Colby at 8 o'clock this morning at his home when the certi-

PROCLAMATION ENFRANCHISES WOMEN OF U. S.

Bainbridge Colby, Secretary of State of the United States of America.

To all to whom these presents shall come, greeting:

Know ye, that the Congress of the United States at the first session, Sixty-sixth Congress, begun at Washington on the nineteenth day of May, in the year one thousand nine hundred and nineteen, passed a resolution as follows, to wit:

Joint resolution, proposing an amendment to the Constitution extending the right of suffrage to women.

Resolved by the Senate and House of Representatives of the United States of America in Congress assembled (two-thirds of each House concurring therein), that the following article is proposed as an amendment to the Constitution, which shall be valid to all intents and purposes as part of the Constitution when ratified by the legislatures of three-fourths of the several states

Headline of the *Washington Star* on Congressional passage of the Nineteenth Amendment. (Library of Congress)

And yet the game was not over. Speaker Walker switched his vote and moved to reconsider. House rules gave the Speaker three days during which only he could call up a move to reconsider, and opponents used that time in a frantic attempt to get one of the 49 to switch. When that did not seem to be happening, the defenders of the status quo reached into their bag of tricks for one more astonishment. At the urging of their lobbyist friends, legislators who had failed to win democratically hid themselves. Skipping out of Nashville in the dark of night, 36 members of the legislature holed up in Decatur, Alabama, for more than a week. They hoped to prevent a quorum while the Speaker pushed away at the positive 49, who, amazingly enough, stayed loyal.

On August 23, Margaret Ford and other Tennessee suffragists sat in the gallery and noted the "conspicuously vacant" chairs. With the runaways absent, freshman legislator Riddick—who had run for office to lead this fight—assumed the de facto leadership. Speaker Walker repeatedly ruled him out of order, but with Walker's allies absent, Riddick eventually won their procedural duel. Finally, by a voice vote, the clerk of the House was instructed to transmit the ratification resolution to the Senate. The opposition desperately called for a court injunction, but Chief Justice D.L. Lansden ruled on the spot, effectively dissolving that delaying tactic.

Governor Roberts—whose support was so uncertain only weeks earlier—had seen the depths to which opponents of female freedom were willing to sink, and he took the certificate of ratification and mailed it off to Washington at noon on August 24. When Secretary of State Bainbridge Colby received it on the morning of August 26, he declared the Nineteenth Amendment to the U.S. Constitution ratified. Women's longest labor was over.

Carrie Chapman Catt summed it up. Since the 1848 Seneca Falls call for the vote, she counted: 480 campaigns in state legislatures; 56 statewide referenda to male voters; 47 attempts to add suffrage planks during revisions of state constitutions; 277 campaigns at state party conventions and 30 at national conventions; and 19 biennial campaigns in 19 different congresses. Literally thousands of times, men cast their votes on whether or not women should vote. Literally millions of women and men gave their entire lives to the cause and went to their graves with freedom un-won. No peaceful political change ever has required so much from so many for so long. None but a mighty army could have won.

Part Two

PROGRESS AND CHALLENGES IN THE FOLLOWING CENTURY

Chapter Eight

Carrying On: Early Ambitions, Small Victories

Women in every state voted for the first time in November of 1920, and the League of Women Voters (LWV) was ready with a long list of intentions for the new Congress in 1921. Many of their goals were not directly feminist, as the LWV differed from its mother, the National American Woman Suffrage Association, in being multi-issue, whereas the NAWSA had the sole aim of winning the vote. With that accomplished, longtime lobbyist Maude Wood Park became president of the League, and it joined other organizations, especially the General Federation of Women's Clubs, to promote dozens of legislative items. Park, in fact, called the agenda "a kettle of eels," as there were so many slippery parts.

Ultimately, only a few federal agenda items directly related to women would come to fruition during the politically conservative 1920s—and those were early in the decade. The nation swung away from the progressive agenda of Democrat Woodrow Wilson after World War I: the Senate rejected his League of Nations, and voters chose three Republican presidents—Warren Harding, Calvin Coolidge, and Herbert Hoover. Harding was deeply flawed, involved in both financial and sexual scandals; indeed, his sudden death fueled rumors of other scandals including malpractice by attending physicians and poisoning by his wife. His vice president, Coolidge, was contrastingly puritanical and taciturn—except for his famous proclamation that the "business of America is business." He wholly supported the demise of the labor, farmer, and consumer organizations that had been successful in the Progressive Era, and the resulting decline in middle-class incomes was a factor in the collapse of the economy soon after Hoover won in 1928. That election was a defining point in America history for another reason: Democrats lost largely because their nominee, New York Governor Al Smith, was Catholic. The nation still was not religiously tolerant enough for a non-Protestant president.

With conservatives firmly in charge in Washington throughout the decade, the liberal goals that the League and other women's organizations had adopted in the first flush of victory became increasingly hopeless—and the one successful legal reform of importance to feminists did not cost any money. That was the 1922 Cable Act, which corrected blatant discrimination against women in immigration law. It was the only progressive change in that body of law, however, as Congress put such severe quotas on newcomers with legislation in 1921 and 1924 that immigration virtually ended—another factor in the coming economic collapse. For women, however, the Cable Act reversed an injustice and was directly related to their recent enfranchisement.

Formally called the Married Women's Citizenship Act (or Married Women's Independent Nationality Act), its sponsor was John L. Cable, a Republican of Ohio. Prior to the Cable Act, if an American man married a foreign woman, she immediately was endowed with his citizenship—but the opposite was true for women: if an American woman married a foreigner, she lost her citizenship, no matter how long she and her ancestors had been in the United States. Few people had cared about this inequality until female citizens were allowed to vote, and then it became important. The legislative victory was especially sweet for longtime feminists because one of their pet peeves from the days of Susan B. Anthony onwards was the frequency with which male immigrants voted without anyone checking on their citizenship.

More than any other public figure, Ruth Bryan Owen was affected by women's inferior position in citizenship. She was the daughter of three-time Democratic presidential nominee William Jennings Bryan of Nebraska, but when she married a British army officer in 1910, she lost her American citizenship. He died soon after World War I, as did her father, who had retired to Miami, and Ruth was left to support four children. With help from her very politically astute mother, Mary Baird Bryan, she became the first congresswoman from the South—yet the incumbent she defeated in 1928 argued on the House floor that she was not eligible because of nuances in citizenship law. The problem arose again in the next decade: President Franklin

any sort was not easily obtainable, and some heavily Catholic states banned the sale of any device to prevent pregnancy or venereal disease. The military and most clergymen were complete opposites on this: his superior officers told the soldier he must use condoms, while the Catholic Church, especially, told him that he must not use them, even within marriage.

Mary Ware Dennett died in 1947, two years after the war ended, and Margaret Sanger would forever replace her as the hero of the birth control movement. While Sanger concentrated on public relations and fundraising, Dr. Hannah Stone and a staff of mostly female physicians fulfilled the court's order to limit contraceptive advice to physicians. Sanger's clinic stayed open, but the importation of diaphragms was another long struggle in the courts. A 1936 decision, however, effectively ruled that birth control and obscenity were not synonymous, and bans on obscenity did not necessarily imply bans on contraception. After that, progressive physicians were able to import contraceptive materials and prescribe their use.

Sanger, along with other activists, transformed the American Birth Control League into the Planned Parenthood Federation of America in 1942, a PR move that enhanced its reputation with middle-class women who were offended by the original name. Some wealthy women, including Katharine Houghton Hepburn, the mother of actress Katherine Hepburn, endowed Sanger's work. Sanger and her husband moved to Arizona in 1937, but she never fully retired. She formed International Planned Parenthood in 1952 and raised money to fund the research that allowed the first birth control pills to go on the market in 1960. When she died a mere six years later at age 87, millions of young women were taking the pill.

Yet some state laws remained regressive, including in heavily Catholic states in the Northeast. Connecticut insisted that pharmacists could not sell contraception to anyone without proof of marriage, and Estelle Griswold bravely challenged it. The head of the state's birth control forces, she opened a clinic designed to bring about her arrest for violating the ban on sales to any but married people. The case went to the U.S. Supreme Court, which ruled in *Griswold v. Connecticut* (1965) that such bans violated constitutional rights to privacy, as well as religious freedom.

Massachusetts was the most illiberal state in the nation on this issue, as its attorney general prosecuted activist Bill Baird for his attempt to purchase birth control pills without evidence of his married state. In *Eisenstadt v. Baird* (1972), the U.S. Supreme Court expanded on its Connecticut decision, saying that the marital status of the purchaser should have no effect on the filling of a legal prescription. With that decision, the long fight over contraception began to end. The Roman Catholic Church continues to view the prevention of pregnancy as a sin, but many studies have shown that Catholic women use birth control at the same rate as other women.

Condoms that would have brought an arrest earlier in the century are now available on grocery-store shelves, as empowered women believe that they have a right to decide for themselves whether or not to become pregnant. The last major judicial challenge to state prohibitions of birth control, *Eisenstadt v. Baird*, was on March 22, 1972—and, less than a year later on January 22, the Supreme Court issued the most important of all decisions on reproductive rights: *Roe v. Wade* (1973).

Abortion

In medical terminology, "abortion" refers to any termination of pregnancy before the fetus is capable of life on its own, with "spontaneous abortion" used as the term for what the public generally calls "miscarriage," and "induced abortion" for the deliberate act. With or without the aid and/or coercion of men, women have terminated pregnancies since ancient times. They have used a number of methods, including violent exercise and deliberate falls, eating and drinking herbal potions to induce menstruation, wrapping themselves tightly in abdominal tourniquets designed to expel the fetus, and inserting any number of instruments into the cervix to induce labor. Knitting needles and wire coat hangers have become the symbolic representatives of such vaginal intrusions, but many other items and purgatives, including turpentine, lye, and castor oil, have been used for centuries. Needless to say, millions of women died.

In the early United States, very little law spoke to the subject, and the evidence is that, from colonial times through most of the nineteenth century, women aborted themselves without feeling that they had done a moral or legal wrong; birth control was considered a greater offense. It was only with the growth of organized medicine that state laws on abortion began to be adopted, usually because of lobbying by physicians. While their arguments were made in terms of protecting patients, it also was true that restrictive legislation seriously disrupted the business of their competitors—midwives—who also practiced as abortionists.

Along with birth control, the right to medically safe abortions slowly became central to the twentieth-century women's movement, as feminists came to understand that there could be no true freedom or equality without the right to control one's own body. Reformist measures introduced in state legislatures during the 1950s and 1960s reflected political compromises by focusing on unwanted pregnancies (rape, incest, and malformed fetuses), as well as the possibility of maternal mortality (extreme youth or age, preexisting disabilities, and most controversial, mental health).

Hospital committees, usually composed of male physicians, decided whether or not to grant a petitioning woman the opportunity to end a pregnancy. This almost invariably limited the option of safe and legal abortions to wealthy and well-connected women—women who, even if refused permission in the United States, could to go to Europe, where the procedure was widely available. Less affluent women went to illegal and sometimes unsanitary abortionists, sometimes paying with their lives. Because they could be arrested, such women also were subject to extortion, especially sexual extortion. Almost every middle-size town had a known abortionist, and law enforcement generally looked the other way, partly because the men who paid for the procedure often were prominent.

Recognizing the injustice of the situation, the National Association for the Repeal of Abortion Laws (NARAL) formed in 1969. The very next year, they succeeded in getting the New York State legislature to adopt a liberalized law that permitted abortions without the necessity of appealing to hospital committees. That women wanted this choice was clear: almost immediately, hospitals were swamped with out-of-state women seeking to terminate their pregnancies legally and safely. The situation was chaotic at first, as physicians were unfamiliar with techniques and equipment was not in stock. Many women endured frustrating and costly delays, but NARAL's point was demonstrated.

Meanwhile, twentieth-century medicine had developed several methods of safe abortions, including the use of labor-inducing vaginal suppositories; the saline method of injecting a salt solution into the uterus via the abdomen; as well as the surgical technique of dilation of the cervix followed by scraping of the uterus, known as D&C (dilation and curettage). Most modern abortion clinics have come to rely on the suction method of removing the contents of the uterus.

Legal permission to use these medical advances became genuine on January 22, 1973, when the U.S. Supreme Court simultaneously struck down two state laws that prohibited abortion as an unconstitutional invasion of privacy. *Doe v. Bolton* (1973) was a Georgia case, where the law required written approval for the procedure by three physicians, as well as a three-member committee. *Roe v. Wade* (1973), a Texas case, also had an anonymous female plaintiff suing the state's attorney general; that it became more famous probably was due to the fact that the lawyer for the petitioner was 24-year-old Sarah Weddington, who was just barely out of law school. She later revealed that as a student, she went to Mexico for an abortion.

The *Roe v. Wade* decision was by a margin of 7–2 of the all-male court; the majority opinion was written by Justice Harry Blackmun of Minnesota. In both the Texas and Georgia cases, the court simply extended the right of individual medical privacy that it had already established in the Connecticut and Massachusetts birth-control cases, *Griswold v. Connecticut* (1965) and *Eisenstadt v. Baird* (1972). It did not bar states from adopting laws and regulations on abortion as a matter of public health, but instead guaranteed a woman's right to privacy in making the early-term decision.

Several more Supreme Court decisions soon reinforced the privacy principle, as *Planned Parenthood v. Danforth* (1976) struck down a Missouri law that required a husband's consent. Massachusetts's Bill Baird, who was not a lawyer, broadened his activism from birth control to abortion and won another victory on the issue of consent with *Bellotti v. Baird* (1979). This U.S. Supreme Court decision again was based in Massachusetts, where state law prohibited abortions for teenagers who did not have parental permission. The ruling allowed a pregnant minor whose parents refused consent for an abortion to appeal her case to a judge.

In the same year as *Danforth*, however, what was known as the "Hyde Amendment" was enacted. With the legislation, sponsored by Henry Hyde, Republican of Illinois, Congress banned the use of Medicaid funds for abortions. For decades thereafter, the Hyde Amendment was debated and re-debated with versions that allowed states to create exemptions on the Medicaid rule, especially for cases of rape, incest, or medical necessity. The Hyde Amendment remains in effect, although a 2017 proposal to make the mandate permanent failed in the U.S. Senate, and the 2016 Democratic platform urged its repeal. It is once again coming into play in the 2020 presidential election.

The election of Ronald Reagan and other conservative Republicans in 1980 led to a public perception that *Roe* was on the verge of repeal. Debate on the Hyde Amendment added to that perception, and as both parties began to focus on the issue from opposite positions, the partisan divide increased. At the same time many thought that *Roe* would be overturned, the Court issued other decisions showing its intent to maintain freedom in this sensitive medical decision. In 1983, it struck down a city ordinance in Akron, Ohio, that required hospitalization for first-trimester abortions. A Pennsylvania law similarly designed to discourage the procedure was struck down in *Thornburgh v. American College of Obstetricians and Gynecologists* (1986). In 1989, the Supreme Court issued a decision that the media portrayed as especially dramatic, even though *Webster v. Reproductive Health Services* only made explicit what had been implicit since *Roe v. Wade*: that states retain the right to regulate abortion, just as all public health is regulated. The result was a confused mixture of attitudes in the public, with neither side of the issue feeling secure in the protection of such an ambivalent, divided, and politicized judiciary.

With more appointees by Republican presidents, Supreme Court justices continued in the 1990s to chip away at the principles established by justices in the 1970s. In *Rust v. Sullivan* (1991), the Court not only attacked the right of privacy established by *Roe*, but also assailed the fundamentals of free speech by ruling that health professionals in clinics receiving government funds could not answer patients' questions on abortion, except to disapprove. Sandra Day O'Conner, the only woman on the Court and a Republican, dissented from the 5–4 ruling that imposed these "gag rules" on physicians. Similar impositions on the free speech of health professionals have been repeatedly repealed and then reimposed, most recently under President Donald Trump.

Beyond the free speech and privacy issues, *Rust v. Sullivan* also threatened to erode the principle of the separation of church and state. Having given up on the issue of birth control and the prevention of pregnancy, the Roman Catholic Church doubled down on its "pro-life" position. Evangelicals and Mormons who had stopped the Equal Rights Amendment in 1982 believed that they could overturn the Court's 1973 ruling, using that to recruit members. Few anti-choice people, however, knew enough about law to understand their leaders' hypocrisy in crusading against *Roe v. Wade* while never even drafting a constitutional amendment—effectively the only way to overturn Supreme Court decisions.

Instead, the issue became a fountain for fundraising, and feminist organizations, too, had to raise money for these battles in court. States usually funded the conservative side of legislators and prosecutors, while liberals had to fund their own defense. Countless politicians—virtually all men—sponsored state laws that they doubtless knew were unconstitutional, but this got their names in the headlines and created a fundraising base. A Louisiana law adopted in 1991 was the harshest of this era: it threatened physicians who performed abortions with ten years of imprisonment at hard labor.

In practice, however, women continued to ignore state laws and sought to safely terminate pregnancies. Clinics, often run by women, were established in even small cities throughout the United States during the 1970s and 1980s, but violence-prone protesters increasingly threatened them. The first case was the kidnapping of clinic owners in 1982, and regular attacks by "pro-lifers" continued, escalating in the 1990s. With only a few exceptions, these attacks were perpetrated by men on other men. Operation Rescue killed a Pensacola physician in 1993, and two more male fatalities followed there the next year. Just after Christmas in 1994, two female clinic receptionists in Brookline, Massachusetts were shot to death. This was the only case of women being killed; although several have been severely injured, neither female professionals nor patients died from other attacks.

The case that may have gotten the most attention was in Birmingham in 1998, when a security guard died in a clinic bombing—and that bomber eventually was convicted of earlier crimes, including a devastating attack when Atlanta hosted the Olympic Games in 1996. Later that year, a physician was shot with a high-powered rifle in his home in Amherst, New York. It was a 2009 case, however, that seemed to chill the anti-choice violence: Dr. George Tiller, who had survived an early shooting by a female activist, was killed by a man while doing his regular duty as an usher at a Wichita church. There were no more fatalities until 2015, when three people were killed in a mass shooting at a Planned Parenthood clinic in Colorado Springs. Non-fatal attacks, however, continued with arson, bombing, and other threats. Two perpetrators whose actions could have been fatal were Catholic priests in Illinois and Alabama.

The March for Women's Lives in 2004, one of the largest protests to date in Washington D.C. was called to protest the ever-growing restrictions placed on women's right to choose at the state and national level. (Wikimedia/Elvert Barnes Photography)

Meanwhile, for the first time in American history, the U.S. Supreme Court had no Protestant justices. It included three Jews and six Catholics when President Donald Trump nominated Brett Kavanagh, a Catholic, to replace another Catholic. Most of the fiery debate on his confirmation centered on allegations of sexual harassment (for more, see Chapter Twelve), but although he averred that he saw *Roe v. Wade* as "settled law," many feminists feared that given the opportunity, he would vote in favor of anti-choice positions. He was confirmed by a Senate vote of 50–48 in October 2018. Only one Democratic senator, Joe Machin of West Virginia voted yes; Susan Collins of Maine, a Republican who claimed to be pro-choice, also voted affirmatively. Voters, especially women, demonstrated their displeasure in the next month's midterm election, giving Democrats a big victory in the House of Representatives.

At the state level, legislators continued to pass bills intended to harass doctors and clinic owners. Laws on parental consent returned, with a new generation of lawmakers unaware that this issue had been addressed by the highest levels of the judiciary decades earlier. States also have mandated that doctors have hospital privileges within a certain distance from their clinics; they have imposed wait times for the procedure; and they have required counseling intended to induce guilt. These laws aimed to raise clinics' operational costs and could be very petty: Texas even regulated the width of clinic hallways. The result of such harassment is that in the five years between 2011 and 2016, more than 150 clinics closed or stopped offering abortions. This led to more court cases, as feminists asked for injunctions to prevent closings and continue access. Several states now have only one clinic, and patients have to drive hundreds of miles for the medically simple procedure.

The closing of clinics may not be entirely due to anti-choice politicians, however, as surgical abortions became less necessary after the Food & Drug Administration (FDA) approved the first dedicated emergency contraception, Preven, in 1998. Many doctors had used combinations of ordinary birth control pills to prevent pregnancy after unprotected sex, but Preven and its 1999 successor, Plan B, were the first medications directly intended for this purpose. Often called "morning after" pills, they prevent pregnancy if taken within a few days of sexual intercourse.

The American Medical Association asked the FDA to consider making the medication available without a prescription in 2000, and that happened in 2006. Initially, the pills were sold only on a "behind the counter" basis, but in a 2009 case, a federal judge ruled that pregnant teenagers could purchase the pills. Just a decade later, all of the major pharmacy chains had online advertisements for low-cost emergency contraception with no prescription necessary.

Meanwhile, an increasing number of people began to see "pro-life" as being "forced birth" instead. Although abortion continues to be a controversial issue at all political levels, the 1973 U.S. Supreme Court decision has stood for more than four decades. During all of this time, opponents have not even drafted a constitutional amendment to once and for all overturn *Roe*. The issue simply is too complex and too individual for "pro-lifers" themselves to agree on wording; instead, the topic is treated with facile slogans and extreme proposals.

Some even seem to openly convey misogyny, as with the Texas Republican who had been married five times—and filed legislation in 2019 that could result in the death penalty for a woman seeking to end her pregnancy. But women who were born when *Roe* became the law of the land in 1973 now are middle-aged, and millions have availed themselves of the opportunity to safely end an unwanted pregnancy. Debates will continue, but ultimately, the liberty to control one's own body hopefully will be seen as simply an extension of other freedoms that women won a century ago.

Chapter Ten

Becoming Full Citizens

Redefining Age, Rape, and Violence–And the Connection to Jury Duty

Patriarchy reigned during the early twentieth century in ways that have been forgotten. Nothing is more revealing of the status of females than laws concerning the "age of consent"—the age at which a male can argue in court that he is not guilty of rape because the female consented. These were (and still are) state laws, and they were abominably low. As the twentieth century began, Delaware had only recently raised the age to ten—from seven! Because of the political activism of the Women's Christian Temperature Union (WCTU), most other states had also recently raised the age, but it remained just ten years old in several, including in the contrasting cultures of Mississippi and New York. In Georgia in 1899, a bill to raise it from ten to twelve was defeated, and in New Hampshire, a "woman" could legally marry at twelve. Although rarely noted by historians, new definitions of age were important to the reforms of the early twentieth century.

Appropriate age was the center of debate on a proposed Child Labor Amendment to the U.S. Constitution, which was under consideration during both the late period of the Nineteenth Amendment campaign and the early phase of the Equal Rights Amendment (see Chapter Eleven). Children routinely were employed in industry, especially textile mills in the South—something that had been done in the North a half-century earlier. After many Northern states passed compulsory school attendance laws, many factories moved to Southern states so that they could employ children without regulation. Congress made attempts at a federal ban, but the Supreme Court struck down these laws as an unconstitutional limit on states' rights. Progressives then drafted a constitutional amendment that would overturn the court and allow a federal ban on underage workers.

Congress passed it by the required two-thirds majority in June 1924, and it went to the states for ratification. Arkansas ratified almost immediately, but no other state did in 1924. Just three did in 1925; none in 1926; and only one in 1927. After the Great Depression began in 1928, more state legislatures ratified, but the motivation was not so much protecting children as it was protecting adults from having to compete with children for menial jobs. The amendment never was added to the Constitution, and child labor ended for economic reasons, not legal ones.

Public debate about child labor, however, opened new thought about appropriate ages in other areas. From the 1920s through the 1940s, most states revised their laws upwards, with higher requirements for age-of-consent laws and marriage licenses. Laws requiring longer school attendance also would be an important factor in liberating young women from family pressure to drop out of school and go to work. During the 1920s and 1930s, it still was very common in both urban and rural areas for education to end with the sixth grade. Many families, especially immigrant ones, expected daughters to begin work in their early teens, often to support the educational aspirations of their brothers. State compulsory education laws—and the reality of truant officers—were important in protecting young women from this sort of exploitation.

A notice about age requirements for child labor published by the Children's Bureau of the Department of Labor in the 1940s. Such regulations would help young women attain higher levels of education. (National Archives and Records Administration)

Age-of-consent laws, of course, were closely related to laws on rape, but governmental responses on the issues were quite different. While age-of-consent laws needed revision, rape laws generally were adequate. That said, enforcement was not, and would not be for most of the century. More than any other issue, this was related to race. In many communities, especially in the South, white men raped black women with impunity, knowing that the victim would not report the crime for fear of further violence. In contrast, black men often were accused of rapes that they did not commit, and far too often, this was used as an excuse for lynching.

The Ku Klux Klan enjoyed a strong revival in the 1920s, and lynching returned—with special terrorism aimed at black men who had gotten "uppity" with their service abroad during World War I. The same was true after World War II, yet no president until Harry Truman even attempted to outlaw lynching. Truman, although he was from Missouri and a member of a family that had owned slaves, asked Congress to pass a federal anti-lynching law in 1948, with the result that he almost lost his election later that year. Despite efforts by both black and white women, no federal anti-lynching law was ever passed. The intersection between race and rape has plagued American society since its inception, but it was not until the 1970s that the problem of rape began to gain traction.

This was directly related to jury duty. Wyoming had introduced female jurors already in 1870, but, almost a century later in the 1960s, three states still completely barred women from juries. All were in the Deep South, but 18 other states strongly discouraged women's participation by giving them automatic exemptions. In these 18 states, a woman who truly wanted to be a juror had to go to the courthouse and actively volunteer to be called, with the result that most juries remained all-male until the feminist revolution of the 1970s. In Florida, for example, State Representative Mary Lou Baker introduced a bill to allow women on juries in 1943, during the midst of World War II when there was a shortage of male jurors. Her fellow legislators rejected it, however, and the bill finally passed after she lost the 1946 election—and even then, the bill required women to actively demand inclusion on juror rolls. In *Hoyt v. Florida* (1961), the U.S. Supreme Court upheld these gender-based exemptions.

Little more than a decade later, the court reversed itself—evidence of the growth of second-wave feminism in the 1970s. Jury exemptions for women remained routine in many states, but in *Taylor v. Louisiana* (1975), the court ruled that these laws violated the Sixth Amendment, which grants defendants the right to an impartial jury of their peers. In the case of rape, it was not likely that the defendant would be a woman, but knowing that her peers would be on the jury made a huge difference in her willingness to report the crime. Female lawyers and judges also were positively affected by the decision, and an end to all-male juries was one of the major, if seldom-acknowledged, reforms of the twentieth century. Court cases on the issue lasted until 1994, however, when the Supreme Court ruled that lawyers could no longer use their peremptory challenges in jury selection to exclude jurors on the basis of gender. Ironically, the decision was based on the plea of an Alabama man who argued that he had been unfairly excluded from a jury deciding a paternity case.

As important as the composition of juries was to the issue of rape, public attitudes were even more important. Most law enforcement officers still were male—the fight to get women hired in police and fire departments was still another goal of countless feminist efforts—and many of those men viewed rape as excusable, especially if the perpetrators were white. Joined by more professional male law enforcers in the 1970s and 1980s, feminists worked hard to change attitudes by publicizing what had been a taboo topic. State bar associations often were helpful in educating judges and lawyers to end trial questioning that blamed the victim for her attack. Some states passed laws demanding that a victim's sexual history be excluded from trial testimony. Feminists used analogies to force people to think about how trials for this crime differed from others: for example, rape victims often were accused of provocation because of dress or behavior, but robbery victims never were faulted for displaying something worth stealing.

Rape also differed from other crimes in that in some states, victims were expected to pay for the evidence to prosecute the case. Again citing Florida, state law in the 1980s required a woman to buy the lab kit needed to prove her rapist's identity. She had to be capable of getting past the trauma and sufficiently informed to know that she should not shower, but immediately go to the county hospital for the evidence collecting, and then pay up to $150 for the necessary lab materials. When Florida's chapter of the National Women's Political Caucus lobbied to abolish these fees, some male legislators had the temerity to say that the fee was necessary because women enjoyed vaginal exams.

Educational campaigns were equally important on the issue of domestic violence, and again, especially education of police officers. Although states had moved past the nineteenth-century laws that spelled out the size of a rod that a husband could use to beat his wife, many people still thought that a marriage license entitled a man to a woman's body, even if violently. When

Kitty Genovese was brutally killed on a New York City street in 1964, almost 40 people later said that they heard her screams but didn't get involved because they assumed it was her husband who was doing the beating. Even when police were called to domestic disturbances, they rarely arrested the man responsible. Again, feminists tackled a taboo topic with publicity.

Encouraged by the increasing numbers of female lawyers, abuse victims began speaking out. A California case proved particularly important: a jury acquitted Idalia Mejia of the 1977 fatal shooting of her husband after she testified to his extreme brutality. Two other cases especially captured headlines in the late 1970s. In Oregon, Greta Rideout charged her husband with rape, and most of the public was amazed that a man could be charged with raping his wife. The jury eventually acquitted him, but the fact that a court accepted the premise of spousal rape was a major milestone. In Massachusetts, a man was sentenced to prison for raping his estranged wife, and within the next few years, about half of the states had passed laws eliminating marriage as a defense against rape charges.

Meanwhile, women at local levels began building domestic violence shelters, and in less than two decades, the nation had some 1,500 sanctuaries for battered women. With some pressure from judges and lawyers, police began to cooperate by taking women and children to safety instead of merely admonishing the family for disturbing the peace. At the beginning, these shelters were staffed by volunteers who also raised private money to maintain them, but soon, feminists successfully lobbied legislatures to include this funding within the established criminal justice system.

The biggest change at the federal level was in 1994, when Congress passed the Violence Against Women Act. By making it a federal crime to cross state lines in the assault of a spouse or domestic partner, Congress enabled the FBI and other law enforcement agencies to work together to capture these criminals. A West Virginia man was the first to be convicted under the act: he spent most of a week driving between there and Kentucky, with his wife beaten into unconsciousness in the trunk of his car. In recent years, the Violence Against Women Act has been especially useful in capturing sex traffickers who sell women's bodies at international events. Because it is a federal law, not merely a state one, criminals can be more easily arrested and prosecuted. It also has been effective with lower-level pimps, who move their young victims frequently to avoid detection by staying too long in any one place. The act expired on the day after Valentine's in 2019, and the Democratic House under Speaker Nancy Pelosi immediately renewed it. As of late 2019, however, the Republican Senate under Senate Majority Leader Mitch McConnell has not taken it up, and the important law enforcement tool remains expired.

Chapter Eleven

The Equal Rights Amendment: An Elusive Goal

The ink was scarcely dry on the Nineteenth Amendment when Alice Paul and the National Woman's Party (NWP) announced plans for a twentieth amendment to the U.S. Constitution. The Equal Rights Amendment (ERA), they pointed out, was necessary because the Nineteenth Amendment granted only the right to vote. Many other laws—both state and federal—routinely discriminated against women, and an amendment ensuring equality would nullify such laws.

Progress on many fronts have been made since the ratification of the Nineteenth Amendment, but a constitutional guarantee of equality before the law has encountered controversy, obstruction, and failure across the twentieth century and into the first decades of the twenty-first.

Nevertheless, the ERA is still a lodestar for most feminists today.

From the 1920s to the 1970s

The ERA that was filed in Congress in 1923 read: "Men and women shall have equal rights throughout the United States and every place subject to its jurisdiction." That was almost a century ago—during the first congressional session to reflect fully the new female voters—yet the ERA never has been adopted. Indeed, many, even most, of the leading feminists in the first half of the twentieth century opposed it.

Opponents did not believe that women were not equal to men, but instead feared that women would lose legal protections that progressives had worked hard to obtain. From their youth in the early twentieth century, women such as Frances Perkins, Eleanor Roosevelt, and their colleagues spent decades laboring for working women's pragmatic needs—and had seen their efforts wiped away by legal maneuvering. Pioneer social workers, for example, succeeded in getting New York to adopt a state law limiting the number of hours women employed in bakeries were expected to work, and in *Lochner v. New York* (1905) the U.S. Supreme Court struck down that law because it violated the women's "contractual freedom." Another court case, *Muller v. Oregon* (1908), reversed that, and by the end of the Progressive Era, most states had limited women's work weeks to no more than six days a week and ten hours a day.

Nonetheless, such gains could be tenuous. In *Adkins v. Children's Hospital* (1923), the U.S. Supreme Court struck down a federal minimum-wage law that Congress had adopted for the District of Columbia. With this decision, state minimum-wage laws throughout the nation were nullified. The Court's majority even had the temerity to use women's recent enfranchisement to argue that there was no longer any need for protective labor laws. A classic cartoon illustrated the case's meaning, picturing a Supreme Court justice handling his opinion to a woman, saying, "This decision affirms your constitutional right to starve."

In a time prior to the existence of Social Security, "Mother's Pensions" were another worthy feminist goal. Many—perhaps most—of the children in orphanages at the time were not actually orphans, but merely fatherless. Their mothers were alive and usually working full-time, but women's wages were so low that widows often were financially forced to place their children in orphanages. Some fathers were dead, of course, but many mothers of "orphans" had been abandoned. The intention of "Mother's Pensions" was governmental support for needy mothers, analogous to pensions paid to military veterans. Feminists worked for this on both the state and federal level. Again, though, conservatives could be expected to challenge such programs as creating a protected class, a class defined as unequal—and an Equal Rights Amendment would further empower this conservative view. The solution, of course, should have been to extend labor laws, parental pensions, and other such legal protections to men as well as women, but that was too visionary for the era.

Even more important, as the twenties roared in, feminism was increasingly seen as passé. Instead of organizing for equal legal rights, young women gained new social liberties—the right to smoke cigarettes, drink illegal liquor, drive fast cars, bob their hair, and wear short skirts while dancing to new jazz. The flapper replaced the suffragist, and private social change became far more important than public political change. The evidence is in the numbers: the National American Woman Suffrage Association had two million members at its high point, but only about one in ten of those chose to join its replacement, the League of Women Voters.

The Roaring Twenties featured three Republican presidents—Harding, Coolidge, and Hoover—and, when the economy burned out after the 1929 Wall Street crash, Democrats won the Congress and the White House with Franklin D. Roosevelt in 1932. Roosevelt's New Deal, much supported by the activism of his wife Eleanor, quickly extended labor protections to men, as new laws on maximum hours, minimum wages, and other reforms were adopted; the new Social Security program covered orphans, widows, and even widowers. Secretary of Labor Frances Perkins, the first woman to be appointed to a Cabinet-level position, implemented these ideas and made them work—ideas that were considered impossibly liberal just a few years earlier. Ironically, these reforms meant less need for the Equal Rights Amendment.

Frances Perkins headed the Department of Labor through both the Great Depression and World War II, when the goals of each era were exactly opposite. It was hard for women to find employment in the 1930s, but after the United States entered World War II in 1941, employers begged them to take jobs, especially in defense plants. Women joined men in building airplanes and ships, in manufacturing weapons and ammunition, trucks and tanks. Many did the same work as men, but rarely were they paid equally. Nor did most demand it, as their biggest motivation was to win the war. The Business and Professional Women's Clubs (BPW), a national feminist organization founded in 1919, did advocate for equal pay—but BPW's monthly magazine, *Independent Woman*, spent more ink on how women could help to defeat fascism.

By 1943, the midpoint of the war, 30 women from 23 states had been elected to Congress, but none had agreed to sponsor the Equal Rights Amendment. Instead of a representative in the House, the first female cosponsor was a senator, Democrat Hattie Caraway of Arkansas. She replaced her husband after he died in office but won the 1932 election in her own right.

Populist Senator Huey Long of Louisiana took a great deal of credit for that, but she again won her seat in 1938, after he had been assassinated. Arkansas men supported her, including labor unions members and veterans of World War I, and this support gave her the political capital she needed to become the ERA's first female sponsor.

Perhaps because she was from Arkansas, neither the National Woman's Party nor any other entity paid much attention to Caraway's unprecedented cosponsorship. Alice Paul, however, did use women's new wartime roles to rework the language of the ERA slightly. The 1943 version read: "Equality of rights under the law shall not be denied or abridged by the United States or by any State on account of sex." This tracked the language of the Thirteenth, Fourteenth, and Fifteenth Amendments that abolished slavery and granted civil rights to blacks after the Civil War. Similar language was used for the Nineteenth Amendment that enfranchised women, and all of these amendments included a second section: "Congress shall have the power to enforce this article by appropriate legislation." That second sentence later would prove a problem for the ERA, as opponents—ignorant of the language of the four earlier amendments—considered it to be a frightening transfer of authority from states to the federal government.

Hattie Caraway, Democratic senator from Arkansas, was the ERA's first female Congressional sponsor. (Library of Congress)

Yet, the war did have some positive effect for the ERA, as the Republican Party included a commitment to equal rights in their 1940 platform and Democrats followed the Republicans at their 1944 convention. Still, many people, including feminists, were concerned about the amendment's rigid language and the negative effect that absolute equality could have on women, especially in divorce and property law. Indeed, the League of Women Voters specifically restated its opposition at national conventions in 1942 and 1944, when the war was continuing to shape the homefront. Continued ambivalence about the ERA was revealed when Congress finally took up the proposed amendment in 1946.

That was the first full year after the war ended, and after Hattie Caraway lost her 1944 reelection. There were no women in the Senate, and senators rejected the ERA with 38 in favor and 35 opposed. That, of course, is a majority, but not close to the two-thirds supermajority that the Constitution requires for amendments. Moreover, the math shows that many senators dodged the issue: the combined total of 73 votes falls far short of the 96 senators who represented the era's 48 states. Because the Senate had rejected it, the House did not bother to vote. Beyond that, even though a number of women held powerful positions in the House during the war years, they agreed with the women of the Roosevelt/Truman administration in opposing the ERA, that it was too simplistic an answer to complex problems.

The war nonetheless brought a new awareness of legal discrimination against women and the wide disparities among state laws. Wartime wives, for example, were shocked to discover that in some states, they could not get their own jewelry out of a safe deposit box in a bank without their husbands' power of attorney: if he had gone off to war without attending to this and other such legal details, she had no immediate recourse. Also, at this time and even later, courts insisted on proven grounds for divorce, and that also varied by state: South Carolina's legal code, for example, had no provision for divorce at all. Men routinely walked away from a marriage, and women were legally helpless.

Dwight D. Eisenhower, commander of the Allied Forces in Europe, had opened opportunities to women in the military, and when he won the 1952 presidential election, ERA supporters hoped for his support. Several proposals with compromise language were considered, but women's organizations could not agree on any substitute; instead, Alice Paul's ERA was filed and refiled every congressional session, never moving out of committee to the floor. After Democrats retook the White House in 1960, John F. Kennedy created the first Presidential Commission on the Status of Women, which aimed to address the dilemma. The National Organization for Women (NOW) grew directly out of this commission, formally organizing in October 1966.

One of NOW's first goals was divorce reform, and unlike the Equal Rights Amendment, this goal was achieved so quickly that few people today remember that there was a time in recent history when the law insisted that married couples stay married. Like marriage licenses, divorce was a matter of state law, and that had plagued women since the beginning of the United States. Early in the twentieth century, for example, future president Andrew Jackson and his wife, Rachel Robards, were accused of bigamy after they married in Mississippi, unaware that Rachel's abusive husband had completed only one of the two steps necessary to end their Kentucky marriage.

In most states at the time, a married woman could not file a lawsuit for any reason, let alone to divorce her husband. This was a primary issue for Elizabeth Cady Stanton and a few others, but many women's rights leaders drew the line at condoning divorce. The greatest factor in whether or not a woman could end her marriage was the social status of her family and the lawyers they could hire. In many states, individual divorce bills had to be passed by the legislature, which again, limited the possibility for ordinary women. In Florida, for instance, millionaire Henry Plant got the legislature to change the law for his personal case; after his divorce was complete, the legislature repealed its recent revision.

The issue languished for decades, and even then, the vital legal reforms were not so much directly related to divorce, but instead were changes to married women's property rights and the guardianship of children. The latter was especially important to women, and as they gained the right to sue and to keep their children, they slowly began to initiate more divorces. That it was women rather than men who were most disillusioned about marriage is clear from the fact that by 1900, two-thirds of divorce cases were brought by women.

After the Nineteenth Amendment was adopted in 1920, feminists who had stayed away from the subject because they prioritized the vote finally felt free to draw attention to the need for divorce reforms. A second factor was World War I, when many men came home with venereal diseases that made their adultery evident. By 1920, there were 3.4 divorces per one thousand married people, up from 0.8 fifty years earlier. Yet far into the twentieth century, a marital partner could stop the legal process of divorce simply by refusing to cooperate.

All divorce cases went to court, and trials often were acrimonious. The only "grounds" for terminating a marriage in many states was long-term desertion (often seven years) or proven adultery. Many detectives made a living by entrapping husbands (and sometimes wives) in compromising situations and taking photos that would provide proof of adultery. Even after World War II, nowhere in the United States could a marriage be dissolved merely by mutual consent and without a civil trial to assign fault, but that became easier in some states than in others.

In a North Carolina case in 1945, the Supreme Court ruled that the Constitution's "full faith and credit" clause meant that states must recognize divorces that were granted in other states. Many lawyers saw the economic opportunity in this, and divorce mills soon popped up in a half-dozen states. Legislatures in Arizona, Arkansas, Idaho, Washington, and especially Nevada amended their laws to make divorce easier and encouraged divorcing couples to place their case in their courts. Arkansas specialized in "divorce by publication." Newspapers ran legal ads telling a defendant that he or she was being divorced, and if the defendant didn't see the ad, judges often would grant the divorce anyway.

More common were the "quickie" divorces that especially prevailed in Nevada, where Reno made an industry of it in the 1950s. Nevada required only six weeks to become a legal resident, and countless women went there, stayed at a resort for six weeks, and returned home with divorce papers. Faced with this competition, other states modified their laws, lowered the cost for divorce, and otherwise smoothed out the process, but it was not until 1969—less than three years after NOW began—that California adopted the first "no-fault" divorce law.

These changes thus were less a result of the organized women's movement than of amendments to state laws that were proposed by male lawyers and legislators. Because the new non-adversarial approach was so obviously superior to the previous situation that encouraged couples to lie, and because the women's movement had other priorities, it was understandable that continued male bias in both law and judicial behavior often was overlooked during the sixties and seventies. By the 1980s, however, feminists were aware of many studies showing that the living standards of divorced women dropped dramatically, while those of men rose disproportionately. The needs of these "displaced homemakers" and the enforcement of child support orders against "deadbeat dads" then became a focus of feminist attention.

"Palimony" entered into the discussion in 1977 when a well-publicized Hollywood case drew national attention. Although they never married, Michelle Marvin had lived with actor Lee Marvin for years and sued for financial support when they broke up. The California Supreme Court ruled against her, but other cases followed in other states, including men who sued women for financial support and same-sex couples who sued each other. By the millennium, however, both palimony and alimony became less common, as women increasingly were seen as capable of supporting themselves—although it was still critical for women of lesser means. The important point is that by the end of the twentieth century, not even the most legalistic of contract lawyers would argue that states had the right to enforce a marital contract that individuals wished to dissolve.

The Next Half-Century

Despite progress in divorce resulting from the Constitution's "full faith and credit clause," at mid-century, state laws continued to insist on regulating other matters and routinely discriminated on the basis of race, gender, and even religion. Democratic President Harry S. Truman used executive orders to racially integrate federal employment, including the armed forces, in 1948. His successor, Republican Dwight D. Eisenhower, went even further in asserting the rights of the federal government over that of the states when he used military troops in the late 1950s to enforce the Supreme Court's 1954 decision that public schools could not exclude students on the basis of race. Sending the Army to displace local police in Arkansas, Mississippi, and Alabama was the death knell for states' rights in terms of race, and gradually the ideal of equality came to be applied to gender, too. Reforms in the century's second half were almost entirely due to replacement of state law with federal law.

Congress passed an Equal Pay Act in 1963, late in the presidency of Democrat John F. Kennedy. Under Democrat Lyndon B. Johnson in 1968, Congress adopted the Consumer Credit Protection Act, which assured women of a right to apply for mortgages and to maintain credit histories separate from those of their husbands. Also in 1968, Congress removed legal limitations on rank for women in the military, and, in 1976, it would mandate the admission of women to West Point and other military academies. Ironically, as more such equalizations occurred in the law, some arguments for the ERA became less relevant. Perhaps even more important, federal agencies began to apply the major civil rights legislation of 1964 and 1965 on the basis of gender as well as race.

The nation was in turmoil not only because of racial integration, but also because of opposition to the war in Vietnam. Some anti-ERA forces were quick to point out that were the ERA in effect, young women would have to submit themselves to the military draft just as young men did, but many newly radicalized people responded that the proper solution should be to end forced military service. Older women's organizations, including the Business and Professional Women, American Association of University Women, and the League of Women Voters began to follow NOW's lead, and even organized labor strongly came on board to work for the ERA.

Coalitions of dozens of organizations, representing millions of people, developed everywhere, and, by March of 1972, there was enough support for the ERA that both congressional chambers passed the proposed amendment by the necessary two-thirds majority. In addition to supermajorities in Congress, however, the Constitution requires that its amendments be ratified by three-quarters of the state legislatures, which means both chambers. Thus 38 states were needed, or a total of 76 positive legislative tallies.

Hawaii ratified almost immediately, and 30 other states followed by the end of 1973. After the first wave of enthusiasm, though, opposition began to strengthen. Probably the most effective argument against the ERA was that women would have to be drafted for an unpopular ongoing war, and even feminists did not know enough of their history to understand that Congress already had that right: indeed, during World War II, it seriously considered drafting nurses, who were inherently defined as women back then. The ERA's negation of protective labor laws—including such issues as a mandate to provide women on assembly lines with chairs and limiting the amount of weight they were expected to lift—remained important to some. Many female lawyers who specialized in divorce opposed the ERA because it would negate laws that favored women in alimony and child custody. When abortion rights entered into the debate after the *Roe v. Wade* decision in 1973, feminists found it increasingly hard to focus attention on the genuine issues, and much of the debate on the ERA degenerated into derisive hyperbole. Public restrooms, not legal equality, generated the most attention.

On the positive side, progress was made in specific state laws, as many legislatures repealed blatantly discriminatory laws and practices. Women, for instance, were admitted to university programs previously closed to them; laws on jury duty were equalized; and property laws reformed. Perhaps the most egregious property case was an Idaho law that gave men superiority in probate: in *Reed v. Reed* (1971), a woman challenged this because, under the state's law, her mentally disabled brother automatically became the executor of their parents' estate. The U.S. Supreme Court struck it down, yet Idaho's attorney general had argued it all the way to the highest level. The case was a perfect example of the complexities of the ERA debate. Moral justice and common sense demanded change—and yet, this reformative Supreme Court decision arguably was a more efficient way of creating change than adding a constitutional amendment that would be applicable to every situation everywhere.

The pattern continued, as other Court decisions seemed to obviate the need for the ERA. During the remainder of the 1970s, the Court struck down numerous state laws with gender bias. Among the examples was an Oklahoma law that set different ages for males and females to buy beer; in an Alabama case, it voided minimum height and weight requirements for police officers as inherently discriminatory against women. In response to a class-action lawsuit brought by the Women's Equity League (WEAL), state-funded medical schools began to drop their quotas on female students, which typically limited women to no more than 10 percent.

The executive branch of the federal government also introduced reforms, often encouraged by FEW, or Federally Employed Women. In 1971, the Civil Service Commission agreed to eliminate references to gender in federal job descriptions, and the Civil Rights Commission expanded the 1964 Civil Rights Act as applicable to women. Title IX of the 1972 education funding act brought more equity in schools and higher education for female students and faculty. The Equal Employment Opportunity Commission also had real enforcement powers, and thousands of women appealed to its regional branches for correction of wrongs in the workplace. And as more women were elected to office, state and local governments reformed discriminatory practices, thus again negating some of the need for a broad constitutional amendment.

More important to the ultimate defeat of the ERA, though, was that conservatives came to see it as an effective rallying tool to build their political organizations. As with the Nineteenth Amendment, most of the states that did not ratify were in the South. Richard Nixon's 1968 "Southern Strategy" of getting conservative Democrats to re-register as Republican proved increasingly successful, especially among white men, and the once "Solid South" of the

Democratic Party split over feminist issues as well as racial ones. Democratic majorities in state legislatures disappeared, greatly hampering the ratification efforts of Democratic President Jimmy Carter. The ERA made little progress during his one term, from the 1976 election to that of 1980, even though he was from the South.

Western states had been liberal earlier in the century, when all but New Mexico had granted women the vote prior to the Nineteenth Amendment, but that was no longer the case with the ERA. Utah, for example, had enfranchised women in 1870, when it suffered from religious persecution, but its political ideology had reversed a century later, and the powerful Mormon Church strongly opposed the ERA. The same was true for evangelical churches, especially in the South. Earlier in the century, clergymen often had supported women's enfranchisement because they believed women would vote for prohibition, but a few decades later, they worried aloud that the ERA might force churches to ordain women.

Conservative groups, including business political action funds, poured money into defeating candidates who supported the ERA. Besides bringing ratifications in the remaining legislatures to a halt, they also managed to persuade some states that had ratified to rescind their approval. Idaho, the home of *Reed v. Reed* (mentioned above), was one of them; its legislature rescinded its ratification in 1977. With the 1980 nomination of Ronald Reagan, the Republican Party took the ERA out of its platform—and Republican women's clubs, ironically, grew stronger. These conservative women marched on legislatures in great numbers, demanding that lawmakers vote against equal rights for women.

Feminists, of course, rallied also. ERAmerica, which formed in 1976, was akin to the earlier National American Woman Suffrage Association in that it was single-issue: the sole goal was to unite women's organizations in support for the ERA. It was effective in some places, and some states that had already ratified the national amendment added equal rights amendments to their state constitutions. In other states, however, such referenda campaigns were lost. Conservatives, of course, played up those electoral losses as proof that women didn't want legal equality. Indeed, the failures were sufficient that time ran out. Congress extended the ratification period from March 1979 to June 1982—but even that was not enough to gain the three additional necessary states. Indiana, which ratified in 1977, was the thirty-fifth and last state to approve it.

First lady, Rosalynn Carter, with former first lady Betty Ford, at a rally for the passage of the Equal Rights Amendment in 1977 sponsored by the umbrella alliance ERAmerica. (National Archives and Records Administration)

With the "Reagan Revolution" of 1980, the country declared itself on a conservative course, and the presidential support that had gone back to Eisenhower in the 1950s was withdrawn. Taking their cues from that, legislatures in Nevada, Oklahoma, Georgia, Missouri, and North Carolina voted down the ERA during the extension period. Phyllis Schlafly, the nation's most influential anti-ERA woman, was from rural Illinois, and even its relatively progressive legislature could not manage the extraordinary majority that its constitution required. In many states, one chamber approved, while the other did not. That was the case in Florida, which turned out to be the last state to vote. Its House repeatedly voted for the ERA, but eight days before the extension expired, the Florida Senate voted against it by 21 to 19, with a Tampa senator deserting the feminists who had campaigned for him because of his promise to ratify.

Yet the decade between 1972, when Congress sent the ERA to the states, and 1982, when the extended expiration period expired, brought tremendous attitudinal change. People who never had considered feminist issues became aware of them, and many hands-on solutions to real problems developed, especially with domestic violence and rape, as well as equal opportunity in employment and education. Gay rights also entered into the debate, particularly after the Hawaii Supreme Court suggested in 1993 that the state ban on same-sex marriage might by unconstitutional. Massachusetts became the first state to authorize such marriages in 2004, and in just a little more than a decade, with the U.S. Supreme Court's decision in *Obergefell v. Hodges* (2015), same-sex marriage became legal everywhere.

Problems, of course, persisted, especially economic issues. A number of governmental entities did comparable worth studies in the 1980s and 1990s, which revealed disparities such as unskilled garbage men whose pay was comparable to credentialed nurses with great responsibilities. Progress was slow, as at the beginning of the twentieth century, women's wages generally were half of that of men—and at its end, the ratio had only risen to about three-quarters. Inequality was especially likely with jobs that traditionally had been segregated by gender, as well as in workplaces that lacked unions, which provide open information on wages. Congress addressed the issue in 2009 with the "Lilly Ledbetter Fair Pay Act," named for a blue-collar woman whose employer used hidden unequal pay scales throughout her working life.

The Lilly Ledbetter case revived the feminist movement to some degree, but it did not revive the Equal Rights Amendment. That continued to be on the back burner, as most leaders saw ERA revival as a legal complication that would impede more tangible causes for women. After Hillary Clinton won the 2016 popular vote for president, and especially after Nancy Pelosi resumed the House speakership when Democrats won a majority in 2018, new enthusiasm arose for another attempt to add the ERA to the Constitution. Illinois retroactively ratified, and many have been led to believe that only one more state was needed to add the amendment to the Constitution.

That sounded simple, but no precedent exists for reviving old ratifications, and the legal ramifications of recisions make the issue even more complex. Court cases predictably would arise from this unprecedented procedure, with current state and federal legislators arguing that they are not bound by actions that occurred almost a half-century ago. Yet Democrat Jackie Speier of California managed to schedule a hearing on the ERA with a subcommittee of the House Judiciary Committee on May 6, 2019, and several feminist organizations testified on behalf of reviving the amendment. A committee of the Virginia legislature also voted affirmatively in 2019, and some of the leading Democratic presidential candidates vowed, if elected, to work for the amendment's adoption. Most importantly, the House Judiciary Committee voted in November 2019 to remove the 1982 deadline. While it seems unlikely that the Senate will do the same, especially by the required two-thirds majority floor vote, if Democrats win overwhelmingly in November 2020, it is possible that the Equal Rights Amendment will be added to the Constitution by 2023, the centennial of its birth.

Chapter Twelve

Taking Power: Milestones and Challenges

Although the ratification of the Nineteenth Amendment was a huge victory, women still had—and have—miles to go in attaining political parity with men. As with early progress in the suffrage movement, local and state milestones largely came first.

Early State Precedents and the U.S. House

Susan B. Anthony and other feminist pioneers were alive and well back in 1892, when the first woman won a statewide office. She was North Dakota School Superintendent Laura Eisenhuth, and other Western states soon followed that precedent—and set new ones. In the next election cycle, 1894, Colorado voters chose three women for their state House. They would continue to do so in the future, and in 1896, Utah voters elected the first female state senator. She was Dr. Martha Hughes Cannon, a physician and the fourth wife of a Mormon elder. As Westerners continued to set these precedents, the first woman elected to Congress was Montana's Jeannette Rankin, an employee of the National American Woman Suffrage Association, in 1916. The second congresswoman, elected in 1920, was a complete philosophical contrast: Alice Robertson of Oklahoma was extremely conservative and had opposed women's right to vote.

Dozens of such precedents had been set prior to the 1920 general election, the first in which women in all states could vote for all offices. There were only a few weeks between the adoption of the Nineteenth Amendment on August 26 and that November election, and some voter registrars tried to hold down women's new rights with debate about implementing the federal amendment. Among the points they considered worth pondering was whether women should register under their husbands' names or their own first names or whatever might or might not demonstrate that they still were considered second-class citizens. Other legalists debated whether the right to vote necessarily implied the right to run for office. In many states, the deadline for candidate filing had passed, and party nominations already had been decided.

Yet in the brief time available, women managed to get on the ballot in several states, mount campaigns, and win their races. The states that elected women to their legislatures for the first time in 1920 were Connecticut, Indiana, New Hampshire, and Vermont. The most remarkable victories doubtless were those in Vermont and Connecticut because both New England states had refused to ratify the Nineteenth Amendment.

Kentucky and New Jersey had off-year state elections, and women won legislative campaigns in both states in 1921. The next cycle, 1922, was the biggest year. With more than the few weeks to organize than they had in 1920, 38 women won legislative seats in 19 states. Pennsylvania had the most, with eight; Minnesota and Ohio followed with four each. Virginia set this milestone in its 1923 off-year election, while the presidential year of 1924 brought seven more states and the Hawaii Territory. The Alaska Territory joined the list in 1936; the last two to elect a woman to their state House were Louisiana in 1940 and South Carolina in 1945. Florida in 1928 was an interesting anomaly: voters not only elected the first woman to its legislature that year, but also the first woman in a statewide race (railroad commissioner), as well as the first congresswoman from the South.

Unlike U.S. senators, who can be appointed to vacancies, all members of the U.S. House of Representatives are elected, even if the election is pro forma. A myth has arisen that the first women in Congress were widows of congressmen and merely placeholders until the next election, but analysis of the first dozen women in the U.S. House shows that generality is less than true. The first two congresswomen, of course, were Jeannette Rankin of Montana and Alice Robertson of Oklahoma, both unmarried women. Rankin won in 1916 and Robertson in 1920, after Oklahoma women got the vote in 1918. The third congresswoman was Winnifred Mason Huck, elected in 1922. An unmarried

Chicagoan, she was so assertive that she ran for the U.S. Senate soon after her election to the House; when she lost, she stayed in Washington and worked for the National Woman's Party.

The fourth, San Francisco's Mae Ella Nolan, did have a husband precede her, but was sufficiently respected that she had the unusual honor of chairing a House committee in her first term. New Jersey's Mary T. Norton was the fifth congresswoman. Elected in 1924, she was married, but her husband rarely was seen in Washington while she rose to tremendous power during a long tenure. Like her fellow San Franciscan Mae Ella Nolan, Florence Prag Kahn was the widow of a congressman; she stayed on the House Military Affairs Committee long enough to have appreciable influence in getting naval bases to California, something that would prove vital in World War II. The first Jewish woman in Congress, Kahn won a special election in 1925, as did Edith Nourse Rogers of Massachusetts. She represented the district north of Boston and is considered the Mother of the Women's Army Corps; her 45-year House tenure set a record for women.

As an estranged wife, the eighth congresswoman, Katherine Langley of Kentucky, was an anomaly. A Republican, she won a special election in 1927 for her husband's seat when he was sent to federal prison for violating prohibition law. She won again in 1928 and successfully negotiated a pardon for him from President Calvin Coolidge, which included John Wesley Langley's promise not to seek office again. He betrayed his vow in 1930 and ran against his wife, with the result that the male Democratic nominee won the seat.

The ninth congresswoman was Florida's Ruth Bryan Owen, a Democrat, elected in 1928 (See Chapter Eight). And in that remarkable year, Illinois elected its second congresswoman, with Republican Ruth Hanna McCormick. Like Ruth Bryan Owen, McCormick came from a powerful political family, but was a strong person in her own right; although known as "Mrs. Medill McCormick," she had worked hard for the vote. Oddly enough, a third woman named Ruth also won in 1928, as voters in the "Silk Stocking" district of Manhattan chose Republican Ruth Sears Baker Pratt. She was wealthy and married but had independent political experience as the first woman elected to the New York City Board of Aldermen. After she seconded the nomination of Herbert Hoover at the 1928 Republican convention, Pratt would be one of many Republicans who lost their elections in 1932, the nadir of the Great Depression.

The last of the women elected to U.S. House in the 1920s, Pearl Oldfield of Arkansas, does fit the image of women who were placeholders after their husbands' deaths, but she nonetheless managed to get a $15 million appropriation for aid in the recovery from the devastating Mississippi River floods in her district. To summarize, of the 12 women elected to the U.S. House during the 13 years between 1916 and 1929, only two—Arkansas's Oldfield and California's Nolan—fit the image of briefly holding the seat of a dead husband. Others indeed benefited from a famous political family, but that ever has been the case for men. Three congresswomen—Montana's Rankin, Florida's Owen, and Illinois's McCormick—were veteran feminists who warmly embraced women's rights. They merit the precedents they won.

Seven of the nine women serving in the House of Representatives on April 15, 1929. From left to right, first row: Pearl P. Oldfield, Arkansas; Mary T. Norton, New Jersey; Ruth Baker Pratt, New York; back row: Ruth Bryan Owen, Florida; Edith Nourse Rogers, Massachusetts; and Florence Kahn, California. Katherine Langley of Kentucky and Ruth Hanna McCormick of Illinois are the two Congresswomen missing. (Library of Congress)

The Great Depression of the 1930s reversed women's progress in every field, including government, but there were more powerful congresswomen during the 1940s and World War II than most people realize. Mary T. Norton of New Jersey chaired the House Labor Committee at a time when labor was crucial to winning the war, and near its end, she led her committee in drafting the extremely significant GI Bill. Frances Bolton of Ohio sponsored important legislation on nurses, who also were key to victory, and after the war, Bolton headed a subcommittee of the Foreign Affairs Committee on Africa and the Near East. Edith Nourse Rogers of Massachusetts led the creation of the precedent-setting Women's Army Corps, and when Republicans held the majority in the postwar years, she chaired the House Veterans Affairs Committee. Margaret Chase Smith of Maine is considered the mother of the Navy's WAVES and would go on to the U.S. Senate.

Eighteen new women joined the U.S. House in the 1940s, and 16 in the 1950s—a slight slip during this postwar "back-to-the-kitchen" decade, but not as regressive as is generally depicted. The most notable may have been Martha Griffiths of Michigan, elected in 1954, who led hearings on economic inequities for women. The counterculture 1960s actually were more disappointing than had been the 1950s, with just ten new women in the House. Two, however, had great feminist impact, and both were racial minorities. Patsy Mink of Hawaii, who won in 1964, was the first Asian American congresswomen, while the first African American, Shirley Chisholm of New York, won in 1968. Chisholm's victory especially would prefigure the intensification of the women's liberation movement of the 1970s.

With support from the National Organization for Women and other new feminist groups, 23 women won their races for the U.S. House during the 1970s; 18 of the 23 were Democrats. The 1970 election brought the fiery Bella Abzug of New York, as well as Ella Grasso of Connecticut, who would go on to be governor. The 1972 election was the most significant, especially with the victory of Patricia Schroeder of Colorado, who would become the strongest congressional leader for women. Two more African Americans, Yvonne Brathwaite Burke of California and Barbara Jordan of Texas, joined the House that year, and Burke would be the first member of Congress to be pregnant in office. New York's Elizabeth Holtzman defeated a 50-year incumbent, Emanuel Celler; he had held the seat since 1922 and was primarily responsible for keeping the Equal Rights Amendment in committee.

Feminists continued to win elections through the rest of the 1970s. Gladys Spellman and Barbara Mikulski gained seats from Maryland; Mikulski later would rise to the Senate. Lindy Boggs of Louisiana especially advocated for women's history, while Mary Rose Oakar of Ohio promoted the idea of "comparable worth." The decade's last cycle, 1978, would bring Geraldine

Ferraro to the House; she would be the Democratic Party's nominee for vice president in 1984, attaining a milestone as the first women to be nominated on a major party ticket. All of the above were Democrats, but two Republicans were notably feminist: Olympia Snowe of Maine and Millicent Fenwick of New Jersey. Fenwick would be the model for mythical Congresswoman Lacy Davenport in the popular comic, "Doonesbury."

The 1980s saw exactly the same number of new women in the House as the 1970s: just 23. The "Reagan Revolution" meant that more were Republicans, and after that party dropped its support for the Equal Rights Amendment from its platform in 1980, efforts for feminist legislation were harder. Perhaps the most significant election of that decade was in 1986, when Californians chose Nancy Pelosi, who would become the first female Speaker of the House after Democrats won a majority in the 2006 midterm elections; she again would become speaker in 2019 after Democrats took back control of the chamber.

The 1990s were a revival of the 1970s, especially as First Lady Hillary Clinton was the strongest feminist ever in the White House. A second factor was the emergence of EMILY's List, which aimed to recruit and fund women who supported women's rights. A total of 61 new women joined the House during the 1990s, more than twice as many as had been elected in any previous decade. The gender gap between parties that pollsters had been predicting became very clear, as just 16 of the 61 women were Republicans. Perhaps the most striking race was that of Los Angeles's Loretta Sanchez in 1996; she defeated a powerful Republican who could not accept that he had lost to a young Latina, but voters further demonstrated their intent by electing her sister, Linda Sanchez, to an adjacent district in 2002.

The decade between 2000 and 2010 brought 63 women, a slight increase from the previous decade. With a Republican president during most of that time, Republican numbers increased significantly, rising from 16 of 61 in the 1990s to 26 of 63 in the new century, but a significant gender gap still prevailed, with Democrats nominating and electing many more women, especially racial minorities. Among the strongest feminists were Debbie Wasserman Schultz and Kathy Castor, both of Florida, and Arizona's Gabrielle Giffords, who nearly died when a right-wing man shot her and others in 2011 at a Tucson shopping center.

The next decade set several precedents in the U.S. House. In the 2012 election, Arizona voters made Democrat Kyrsten Sinema the first openly bisexual woman representative. She would go on to the U.S. Senate, while Utah's Mia Love, the first Republican African American woman, would win in 2014, but lose in the next cycle. The 2016 election brought the first woman of Vietnamese heritage, Florida's Stephanie Murphy, and the first Indian American, Pramila Jayapal of Washington; both were Democrats, and Jayapal later would make headlines by speaking in committee about the discrimination that her transgender child endured.

The 2018 midterm cycle was another revolution: not only did 28 new women enter the House, but also Speaker Nancy Pelosi returned with a firm Democratic majority. All but one of the new victors were Democrats; the only Republican was Carol Miller of West Virginia, whose father had been in politics. Among the precedents set in 2018 were the election of the first Native American women, Deb Haaland of New Mexico and Sharice Davids of Kansas; and the first two Muslim women, Ilhan Omar of Minnesota and Rashida Tlaib of Michigan.

Krysten Sinema, Democrat of Arizona, the first openly bisexual woman in the House of Representatives, was elected to the Senate in 2018. (Wikimedia/U.S. House)

The most attention-getting was Alexandria Ocasio-Cortez of New York: after defeating a longtime powerful white man in the Democratic primary, Democratic caucus chair Joe Crowley, she, at age 29, was the youngest woman ever elected to Congress. Ayanna Pressley of Massachusetts was far from the first African American congresswoman, but President Donald Trump nonetheless included her when he attacked Omar, Tlaib, and Ocasio-Cortez in a speech that led to these four freshmen being dubbed "The Squad." Veronica Escobar, also elected in 2018, soon drew attention because of a mass shooting in her district; the gunman said he had driven hundreds of miles to El Paso because it would give him a better chance to kill more Hispanics. Escobar was elected to the Democratic House leadership team in November 2019.

As of 2019, 102 women were serving in the 435-member House, making up just less than one-quarter of the whole; 89 were Democrats and 13 Republican. Although the total number is far from the 50 percent that a truly representative House of Representatives should be, it nonetheless showed tremendous recent progress. That number is an important milestone—representing approximately one-third of the total number of women, slightly more than 300, who have *ever* served in the House.

Just four states—Alaska, Mississippi, North Dakota, and Vermont—never have elected a woman to the U.S. House. Three of the four—Alaska, North Dakota, and Vermont—have populations so small that they are entitled to only one seat, and campaigning in their statewide races is the equivalent of campaigning for the U.S. Senate. Alaska has chosen women as both governor and U.S. senator; Vermont has had a female governor; and North Dakota elected the first woman to statewide office, back in 1892.

The U.S. Senate

The U.S. Senate was much slower to include women than the House, which had its first in 1916. The ostensible first in the Senate was in 1922—and Georgia's Rebecca Latimer Felton merely was appointed to a vacancy. Although 1922 was a tremendous year for electing women to state legislatures, Felton's appointment simply honored the elderly woman for her lifelong work as a populist writer. She went to Washington, took the oath, made a short speech, resigned, and returned home. The second, Hattie Caraway, Democrat of Arkansas, was intended as a placeholder for her recently dead husband, but she had lived in Washington for years, decided that she liked being a senator, and won a triumphant reelection in 1932. She defeated a string of well-qualified men and again won in 1938.

Four more women served between 1937 and 1948, but all were appointed or won special elections in which they were known to be placeholders for men. South Dakota had the distinction of doing this twice, with women in both 1937 and 1938; the other two states setting the precedent were Alabama and Louisiana. Thus, the second "real" female U.S. senator was Margaret Chase Smith, a Republican of Maine. She had replaced her husband in the U.S. House in 1940 and went on to the Senate after winning the 1948 election. Known as the Mother of the WAVES, the naval branch for women in World War II, Smith was extremely popular. In 1964, she became the first woman to mount a serious presidential campaign for a major party; Republicans nominated Arizona Senator Barry Goldwater instead, who lost in a landslide to incumbent Democrat Lyndon Johnson. Smith served 32 years, from 1940 to 1972, when she lost partly because of her support for the Vietnam War and partly because of ageism—she would have been 80 when her term ended.

Another five placeholders represented their states in the U.S. Senate during the 1950s and 1960s. Alabama and Louisiana repeated their precedents, and Nebraska had two during that era, but the only significant woman was Maurine Neuberger, Democrat of Oregon. She also replaced her husband but was elected in her own right when he died two days before the filing deadline in 1960. She sponsored legislation to ban billboards on then-new interstate highways, to allow working women to deduct the cost of childcare on their income tax, and to end television ads for liquor and cigarettes. These stances were too far ahead of their time, and Neuberger announced her retirement in 1965, more than a year before her term would end.

Thus, over a half-century passed between 1920, when women got the vote, and the 1978 election of the first female senator who had not been preceded in office by her husband—and even then, Nancy Landon Kassebaum of Kansas was the daughter of Republican presidential nominee Alf Landon. Although her only previous electoral experience was a small-town school board, she defeated eight men in the primary and won the 1978 general election with a comfortable majority. Like Margaret Chase Smith, she was a progressive Republican who became popular with women in both parties. Kassebaum served until 1996 and might have been a presidential contender had she not been from Kansas, where fellow Republicans long supported Senator Bob Dole, the party's nominee in 1996.

Minnesota elected Muriel Buck Humphrey, widow of Vice President Hubert Humphrey, to fill a vacancy in 1978. The last woman to fall into this category would be North Dakota's Jocelyn Birch Burdick, who was appointed to her late husband's seat in 1992 and served only briefly. Instead, it was the 1980 election that marked the beginning of the end of the Senate as an exclusive men's club. After that, women would be seen as contenders in their own right.

Paula Hawkins was the first female U.S. senator with no connection to a man in Congress. Floridians elected her in 1980, even though she was a

Republican, while Florida still was dominated by Democrats. Although she opposed the Equal Rights Amendment, Hawkins ran very much as a woman, dubbing herself "the housewife from Maitland." She had successfully used that mantra to win election to the state's Public Service Commission, which regulated utility rates. In the Senate, however, she soon lost support, especially after she served steak at a press conference demanding cuts to food stamps. Similar gaffes followed, and she lost the 1986 election by a wide margin to Democratic Governor Bob Graham.

The year that Hawkins lost, 1986, brought Maryland's Barbara Mikulski to the Senate; she had been elected to the House in 1976. The race was notable because it was the first time that both major parties nominated a well-known woman. Republicans had high hopes for Linda Chavez, but Mikulski defeated her with 61 percent of the vote. Mikulski championed women's rights, childcare, customer protection, and even national health insurance. Despite what some would see as these controversial positions, she easily won reelection in 1992, 1998, 2004, and 2010. When she retired at the end of 2016, she had the longest tenure of any woman in the Senate.

Mikulski would welcome four new female colleagues in 1992, often dubbed "The Year of the Woman." All were Democrats, and California set a precedent by electing Dianne Feinstein and Barbara Boxer to both of its Senate seats. Illinois elected the first African American woman, Carol Moseley Braun, while voters in Washington State chose Patty Murray. The media particularly was stunned by Murray's victory, as she won on an average campaign contribution of a mere $35; she was motivated to run after a local lawmaker dismissed her as "just a mom in tennis shoes." With incumbents Mikulski and Kassebaum, the Senate zoomed from two women to six. Although this was a mere 6 percent of the upper chamber, it was seen as revolutionary and set the stage for women as genuine players.

During the remainder of the 1990s, six women from five states won Senate races. Republican Kay Bailey Hutchison won a special election in Texas in 1993. In 1996, Maine joined California in electing two women, Republicans Olympia Snowe and Susan Collins, to serve simultaneously. Near the end of the decade, Arkansas had its second woman, Blanche Lincoln, while Louisiana voters elected Mary Landrieu. Both were Democrats.

Some called the 2000 election "The Second Year of the Woman," as the Senate had four new women. Washington became the third state to have women simultaneously holding both seats when Maria Cantwell, a Democrat, joined incumbent Patty Murray. The others were Jean Carnahan of Missouri and Debbie Stabenow of Michigan, also Democrats, and—with far more attention—former First Lady Hillary Clinton, who became the first female U.S. senator from New York. As the new millennium began, the Senate had 13 women, three Republicans and ten Democrats. It was a historic high—although at 13 percent of all seats, still low by any standard of equity.

The 2002 election brought two new women, Alaska's Lisa Murkowski and North Carolina's Elizabeth Dole, both Republicans. The year 2004, when Republican George W. Bush defeated Democrat John Kerry to retain the White House, was notably unsuccessful for women; no new ones joined the Senate. That negative would not be repeated, however, as women did better in the next years. In 2006, Minnesota's Amy Klobuchar and Missouri's Claire McCaskill, both Democrats, won their races. The 2008 cycle brought two precedents: Democrat Jeanne Shaheen of New Hampshire became the first woman to move to the Senate from a governorship, and in North Carolina, Democrat Kay Hagan became the first woman to defeat an incumbent woman, Republican Elizabeth Dole. In the last cycle of the decade, New York's Kirsten Gillibrand, who initially was appointed, won her 2010 campaign. That election year set another precedent as New Hampshire became the first state to have female senators of differing parties; Kelly Ayotte, a Republican, joined Democrat Jeanne Shaheen.

The next decade saw the election of the first Asian woman, Democrat Mazie Hirono of Hawaii, in 2012. That year also brought Democrats Elizabeth Warren of Massachusetts, Heidi Heitkamp of North Dakota, and Tammy Baldwin of Wisconsin, the Senate's first open lesbian. All were the first female senators from their state, as was Republican Deb Fischer of Nebraska. The 2014 cycle also was successful for women, despite being an off-year election in terms of the presidency: two Republicans and four Democrats won new seats. The Republicans were Shelley Moore-Caputo of West Virginia and Joni Ernst of Iowa; the Democrats were Catherine Cortez Masto of New Mexico, Tammy Duckworth of Illinois, Kamala Harris of California, and Maggie Hassan of New Hampshire. Like Jeanne Shaheen, Hassan had previously been governor, a precedent that as of 2019, had not been replicated by another state.

Two women, Democrat Tina Smith in Minnesota and Republican Cindy Hyde-Smith in Mississippi, were appointed to fill vacancies during 2018, and both won their races in the fall. The 2018 election also brought Republican Marsha Blackburn in Tennessee and Democrat Jacky Rosen in Nevada, while Arizona had women of differing parties in its two seats: Republican Martha McSally was appointed, while Democrat Kyrsten Sinema was elected.

In total, since the ceremonial appointment of Georgia's Rebecca Felton in 1922, just 56 women ever have served in the U.S. Senate. Including both elected and appointed women, 36 have been Democrats and 20 Republicans. None ever has come close to winning—or even campaigning for—the Senate presidency, and they have chaired many fewer important committees than women in the House. Eighteen states, as of 2019, have either never appointed or never elected a woman to the upper chamber of Congress: these are Colorado, Connecticut, Delaware, Idaho, Indiana, Kentucky, Montana, New Jersey, Ohio, Oklahoma, Oregon, Pennsylvania, Rhode Island, South Carolina, Utah, Vermont, Virginia, and—ironically, Wyoming, which was the first to grant women the vote back in 1869.

Precedents as Governors

The close connection of the words "governor" and "government" demonstrates the power that rests in that position. Except for the president, state governors enjoy more political muscle than any other office. Women won elections as governors soon after the Nineteenth Amendment, and then failed to follow up on these precedents. Wyoming's Nellie Tayloe Ross is considered the first, as she was inaugurated a few days prior to Miriam "Ma" Ferguson in Texas. Both Democrats, they were preceded by their husbands in the office. Both won in 1924, but Ross lost her reelection. Ferguson won twice, once in 1924 and again for another non-consecutive term in 1932.

No woman followed until 1966, when Lurleen Wallace replaced her husband George in Alabama. Like the first female U.S. senators from Georgia and Arkansas, the first three female governors did not hail from progressive states. While Wyoming's Ross gained some national respect as head of the U.S. Mint, the media treated Ferguson and Wallace with the disdain generally held for what was viewed as the less literate South.

The fourth precedent came when the affluent state of Connecticut chose another Democrat, Ella Tambussi Grasso, in 1974. The first woman elected in her own right, she also overcame an immigrant heritage in a place where people proudly call themselves "Yankees." Grasso was very much an independent person; indeed, her husband stayed so far in the background that when he died later in her career, many people were surprised to discover that she was married. Everyone knew that Dixy Lee Ray, who was elected governor of Washington in 1976, was unmarried. A conservative Democrat and scientist who taught at the University of Washington, her victory took political pundits by complete surprise. The era was too early for even hints of lesbianism, but Ray's image in the media was shaped around the fact that she gave herself a chainsaw for Christmas.

While women joined Congress in unprecedented numbers during the 1970s, only Grasso and Ray were elected governors during that decade. Progress continued to be slow, as the 1980s brought five female governors, although two, in New Hampshire and Arizona, rose from lieutenant governorships and were not elected. The elected ones were Kentucky's Martha Layne Collins in 1983 and Vermont's Madeleine Kunin in 1984. Like all previous female governors, they were Democrats, but in 1986, Nebraska's Kay Orr became the first Republican.

The biggest jump came in the 1990s, when six women won gubernatorial races. Three were just in the year 1990, and all were Democrats: Joan Finney in Kansas, Barbara Roberts in Oregon, and the most famous, Ann Richards in Texas. When voters chose her over a billionaire, Texas became the first state to twice elect a woman. On the negative side, while 1992 was dubbed "The Year of the Woman" because of the U.S. Senate, not one woman won a governorship that year. The next election cycle, 1994, brought the second Republican, as pro-choice Christine Todd Whitman won in New Jersey. The last victory of the decade was in 1996, when Jeanne Shaheen became governor in New Hampshire. She would go on to the U.S. Senate, setting another precedent.

No women won gubernatorial elections in 1998, but two did in 2000: Democrat Ruth Ann Minner in Delaware and Republican Judy Martz in Montana. The 2002 election brought four women, the most ever. They were Republican Linda Lingle in Hawaii, as well as Democrats Janet Napolitano in Arizona, Jennifer Granholm in Michigan, and Kathleen Sibelius in Kansas. Kansans thus joined Texans as having twice elected women to their top job. Another Southern state demonstrated willingness to elect women in 2003, when Democrat Kathleen Blanco won the Louisiana governorship. In 2004,

Washington set another precedent by having women in all three of its top offices, as Democrat Christine Gregoire became governor, joining U.S. Senators Patty Murray and Maria Cantwell. Gregoire's race was very close and bitter; with recounts and lawsuits, it wasn't until the following June that her 129-vote victory was upheld.

One woman won in 2006, as Alaskans elected Sarah Palin; her rise and fall was meteoric, as she would be the Republican nominee for vice president with presidential candidate Senator John McCain, just two years later. Soon after losing that national 2008 election and amid family scandals, she would resign the governorship. That year also brought victory for a woman in the Senate, Democrat Bev Perdue of North Carolina; she served one six-year term and did not run for reelection. The 2010 cycle was the first in which all the winners were Republicans: Mary Fallin in Oklahoma, Susana Martinez in New Mexico, and Nikki Haley in South Carolina. In a race closely watched by women, Martinez defeated Democrat Diane Denish, making Martinez both the first woman to be governor of New Mexico and the first Hispanic woman to serve as a governor in the country. Both she and Oklahoma's Fallin, a former congresswoman, started out with high approval ratings, but various controversies cost them support. When they were term limited in 2018, polls showed Martinez to be the third least-popular governor in America, while Fallin topped that unfortunate list. Nikki Haley, whose family emigrated from India, proved by far the most successful, but after President Donald Trump appointed her as ambassador to the United Nations in 2017, she resigned less than two years later.

New Hampshire elected Democrat Maggie Hassan as governor in 2012, and, like her predecessor, Jeanne Shaheen, Hassan would go on to the U.S. Senate. Rhode Island chose its first woman, Democrat Gina Raimondo in 2014, and, the following year, Oregon had its second with Kate Brown. She became governor due to a resignation but won an election in 2016 and again in 2018. Brown is the nation's first openly bisexual governor. Two Republican women, Kay Ivey in Alabama and Kim Reynolds in Iowa also became governors by default in 2017 but won election 2018. Ivey is Alabama's second female governor, while Reynolds is the first in Iowa.

Along with the wave of women elected to Congress in 2018, five won gubernatorial races; four of the five were Democrats. The Republican was Kristi Noem in South Dakota, the first woman to lead that state. Gretchen Whitmer became the second female governor of Michigan, while Michelle Lujan Grisham was the second for New Mexico. A Democrat, she succeeded Republican Susana Martinez; the two of them were the nation's first Latinas to be governors. Although Maine had an excellent record of sending women to Congress relatively early, it elected its first female governor only in 2018 with Janet Mills. Finally, Kansas elected its third woman as governor, as Laura Kelly followed the earlier Joan Finney and Kathleen Sebelius; all were Democrats.

Including women who rose to governorships because of vacancies as well as those who have been elected, 44 women in 29 states have served in this top job, as of 2019. Those states that have never had a female governor are Arkansas, California, Colorado, Florida, Georgia, Idaho, Illinois, Indiana, Maryland, Minnesota, Mississippi, Missouri, Nevada, New York, North Dakota, Ohio, Pennsylvania, Tennessee, Virginia, West Virginia, and Wisconsin. Despite great gains, this list—including some of the most demographically, politically, and economically influential states—demonstrates how women have yet to share fully in the power to govern.

Precedents in State Judiciaries

At its 1920 height, some two million people belonged to the National Association Woman Suffrage Association, and several hundred thousand belonged to other organizations devoted to female enfranchisement. That is an enviable political base, even in today's much larger population. And yet relatively few women took advantage of that established network to win judicial contests. The judiciary traditionally is more conservative than the executive and legislative branches of government, and women may have been further discouraged by their decades-long struggle to become lawyers. But women might have won more judicial seats earlier in the century had more of them taken the risk, as demonstrated by the amazing Florence Allen of Ohio.

Both she and her mother were active for the vote; indeed, her mother, Corrine Tuckerman Allen, was the first to enroll in Smith College when that single-sex institution began in 1875, a time when higher education for women was considered radical. Daughter Florence was well educated, too, yet was rejected by several law schools on the grounds of gender. She finally won admission to the law school of New York University and was admitted to the Ohio bar in 1914. In 1919, before Ohio women could vote, she was appointed as an assistant prosecutor for Cuyahoga County. In the very next year, 1920, she won election for a Cleveland judgeship. Showing remarkable confidence in both herself and the voters, she again organized her feminist network in 1922, and won election to the Ohio Supreme Court by a wide margin.

Yet despite this early precedent, decades passed before another woman was elected to a state supreme court. That was Lorna Lockwood in Arizona in 1960. Her colleagues would elect her as chief justice in 1965, setting a national precedent for that position. Not all states elect their highest court, of course, and the third woman on a state supreme court was appointed; she was Susie Marshall Sharp, appointed to the North Carolina Supreme Court by Governor Terry Sanford, a Democrat, in 1962. Sharp had endured a great deal of ridicule by her male colleagues in law school, but like Arizona's Lockwood, her colleagues would subsequently choose her as chief justice.

Thus, despite Florence Allen's early success, only a mere three women had served on the supreme court of the 50 states during the half-century between 1922 and 1972. The 1970s brought a feminist revolution, however, and in that decade alone, a dozen states set this precedent. Michigan's Mary Stallings Coleman became the fourth in 1972, when she won the elected office there. Alabama voters followed in 1974, electing Janie Shores. The ten other women were appointed, and with the exception of Kansas, all were by Democratic governors. Governor Ella Grasso became the first to name another woman when Ellen Ash Peters joined the Connecticut Supreme Court in 1978.

The pattern continued in the 1980s, as 15 women became the first on the highest court in their state. Again, only two were elected, in West Virginia and South Carolina, both in 1988. Of the 13 women who were appointed, eight were named by Democratic governors and five by Republicans. In 1981, Washington Governor Dixie Lee Ray, a Democrat, became the second woman to appoint another woman. Another 16 women set the precedent in the 1990s. Six were in states that elected their supreme court: alphabetically, women won elections during the 1990s in Illinois, Kentucky, Louisiana, Nevada, and Texas. Of the ten who were appointed, three were chosen by Republican governors, while seven were appointees of Democrats.

As the new millennium began, just four states had not yet had a woman on their highest court. Governors rectified this with appointments in Delaware, New Hampshire, South Dakota, and ironically again, Wyoming, which had been the first to grant the vote back in 1869. Three of the four appointments were in 2000, and the last was South Dakota in 2002, 80 years after Ohio's Florence Allen set the precedent in 1922.

Precedents in the Federal Judiciary

After being the first woman on a state supreme court, Florence Allen also went on to be the first woman on a federal court. She was appointed by Democratic President Franklin Roosevelt to the appellate court in Cleveland in 1934, his second year in office. Thus, during the years of Republican presidents from 1920, when women got the vote, to 1932, when the party lost the White House, none had appointed a woman to any of the many federal courts across the nation. And another 14 years would pass before another woman was appointed to the federal judiciary, when in 1949, Democratic President Harry Truman named Burnita Shelton Matthews to the federal district bench in Washington D.C.

Four women won appointments in the 1960s, all of them by Democratic presidents John F. Kennedy and his successor, Lyndon B. Johnson. Kennedy had appointed Sarah T. Hughes to the district court based in Dallas, and, after he was assassinated there in 1963, she administered the oath of office to the new president. Millions of people saw Judge Hughes on television, and the image created new aspirations for girls. President Johnson also deserves credit for appointing Constance Baker Motley to the federal court in New York. She was the first African American woman in this position, and for decades, feminists hoped that she would go on to the U.S. Supreme Court. Motley, who was born in 1921 to immigrants from the Caribbean, set a number of other records for women prior to her 2005 death, but, as of 2019, no African American woman ever has been on the U.S. Supreme Court. (For more on political milestones for women of color, see Chapter Thirteen.)

California Republican Richard Nixon, who succeeded Lyndon Johnson with his 1968 election, appointed just one woman to the federal judiciary prior to his forced resignation in 1973; his successor, Republican Gerald Ford of Michigan, also appointed one. Ford lost the 1976 election to Georgia Democrat Jimmy Carter, who, in turn, would lose to California Republican Ronald Reagan in 1980. There were no vacancies on the highest court during Carter's tenure, but he nonetheless had great—yet largely unrecognized—impact on the federal judiciary. During his four years in office, President Carter appointed 36 women as judges on district and appellate courts, more than four times as many as the seven previous presidents. Federal judges, of course, must be confirmed by the U.S. Senate, and they serve for life. The long-term effect of Jimmy Carter's appointments merits more recognition.

By the time that Ronald Reagan took office in 1981, a great deal of pressure had built to have a woman on the U.S. Supreme Court. Two centuries had passed, and more than a hundred men had served before the first woman, Arizona's Sandra Day O'Connor, joined the court in 1981. Her career shows the effect of feminism in the 1960s and 1970s: although she was at the top of her class at Stanford University, she was offered only jobs as a legal secretary after graduation in the 1950s. O'Connor's confirmation was unanimous, and she served with distinction until retirement in 2005. First Lady Laura Bush was on record as asking her husband, President George W. Bush, to name another woman to a Supreme Court vacancy during his term, but he did not.

The partisan difference between presidential appointments of women became very clear in the decades after 1981, as the numbers rose and fell depending on which party held the White House. By the share of women appointed compared to their total appointments, Republican presidents lag behind their Democratic counterparts. Ronald Reagan was 7 percent; George H.W. Bush came in at 18 percent; and George W. Bush at 21 percent. Democrat Bill Clinton was 28 percent, while Barack Obama holds the clear record at 42 percent. As of early 2019, 28 percent of Republican Donald Trump's appointments have been women.

In the nearly four decades after the appointment of Sandra Day O'Connor, no Republican president has named a woman to the U.S. Supreme Court—and, even more telling, Senate confirmation votes indicate increased partisanship. Even though O'Connor had been active in the Republican Party, no Democratic senator voted against her in 1981. Three senators voted against Ruth Bader Ginsberg, appointed by Democrat Bill Clinton in 1993. The women named by Democrat Barak Obama faced significantly more hostility, even though their records were flawless. Sonia Sotomayor, whose family roots are in Puerto Rico, was confirmed by a vote of 68–31 in 2009, while the 2010 tally on Elena Kagan, the second Jewish woman on the court, was 61–37. Those three women—Ginsberg, Sotomayor, and Kagan—remained justices in 2018, when in a very contentious hearing that centered on his treatment of women, Brett Kavanaugh was confirmed by the Senate. He was the second white man appointed by Donald Trump, bringing the total throughout American history to 110 men and 4 women.

Sexual Harassment Takes Center Stage

Just as Kavanaugh had been credibly accused of sexual harassment when he was in prep school, that difficult topic had been rising on the feminist agenda. Sexual harassment, of course, had been a problem for women from time immemorial, but as with rape and domestic violence, it was a taboo topic and a problem that had no name. Although countless women in all periods of history lost opportunities because they refused to give sexual attention to men, a new vocabulary had to be invented when the Equal Employment Opportunity Commission (EEOC) declared sexual harassment to be unlawful in 1980. The reality of such attitudes was reinforced that year when it was revealed that Chicago policemen had strip-searched almost 200 women arrested for traffic violations and similar minor offenses.

The Supreme Court did not rule on the EEOC's decision until 1986, but it was unanimous. In unambiguous language, the court declared that demands for sexual favors in the workplace violated the 1964 Civil Rights Act. Women responded with alacrity, and cases filed with the EEOC soared from just 10 in 1985 to 624 the next year. That the problem was common could be seen in a 1988 survey of federal employees that showed 40 percent of women had experienced sexual harassment at some point during their careers. The worst statistics were at the State Department, and international disparagement of women seemed confirmed in 1994, when the United Nations settled a lawsuit brought by an American woman for $210,000. By then, Madeleine Albright had become the first female secretary of state, and she confirmed the pervasiveness of the problem, saying "this is still a very male organization."

The 1991 Senate confirmation hearings of Supreme Court nominee Clarence Thomas especially focused attention on sexual harassment. A conservative Republican, he would become the second black man on the court, following the retirement of civil rights hero Thurgood Marshall. Anita Hill, a graduate of Yale Law School, testified that Thomas had sexually harassed her when they worked together earlier. Senators, including some Democrats, were offensive in challenging her credibility and voted Thomas onto the court, where he has not promoted the interests of either blacks or women.

A second incident in 1991 brought additional attention to the issue. Sexual harassment in the military came to public attention with the "Tailhook" convention of the Navy and the Marine Corps, when more than a hundred men openly assaulted women in a Las Vegas hotel. The Pentagon deplored that, of course, but took the offenses less than seriously. When a 1995 survey of female veterans found that 90 percent of those under age 50 reported experience with sexual harassers, military leaders criticized the study's methodology and said that "only" 64 percent of active-duty women reported such problems.

Also in 1995, Republican Robert Packwood of Oregon was forced to resign from the U.S. Senate after almost two dozen women testified that he had harassed them. He initially denied it, but his own diary entries spoke to the truth. Congress responded with the 1995 Congressional Accountability Act, which outlawed this behavior, but similar cases continued to spring up on a regular basis. Late in 2018, the House passed a bill requiring members to pay settlements of such suits out of their own pockets, but as of 2019, the Senate has not followed.

"Hostile workplace" entered the language in 2010, when the Supreme Court ruled that an environment that allows pornography or obscene language can be a civil rights violation, even if no particular person is targeted. It had ruled earlier that employers were responsible for employee behavior, and because of this, many corporations began education programs to change male attitudes about their female coworkers. Women in the entertainment industry particularly came forward in 2017 to talk about the long-whispered reality of the casting couch, and famous men in film and other media lost their jobs. The "#MeToo" movement came out of this, and with the ease of organizing on social media, it had a tremendous effect in the 2018 congressional elections. Sexual harassment became a major issue in many races, and its victims helped elect dozens of feminists to Congress and other offices. Real change already had occurred, and more is sure to follow.

Chapter Thirteen

"We Shall Overcome": Minority Women's Long Road to Progress

Political progress is not necessarily a straight line, as shown by the fact that women of color were more active in the feminist movement during the mid-nineteenth century than in the early twentieth century. Former slave Sojourner Truth spoke at the 1851 women's rights convention in Akron, Ohio, a mere three years after the first meeting in Seneca Falls, New York. As long as Quaker women such as Lucretia Mott and Susan B. Anthony headed the movement, black women were welcome. Later leaders, however, did not encourage efforts by non-white women. (See Part One for discussion of many of these black leaders, such as Frances Watkins Harper, Lottie Wilson Jackson, Harriet Forten Purvis, Sarah Remond, Josephine St. Pierre Ruffin, Ida B. Wells-Barnett, and Fannie Barrier Williams).

When, for example, the National American Woman Suffrage Association met in New Orleans in 1903, only three white women accepted an invitation from a black women's organization, the Phillis Wheatley Club—an aging Anthony, Alice Stone Blackwell of *Woman's Journal*, and dress reform leader Elizabeth Smith Miller. The dress reform issue is rather illustrative of the gap between white and black women: black women were in many ways more conservative, especially in terms of feminist visibility. They had no interest in wearing pants or otherwise challenging male social prerogatives; instead, their political action often was driven by protecting their men, especially from the real possibility of lynching. Another round of racial terrorism appeared after

World War I, during the same years when the Nineteenth Amendment went into effect, and for black women, exercising their new rights became dangerous.

Nevertheless, they showed courage. As soon as the Nineteenth Amendment was ratified, Florida educator Mary McLeod Bethune began registering voters, and the Ku Klux Klan responded with a night attack on her Daytona boarding school. Bethune, however, had been astute enough to recruit trustees such as John D. Rockefeller Jr., and after she went public about the attempted terror, the Klan never bothered her again. Farther north, Richmond banker Maggie Walker campaigned for the statewide office of superintendent of instruction in 1921; although she did not come close to winning, she made the point that black women could be political activists.

In another case of changed status for ethnic minorities, the Seminole tribe of Oklahoma chose Alice Brown Davis as their first female chief in 1922. In that same year, voters in New Mexico chose Soledad Chavez Chacon as secretary of state; in the first election in which New Mexican women could vote, an all-male delegation of Democrats came to her home and recruited her. During the same era, Republican Blanche Armwood of Tampa, who was so brilliant that she passed the Florida State Teachers Examination at age 12, traveled throughout the South for the Urban League, registering voters and teaching the new field of home economics. Racism, however, remained on Florida's west coast to such an extent that in 1923, a white mob completely annihilated the African American town of Rosewood.

Washington D.C. still was very much a Southern city in this era, and Anna Julia Cooper would lead efforts for African Americans from the 1920s on through the 1960s. Born in slavery and probably fathered by her "master," she became perhaps the world's best educated black woman: after a career as a principal in segregated schools, Cooper earned a doctorate from France's prestigious Sorbonne in 1925. Her longtime local ally was Mary Church Terrell; having spoken to the 1904 International Woman's Suffrage Alliance in three languages, Terrell would become even more radicalized as she aged. Another black woman in Washington with a very feminist viewpoint was Nannie Burroughs, who ran a boarding school for girls. She candidly attacked black men for their failure to support women, writing in her autobiography: "the men ought to get down on their knees to the Negro women. They've made possible all that we have." In the same era, Gertrude Bonnin (Zitkála-Šá), a member of the Yankton Dakota tribe, spent much of her life lobbying for American

Indians. In 1926, she helped to establish the National Council of American Indians, which she would lead as its president until her death. When she died in 1938, she was honored with burial in Arlington National Cemetery.

Education remained key to advancement, minority women knew, and better educational opportunities remained the highest priority of most black women. In 1926, Atlanta's Selena Sloan Butler founded the National Congress of Colored Parents and Teachers, but the slowness of progress was indicated by the fact that it would not fully merge with white PTA units until 1970. Professional education also was a concern of African Americans in an era when opportunities were closed to many. A 1926 study, for instance, of the nation's 1,688 accredited nursing schools showed that only 54 accepted African American students.

A photograph of African American activist Anna Julia Cooper published in her 1892 book, *A Voice from the South*. (Wikimedia)

Across the spectrum, black women faced discrimination. In a high-profile 1929 case, First Lady Lou Henry Hoover invited the wife of a black congressman, New York's Oscar De Priest, to a luncheon for congressional wives, resulting in a huge uproar. A Washington newspaper raged that Hoover was "defiling the White House," and several state legislatures passed resolutions condemning her.

The Great Depression of the 1930s hurt minorities even more than most Americans, but the New Deal that began in 1933 would ultimately improve the lives of many. When, in 1935, Democratic President Franklin Roosevelt appointed Mary McLeod Bethune to head the Office of Minority Affairs in the National Youth Administration, she became the federal government's first African American of either gender in an executive position. She traveled thousands of miles across America, working for opportunities for needy young people, including Mexican Americans and Native Americans. Later, she would be the only woman of color in the entire world who had an official status at the founding of the United Nations.

Several organizations merged into the National Council of Negro Women (NCNW) in 1935, and the NCNW soon had some 800,000 members. They focused on creating employment opportunities, ending state poll taxes, and securing a place for black women in the military. Another milestone came in 1938, when the first African American woman was elected to a state legislature. Quaker women in Philadelphia organized a phone bank—then a new campaign technique—to elect Democrat Crystal Bird Fauset in a largely white district. She soon disappointed her supporters though: she resigned before her term was over, switched parties, and worked in the 1940 presidential election for Republican nominee Wendell Willkie against Democrat Franklin Roosevelt. Republicans did not keep her on the payroll after they lost, and Fauset spent the rest of her life seeking another political position in vain.

The decade's closing year brought another national debate on race, when the Daughters of the American Revolution refused to rent their Washington hall to celebrated soprano Marian Anderson. Hundreds of white people signed petitions objecting to this race-based insult, including two Supreme Court justices and several Cabinet members—who, of course, were white men. Eleanor Roosevelt resigned her DAR membership, and New York Congresswoman Carolyn O'Day headed a committee that moved the concert to the Lincoln Memorial, greatly enhancing the attention it drew and leading to its renown as a historic event.

That some racial progress was being made is indicated by the fact that 1940 was the first year in which there were no recorded lynchings. However, Congress consistently rejected federal anti-lynching law as it did throughout Roosevelt's administration, including after Democratic President Harry Truman put it at the top of his civil rights agenda. He did manage to get the Pentagon to accept racial integration of the armed forces in 1948, but it was done by executive order, not congressional act. The military also was gender-integrated in 1948, after black women had proven their worth during World War II. Again, this was largely due to the ubiquitous Mary McLeod Bethune.

She served on the advisory board that formed the Women's Army Corps in 1942, and the corps, headed by a white Texan, Oveta Culp Hobby, accepted black women from the beginning and even promoted them as officers. This was in contrast to the women's corps of the naval branches: although they could have followed the Army's precedent, they initially excluded blacks, despite the corps' leadership under Northern white women. Nor did the older nursing corps of either the Army or Navy include black women until late in the war, even though there was a desperate need for nurses. Mabel K. Staupers of the National Association of Colored Graduate Nurses led congressional lobbying to force the corps to accept black applicants.

Women did hold top editorial positions at newspapers and magazines aimed at black readers, and Jessie Vann was owner and publisher of the weekly *Pittsburgh Courier* from 1940 to 1963. It had a national circulation, and Vann may have been the wealthiest black woman in America. *The Crisis*, published by the National Association for the Advancement of Colored People (NAACP), featured Jessie Redmon Fauset as its literary editor; a 1905 graduate of prestigious Cornell University, she was probably the first black woman in the world to earn Phi Beta Kappa membership. Ethel Payne of the nationally circulated *Chicago Defender* reported from every inhabited continent except Australia during World War II, and soon was known as "the first lady of the black press."

The war's 1945 end marked the beginning of the modern civil rights movement—and that was not limited to Southern blacks. Alaskan natives also lived in a segregated society, with businesses even posting notices that banned Indians. When the territorial legislature met in 1945, Elizabeth Peratrovich of the Tlingit nation delivered such moving testimony on the discrimination she encountered that the legislature overwhelmingly passed bills assuring natives access to public accommodations and the right to live in a neighborhood of their choice. It would be another two decades, however, before similar legislation passed on a federal level—and even when it did, there would not yet be any female minority in Congress.

With segregation still the rule in the nation's capital, a nearly 90-year-old Mary Church Terrell led other blacks in a 1953 sit-in at a Washington restaurant. When they were refused service, she sued on the basis of never-repealed Reconstruction laws, and the Supreme Court conceded that she was right. Even more creatively, Terrell surreptitiously bought up theater tickets and distributed them to African Americans, thus forcing management either to admit them or play to an empty house.

The next year was a big turning point. In *Brown v. Board of Education of Topeka* (1954), the Supreme Court ruled that young Linda Brown could not be excluded from her neighborhood school because of race. The decision was the result of legal research and careful planning by black parents, and other, lesser known school discrimination cases would dominate the next decades as millions of white parents refused to send their children to integrated schools. The nation's attention especially focused on Little Rock's Central High School in 1957, when NAACP leader Daisy Bates led nine students—the majority of them girls—who undertook the difficult task of being first. President Dwight D. Eisenhower sent federal troops to protect them, and the school was integrated, but the lives of Bates and other leaders were threatened, and they routinely were denounced by newspapers and politicians as "communists."

Outside of education, other women worked to integrate other institutions. The most famous action was on December 1, 1955, when seamstress Rosa Parks refused to give up her bus seat to a white man. That was the law in Montgomery, the capital of Alabama, and she was arrested and jailed. Her passive resistance not only forced many white people to think about issues they had never considered, but also inspired countless African Americans to emulate her. Blacks in Montgomery boycotted buses, which meant missing work and paychecks, but they brought the economy to a halt and ultimately made progress.

Rosa Park's action, which helped build the career of young Martin Luther King, Jr., overshadowed another tragic incident that occurred a few weeks later on Christmas Day in 1955. Harriet and Harry Moore were Florida educators who had been fired from their jobs for civil rights activity. When they continued to register black voters, racists planted a bomb in their home in a rural African American community near today's Kennedy Space Center in Florida. After returning from a Christmas Eve dinner with family, they went to bed, and a bomb exploded that could be heard four miles away. No ambulance service was available for blacks, and Harry died on his way to a segregated hospital in Orlando. Harriet lived long enough to tell federal officials not to trust the local police, but their killers were not convicted.

Racist resistance to integration remained strong for years, and, like Harriet Moore, other unheralded women played important roles. Autherine Lucy successfully went to court to be allowed to enter graduate studies in library science at the University of Alabama, but when she appeared on campus to enroll in February 1956, a large mob greeted her. She went back to court to have the ruling enforced, but the university's administration trumped up technical violations of school rules to expel her.

During the same period, South Carolina passed a law forbidding government employees from joining civil rights organizations, and Septima Poinsette Clark, who had taught in black schools in the Charleston area for 40 years, was fired when she refused to deny that she was a member of the NAACP. In 1960, six-year-old Ruby Bridges was greeted by a yelling mob when she became the only student at a previously all-white elementary school in New Orleans. She and her white teacher spent her first grade alone, as no one else enrolled. Some, including black students, did the next year.

Rosa Parks (left) and Septima Poinsette Clark (center) with Parks's mother, Leona McCauley, outside the Highlander Folk School in 1956.

Dorothy I. Height became president of the National Council of Negro Women in 1957 and held that position in Washington for the next 30 years, working on countless campaigns for equality. Atlanta-based Ella Baker mentored young people in the Student Nonviolent Coordinating Committee, which conducted sit-ins at restaurants and other public businesses, and she would become a leading force in the civil rights movement. A young Marian

Wright Edelman, later the founder of the Children's Defense Fund, used the legal skills she acquired at Yale to free civil rights workers from Mississippi jails. In South Florida, Eula Johnson led young people with "swim-ins" to integrate beaches in 1961. Previously, there had been only one beach along the five-hundred-mile peninsula where blacks could legally swim.

Racists continued to resist, however, and what may have been the most heartless attack came in September 1963, when four black girls died in the bombing of a Birmingham church. Local police did not investigate, and no one would be convicted of these murders until 1977. Instead, police attacked nonviolent African Americans, including Fannie Lou Hamer of rural Mississippi. The twentieth child of sharecroppers, Hamer began registering black voters in 1962 and was repeatedly beaten. At one point, policemen had the temerity to arrest and jail her for "driving a bus of the wrong color." She courageously continued, though, and challenged Mississippi's all-white delegation at the 1964 Democratic National Convention. Business was held up for days while the credentials committee debated; its compromise satisfied neither side, but that convention marked the end of "Dixiecrats" who claimed to be Democrats.

Fannie Lou Hamer at the Democratic National Convention in Atlantic City in 1964.

A less-noted 1964 milestone was the election of the first Asian American in Congress, Patsy Takemoto Mink of Hawaii. Mink went on to decades of feminist leadership and was nationally known, but Verda Freeman Welcome's precedent was much less known: she was quietly elected as the nation's first black female state senator in 1962. Welcome had won election to Maryland's lower chamber in 1958, and, four years later, moved up to represent part of Baltimore as a senator. In April 1964, five pistol shots were fired at her, slightly wounding her and shattering the glass in her car. An investigation revealed that one of the two shooters was a member of the legislature. Unintimidated, she went on to serve in the Maryland Senate for 20 years, from 1962 to 1982.

Welcome was the first black female state senator, but oddly enough, her precedent was preceded by an even more difficult election. The first black woman to win a statewide office was in 1960, when Wisconsin voters chose Velvalea Rodgers Phillips, called "Vel," as secretary of state. A Milwaukee native, she had won earlier races for city council—and yet, police wrongfully arrested her during the riots that followed Martin Luther King's 1968 assassination. Making progress in statewide offices was slow, though, and more than a decade would pass before California voters made March Fong Eu the first Asian American woman to win a statewide office in 1974, when she was elected as secretary of state; she had won election to the legislature in 1966.

President Lyndon B. Johnson, a Democrat, won the 1964 election by a landslide, and he enabled other precedents for women. Patricia Roberts Harris, a civil rights attorney and professor at Howard University, became the nation's first female African American ambassador when she went to Luxembourg. Johnson named the first black woman on the federal judiciary: Constance Baker Motley served as a judge for the district court in Manhattan and was a role model for countless aspiring attorneys. A Texan, Johnson also mentored Houston attorney Barbara Jordan; in the 1966 election, she became the only woman and the only African American in the Texas Senate. Jordan, later as a congresswoman, would be a major player in President Richard Nixon's impeachment hearings.

The National Education Association elected North Carolina teacher Elizabeth Koontz as its president in 1967; she was the first African American of either gender to preside over the 106-year-old organization. The next year, however, brought the biggest milestone, when Shirley Chisholm of New York City became the first African American congresswoman. Her win was especially impressive because she not only defeated Tammany Hall's preferred candidate in the primary, but also a popular black man who ran on a Liberal Republican ticket in the general election. Millions of women, both white and black, followed Chisholm's feminist leadership, and in 1972, she would become the first African American woman to wage a serious campaign for president.

Chisholm was joined by Houston's Barbara Jordan in the 1972 election, as well as Yvonne Brathwaite Burke of Los Angeles; Burke would be the first member of Congress to be pregnant in office. The next year, Cardiss Collins of

Chicago became the fourth black congresswoman; she won a special election to replace her recently dead husband. Democratic President Jimmy Carter of Georgia, who won in 1976, was the first to appoint a black woman to the Cabinet. He named former ambassador Patricia Roberts Harris as head of the Department of Housing and Urban Development in 1977. Two years later, he asked her to move to Health and Human Services, and Harris thus became the first woman to have held two Cabinet positions.

The 1980 election of Republican Ronald Reagan signaled a return to conservatism, and that continued with his successor, George H.W. Bush in 1988. No black women held high-level positions in either administration, and the numbers in Congress fell compared to the 1970s. Even icon Shirley Chisholm lost reelection in 1982, partly due to gerrymandering after the 1980 census. One exception to this backtracking on progress for minority women was Antonia Novello, a Puerto Rican who was appointed by Bush in 1990 as the first female surgeon general; Dr. Novello was truly novel in viewing violence as a national epidemic.

Just three minority women were elected to the U.S. House during the Reagan years of 1980s, and two of the three were Republicans. The only Democrat was Katie Beatrice Hall, an African American elected from Indianapolis in 1982. The Republicans were Patricia Fukuda Saiki of Honolulu, in 1986, and Miami's Ileana Ros-Lehtinen, the first Cuban American congresswomen, in 1988. Although minority political achievements were rare during the Reagan/Bush administrations, NASA set precedents with Dr. Mae C. Jemison as the first black woman in space; Dr. Ellen Ochoa became the first Hispanic woman.

Lottie H. Shackelford, a black woman, became mayor of Little Rock, Arkansas, in 1987, but in that city's system, the mayor is elected to a one-year term by the city council, not by voters. In 1990, voters in Washington D.C. chose African American Sharon Pratt Dixon (later Kelly) as mayor; she was the first woman to hold that position. Her tenure was tumultuous, however, and she lost the next election to former mayor and convicted drug dealer Marion Berry.

The most noted achiever of the era doubtless was Carol Moseley Braun of Chicago. Illinois voters made her the first black woman in the U.S. Senate in 1992, but after revelations of financial corruption, she would lose in 1998. Controversy also chased Dr. Joycelyn Elders of Arkansas, who was appointed as surgeon general by Democratic President Bill Clinton in 1993; conservatives would force her resignation when her proposals on sex education proved too candid. Other minority women, however, did well during the years of the Clinton administration, especially in the U.S. House.

Los Angeles voters elected Congresswoman Maxine Waters by a huge margin in 1990, and as of 2020, she still leads the way for other black women, especially on issues of poverty. More than a dozen minority women won elections to the U.S. House during the 1990s, including African Americans Barbara-Rose Collins of Detroit, Carrie Meek of Miami, Eddie Bernice Johnson of Dallas–Fort Worth, Cynthia McKinney of Atlanta, Sheila Jackson Lee of Houston, Julia Carson of Indianapolis, and Juanita Millender-McDonald of Los Angeles. Eva Clayton of coastal North Carolina was the first black woman elected from a non-urban district.

Other minority congresswomen elected in the 1990s were Anna Eshoo, of Armenian ancestry, who won California's Silicon Valley; Lucille Roybal-Allard, a Mexican American in Los Angeles; Nydia Velázquez, a Puerto Rican representing parts of New York City; and—greatly to the shock of the Old Guard—young Loretta Sanchez, who narrowly defeated a powerful white man in Los Angeles. Her sister, Linda Sanchez, soon would join her, representing an adjacent district.

Although Minneapolis's minority population was small, voters elected African American Sharon Sayles Belton as mayor in 1993. A city council member since 1983, she also had served as president of the National Coalition Against Sexual Assault. Another unexpected development was the American Bar Association's choice of Roberta Cooper Ramo as its president for 1995. A New Mexican of Native American descent, she was the first woman of any ethnicity to preside over this prestigious organization of attorneys. Ramo, who could not get a job when she graduated from the University of Chicago in 1967, said that her most satisfying cases involved freeing civil rights workers from jail, even when she had to borrow cab fare from her clients.

Atlanta elected Shirley Franklin as the first black female mayor in a major southeastern city in 2001, and she did such a good job that she was reelected in 2005 almost without opposition. Baltimore had its first female mayor when Sheila Dixon, an African American, assumed the office in 2007. No kin to Washington mayor Sharon Pratt Dixon, she defeated more than a half-dozen candidates, but was forced to resign in 2010 because of a corruption scandal.

Baltimore then became the first major city to have a woman replace another woman, as Stephanie Rawlings-Blake, also an African American, became mayor. As of 2020, black women are mayors of seven large cities, and, except for San Francisco, all are in the South.

One of the most important advances in this period was the appointment of Sonia Sotomayor to the U.S. Supreme Court by President Barack Obama in 2009. The third woman to join the ranks of the nation's highest court, Sotomayor was born and raised in the Bronx, New York, by parents born in Puerto Rico, and graduated from Princeton University and then Yale Law School. Her milestone as the first Latina Supreme Court Justice has been celebrated as a major advance for women and people of color.

Upwards of a dozen women who were racial minorities joined Congress during the first decade of the new century, and the 2010 election marked an important milestone with gubernatorial races. Two states chose women of minority backgrounds as governors: both Republicans, they were New Mexico's Susana Martinez, a Latina, and South Carolina's Nikki Haley, an Indian American, who would go on to serve as UN Ambassador. As of 2020, however, no state had elected an African American woman as governor, although Stacey Abrams, the Democratic nominee in Georgia in 2018, came very close.

Numbers in the U.S. House continued to climb during the century's second decade, and by 2020, more than a third of its women had an ancestry that defined them as an ethnic minority. One highlight is the first-ever election of Muslim-American women to the House in the 2018 midterms—Congresswomen Ilhan Omar of Minnesota, who was born in Somalia, and Rashida Tlaib, who is the first Palestinian American. Also, Washington sent Pramila Jayapal, an Indian American, to the House in 2016. The U.S. Senate, is designed to be more conservative than the House. It had no minority women for 14 years after Illinois's Carol Moseley Braun lost her seat in 1998, as none won until 2012. Hawaii's Mazie Hirono, a Democrat of Japanese ancestry, then became the second female senator who did not identify as white. Two more women joined her in 2016: Catherine Cortez Masto, a Hispanic Democrat of Nevada, and Kamala Harris, Democrat of California, who considers herself to be mixed race.

It was with remarkable speed that gay rights were achieved in terms of marriage equality: not even a dozen years passed between the first big victory for LGBTQ equality, when Massachusetts granted the right to marry in 2004, and the 2015 Supreme Court decision in *Obergefell v. Hodges* that states could not ban same-sex marriage. But electoral success for a gay woman preceded that milestone achievement by three decades when Elaine Noble, who was openly gay, won her race for the Massachusetts legislature back in 1974.

In addition to legislatures, local governments—even large ones in the South—have opened their ranks to lesbians. Cathy Woolard joined the city council in Atlanta in 1998 and won a citywide race for council president in 2002. Voters in the cowboy-image city of Houston chose Annise Parker as mayor in 2010. In 2017, Jenny Durkan won election as Seattle's mayor; Seattle had been the first big city to elect any woman as mayor, with Bertha Landes back in 1926. Jane Castor, the former police chief in Tampa, won its 2019 mayoral race. She was Tampa's third female mayor and the city's first to openly identify as LGBTQ; she defeated her billionaire opponent with 73 percent of the vote. At the same time, Chicago elected its second female mayor and first lesbian, Lori Lightfoot, who also is African American.

On the federal level, Tammy Baldwin of Wisconsin became the first lesbian in the U.S. House in 1998, and voters promoted her to the U.S. Senate in 2012. Democrat Kyrsten Sinema of Arizona, who is bisexual, followed the same career path, winning a House seat in 2012 and moving to the upper chamber in 2018. Although Kansas has elected Democratic women as governor three times, it is akin to Wisconsin and Arizona in often being portrayed as conservative; however, Kansans elected Sharice Davids, a lesbian and Native American, to the U.S. House in 2018. That revolutionary midterm election also saw Angie Craig of Minnesota join the House, as well as Katie Hill of California; both identify as LGBTQ.

Kate Brown became the third female governor of Oregon in 2018 and the first open bisexual to win a governorship anywhere in the nation. As of 2019, all 50 states have elected openly gay people to some office—be it local, state, or national. Most are men, but women quickly are catching up. Prejudices against both groups are dying, and the future looks positive.

Although the women's movement of the early twentieth century did not especially welcome assistance from racial or gender minorities, that situation had changed by the beginning of the next century. The demand for an intersectional feminism, one that recognizes the defining importance of class, race, ethnicity, and multi-gender identities, has become a new banner under which new groups are organizing to advance the political equality of all women.

This was on full display in the Women's March on Washington in January 2017, organized in just three months following the election to the presidency of Donald Trump. And while some traditional feminists have struggled with these new definitions and directions, the challenges have fortified a new wave of women's activism that is clearly making a mark on—in many ways, at the helm of—the politics of the country.

Appendix: Foreword to the First Edition, Part One

By Geraldine Ferraro,
former member of the U.S. House of Representatives

(Part One of *Victory for the Vote* was first published as *A History of the American Suffragist Movement* on the occasion of the 150th anniversary of the Seneca Falls Convention.)

Knowing what to write about something that happened 150 years ago in a small New York town is not easy. I was asked to reflect on the events at Seneca Falls and describe just what they have meant to me and more generally what they have meant for American women. Evaluating the impact of those days reminded me of the many celebrated achievements of women. But the exhilaration of those triumphs is bittersweet when I consider how much we stand to lose if we are complacent. One thing is certain: that remarkable occasion and the courageous leaders who challenged the status quo deserve more than a footnote in American history.

In the middle of a hot summer in 1848, 68 women, with the encouragement of some enlightened men, staked claim to rights bestowed upon them by their Creator. History has called it a defining moment, a great moment—claims I won't dispute. It was a great moment for everyone who cherishes justice and human dignity. Those assembled in that tiny upstate New York church advocated for fundamental rights. They rejected men's power over women and invited others to work with them to ensure that women would no longer be deprived of property, economic security, and the right to vote.

Unlike the American revolution, which began with the "shot heard round the world," the rebellion of Seneca Falls—steeped in moral conviction and rooted in the abolitionist movement—dropped like a stone in the middle of a placid lake, causing ripples of change. No governments were overthrown, no lives were lost in bloody battles, no single enemy was identified and vanquished.

The disputed territory was the human heart and the contest played itself out in every American institution: our homes, churches, schools, and ultimately in the provinces of power.

The delegates of Seneca Falls believed they were entitled to participate in public life as first-class citizens, and they mobilized quickly to secure a number of rights related to property and education. Even so, there were those who doubted that women would work so steadily and fight so long to secure all the privileges they sought, including the right to vote. Detractors seemed convinced that lack of political experience, internal disagreements, and feminine frailty of every conceivable variety would doom suffragist efforts. Instead, the women prevailed. It took a combination of conviction, tenacity, and plain old roll-up-your-sleeves hard work. And, although courage and commitment cannot be measured, I would guess that the long-term successes of the movement that began in Seneca Falls came from an unspoken understanding among the leaders that fighting for human rights is never for the fainthearted. It is a difficult journey, in which achievements are tempered by unexpected setbacks and false starts.

The movement launched at Seneca Falls was no exception. Despite its quick initial successes, there were lengthy delays. I am saddened when I am reminded that only one of the Seneca Falls pioneers lived to cast a vote in a federal election. Certainly, the victories would be sweeter if more of the original visionaries could have benefited. Nevertheless, their example of dedication, which guaranteed the full participation of future generations, is an expression of love and leadership worth emulating.

Long before I ever heard about Seneca Falls, my mother demonstrated similar determined devotion to my brother and me. When my father died, I was just eight years old. His heart attack was a shock that changed my life. The emotional loss was devastating, and his sudden absence threatened my family's solid working-class existence. But my mother was not to be deterred from her goal of giving me and my brother a better life than she had. Though she had no formal education past eighth grade, she did have a skill learned when she was a teenager that had helped her support her younger brothers and sisters. So she went back to work as a crochet beader, often bringing piecework home at night to make the extra money she needed to make ends meet. I remember as a little girl kissing her goodnight as she worked on into the early hours of the morning, hunched over a wooden frame crocheting tiny beads in beautiful patterns on material that would be part of a fancy and expensive gown.

Not a day goes by that I don't think of the sacrifices my mother made for me. It was her vision that built the foundation for my life. And because of her example, I have been able to bring into my public life the values she treasured: hard work, love of family and community, and a determination not to waste the opportunities I have been given. This is where my life and the legacy of Seneca Falls intersect. Just as my mother provided me with the chance to develop my talents, the founders of the women's suffragist movement gave me a world where I could apply those talents.

I happened to make my way in politics, but before that I taught grade school. I raised a family and prosecuted crimes. I have been a teacher, a mother and grandmother, an attorney, a wife, a legislator, a media commentator, and a human rights advocate. I have sponsored legislation in the House of Representatives to ensure that women would not be deprived of pension benefits, led the United States delegation to the United Nations Human Rights Commission, and, when my children were in school, I even taught classes on how to make macramé holders for hanging plants.

And of course, in the middle of a hot summer, 136 years after Seneca Falls, I stood proudly before this nation to accept my party's nomination for the second-highest elective office in the land. All of these things large and small, public and private, were possible because the women and men of Seneca Falls made certain that laws would not limit women's dreams nor dictate their deeds. (Although there are still those who would outlaw macramé.)

You might conclude, then, that I think the work is over, that women have arrived. Nothing could be further from the truth. Challenges will always remain because securing rights, women's rights, any rights is an activity, not a destination. If you doubt that, take a look around the world. Surely, the struggle for justice is seen daily in the emerging democracies of the former Soviet Union, in Africa, in Latin America, in China—anywhere people are still standing outside the reach of the liberties we enjoy.

But we needn't look so far from home. Current social and political debate still grapples with the question heard at Seneca Falls: "Can we truly afford to exclude anyone from contributing their fullest to society?" Certainly, that question remains at the root of the women's movement, and it resonates when we oppose severe restrictions on immigration, advance the rights of lesbians and gays, and object to dismantling affirmative action. Of course, we still can celebrate achievements and revel in progress made, but our obligation now is not simply to congratulate ourselves on how far we have come but to shoulder our responsibility together and continue the journey.

In any number of real ways, women still struggle. Women's wages are rising, but men still make more money. More women run statehouses and sit in corporate boardrooms than ever before, but not in numbers that reflect half the population. The majority of people living in poverty continue to be women, and for many the economic promise of Seneca Falls is only that, just a promise.

Women have been able to vote for more than 75 years, but many express the same disturbing indifference to politics as many men. I say this not as chastisement but as a reminder of the power of the ballot box. At Seneca Falls women rejected passivity in favor of action. Voting is an action that asserts that no one is entitled to make decisions for us without considering our opinions. You may doubt the effect voting has on what politicians do but I assure you, my colleagues would be doing cartwheels to win your approval if they knew 85 percent rather than 55 percent of voters would turn out election day.

Rejecting passivity, the leaders at Seneca Falls outlined the Declaration of Principles that called for changes in the law. Starting in the 1850s, with the passage of legislation in New York and Massachusetts guaranteeing women control over their own property and wages, many laws rooted in the declaration were enacted. By 1900 most states had similar laws, and more colleges had begun enrolling women, opening the way for women to pursue law and other professions. Progress toward pay equity began as early as 1872. States and new territories began passing suffrage laws in 1869, with Wyoming leading the way. It must have been a heady experience to witness those achievements, but it also must have been discouraging to encounter the waves of resistance in response to change.

Even a casual political observer knows that passing legislation is not an easy process. But compared to changing attitudes, sweeping legislative reform is a breeze. To change attitudes in 1848, men had to acknowledge that the rights they enjoyed belonged to their sisters as well as their brothers. And women needed to take the power they claimed, recognizing that passivity would never be as persuasive as organizing. As a legislator, I know that to change law, you define the issue, craft legislation, build consensus, determine if you have the votes needed to pass the measure, and take the vote. To change attitudes, the intangibles we call the "spirit of the law," requires more—a toughness anchored by unwavering principles.

I keep a few stories tucked away as personal reminders that achieving equality requires a sustained willingness to enforce what is fair. That way, I'm never tempted to declare discrimination extinct. It was 1978 and I was starting my first term in Congress. In order to keep my personal expenses separate from work-related ones, I applied for an airline credit card to pay for travel between Washington and Queens. I completed the form, ticking off each item: yes, I was employed; yes, I paid my bills on time; gender?—female. I detailed my work history, including the years I spent as a homemaker. I added that my annual salary was $60,000 and proudly wrote in the box labeled "occupation," member of the United States House of Representatives. My credit application was promptly denied—twice.

The Equal Credit Opportunity Act, which prohibited sex discrimination in all consumer credit practices, was four years old and obviously not sufficient to keep a member of Congress from facing discrimination. Given that realization, what hope was there that others without any access and little recourse could insist on the protections of the law?

This is only one instance in my life when I have experienced gender discrimination, but there were many others. And it would be foolish to conclude that such practices have disappeared. The work continues. The moral imperatives and practical necessities that have been the underpinnings of the women's movement since Seneca Falls are still vital to our nation today. The celebration of this anniversary is an opportunity to rededicate ourselves to those principles.

Bibliographic Note

Early feminists were uncommonly insightful in many ways, not least of which was their awareness of their role in history. They knew that what they were doing was important; more important, indeed, than many political scientists and historians have yet truly recognized. Because of this, they kept records. Few other political movements have been equally conscientious about documenting their legacy—at the same time they were creating it.

Early on, long before success was in sight, the pioneers of the women's movement began publishing their records. Many left autobiographies and reminiscences, as well as journals, speeches, letters, and other documentation of their work. They clipped and later republished literally thousands of newspaper stories and editorials, both supporting and opposing them. Their own periodicals, in particular the *Woman's Journal* but also other, less long-lived papers, also provide a lively record. None of these records, however, can compare to the massive *History of Woman Suffrage.*

The collective memory-book of the right-to-vote movement, it actually had many more authors than the four whose names appear on the covers of its six volumes. The title pages in the first three volumes read, "edited by Elizabeth Cady Stanton, Susan B. Anthony, and Matilda Joslyn Gage." The use of "edited by" clearly was intended to spell out their aim to compile and express the thoughts of many others, along with their own. "Scrapbook" is a particularly applicable term for the first volume, for it is a diverse source of unusual information. Its pages are often a curious combination of opposites, as the unsophisticated style of novices contrasts with astonishingly original philosophy.

The National Woman Suffrage Association was less than a decade old when the three women began collecting their documents, and the editors felt obligated to explain why they were writing a "history" of something that was far from achieved. They met this pre-publication criticism head on, saying that it was important to have "an arsenal of facts" before "all who could tell the story will have passed away." They understood, too, that as "historians of a reform in which we have been among the chief actors," they would be accused of a lack of objectivity. They also were ready to answer that charge: "As an autobiography is more interesting than a sketch by another, so is a history written by its actors, as in both cases we get nearer the soul of the subject." They anticipated criticism, too, because Stanton, Anthony, and Gage headed one of the two rival suffrage associations, but they dismissed that point: "We have felt no temptation to linger over individual differences. These occur in all associations and may be regarded as an evidence of the growing self-assertion and individualism in woman."

They had begun compiling memorabilia in Stanton's New Jersey home in the late 1870s, and Gage did most of the work of pulling disparate sources together into book form. Like everything else they did, the women also had to finance publication themselves, but by 1881, the volumes began to roll off the press. The first covered the years 1848 to 1861, between the Seneca Falls Convention and the beginning of the Civil War. The second came out the next year and dealt with the period from 1861 to 1876, when the nation celebrated its centennial. The first volume ran 878 pages; the second was even larger with 952; and the third part of the series was 1,012, including an index that the first two volumes lacked.

The third was published in 1885 and brought the activists' history current with their own lives. They began its preface: "the labors of those who have edited these volumes are not only finished as far as this work extends, but... all our earthy endeavors must end in the near future." Actually, the future held much more for them, as Gage and Stanton would write their most important books after this. The assessment was correct, however, in that it was the last work that they did together.

The fourth volume, which listed Susan B. Anthony and Ida Husted Harper as editors, was the biggest of all at 1,144 pages. It was published in 1902, the year that Stanton died, and covered the history between 1883 and 1900. The influence of Harper's journalistic training is clear in this volume: it systematically detailed information on a year-by-year basis and featured the first alphabetically listed reports from every state and territory, as well as from many nations and fields of endeavor. Because each of these reports was written by at least one person, the volume included writing by significantly more than 50 authors.

The last two volumes, which were published in 1922, also had multiple authors. Harper was the sole editor and had intended it as one volume covering 1900 to 1920, but the era included so much information that it was simply impossible to hold it to one: volume five has 817 pages and six runs to 899. Especially in volume six, Harper acted almost exclusively as an editor rather than an author. It is a very democratically written history of the final success (or failure) in each state, including reports from rival organizations. These summaries were written by people who were closest to the action, and they ring with the validity of insiders.

Reading the 5,702 pages of *History of Woman Suffrage* is like exploring some long-locked grandmother's attic. It is an adventure in discovery that can be both wondrously significant and tiresomely trivial and duplicative. Especially in the early volumes, treasures and trash are thrown together, and it sometimes demands dedication to separate them. Even in the later volumes, its pages contain bias, occasional omissions of facts, and some shading of the truth to feature the authors' views in the best possible light—but these accusations may be made of virtually all authors and books.

The larger point is that history is complex, and women's history in particular requires a great degree of thoughtfulness, open-mindedness, and fact-seeking. Although *History of Woman Suffrage* has its faults, it is by far the most important reference we have, and too much of the information in its nearly 6,000 pages has been neglected. The methodology of Part One of this book, then, has been to use other sources for balance when needed, but to take most quotations from the official history of the chief suffrage organization. Obviously, many quotes did come from other sources: the first one of the book, for example, is from Massachusetts Governor John Winthrop, when he called Lady Deborah Moody "a dangerous woeman." While a few readers might want to know that these words can be found in volume four, page 456 of Winthrop's papers, it seems a higher priority instead to use the available space for more of the exciting details of the complex suffrage story.

History of Woman Suffrage is in many ways analogous to the Bible: both feature many writers with individualistic styles who may exhibit bias, make omissions, and contradict each other. But both tomes are such mother lodes of beginning points that countless books have been and will be written to explore and expand on them. Because there is so much to be gleaned from this one treasure, no quotations from secondary sources were used. The same methodology was used for the chapters on issues and people during the century between 1920 and 2020. Because *Victory for the Vote* is aimed at a wide audience, not particularly for scholars, visual appeal took priority over citation notes.

Clues for finding the further details on quotes are included in the text, as for example, "the Associated Press reported on June 21, 1937," which is enough information for the curious reader to find the full source in today's online world. Other books that have been published during the two decades since the original work, *A History of the American Suffragist Movement* (ABC-CLIO, 1998), are included under "Secondary Sources." To keep the sales price low for a mass audience, it was necessary to limit the bibliography's secondary sources to one book per author—but in most cases, an online search for that author will bring up additional relevant titles.

Other books have been added to the bibliography for subjects that were extraneous to the first version, which ended with the ratification of the Nineteenth Amendment in 1920. Thus, subject areas such as the Equal Rights Amendment and the birth control movement have been added—but not nearly every title that could have been included. This is especially true for people whose activism was post-1920. Instead of listing for example, biographies of Ruth Bryan Owen (the first congresswoman from the South) or Hattie Caraway (the first woman elected to the U.S. Senate), we hope that you simply will do a search for their names.

Literally thousands, perhaps tens of thousands, of sources could be included for further reading. That denotes a wonderful new world, one that provides us with massive amounts of material on women's history and the issues we deal with daily. This was not the case when I published my first book in 1986, and I am so grateful to have lived to see the day.

—Doris Weatherford

Sources and Further Reading

Primary Sources

Addams, Jane. *Democracy and Social Ethics.* New York: Macmillan, 1902.

Anthony, Susan B., and Ida Husted Harper, eds. *History of Woman Suffrage,* vol 4. 1902. Reprint, New York: Arno Press, 1969.

Beard, Mary Ritter. *Woman as a Force in History.* New York: The Macmillan Co., 1945.

Blackwell, Alice Stone. *Lucy Stone: Pioneer of Women's Rights.* Boston: Little, Brown & Co., 1930.

Blatch, Harriot Stanton, and Alma Lutz. *Challenging Years: The Memoirs of Harriot Stanton Blatch.* New York: G.P. Putnam's Sons, 1940.

Bloomer, Dexter C. *Life and Writings of Amelia Bloomer.* Boston: Arena Publishing Co., 1895.

Brown, Olympia. *Acquaintances, Old and New, Among Reformers.* Milwaukee: S.E. Tate Press, 1911.

Burroughs, Nannie Helen. *A Documentary History of an Early Civil Rights Pioneer, 1900–1959.* Notre Dame: University of Notre Dame, 2019.

Catt, Carrie Chapman, and Nettie Rogers Schuler. *Woman Suffrage and Politics: The Inner Story of the Suffrage Movement.* New York: Charles Scribner's Sons, 1923.

Congress of Women. *The Congress of Women Held in the Woman's Building, World's Columbian Exposition, Chicago, U.S.A.,* 1893. Philadelphia: C.R. Parish, 1894.

Croly, Jane Cunningham. *History of the Woman's Club Movement in America.* New York: H.G. Allen & Co., 1898.

Dennett, Mary Ware. *Who's Obscene?* New York: Vanguard, 1930.

Doress-Worters, Paula, ed. *Mistress of Herself: Speeches and Letters of Ernestine Rose.* New York: City University of New York, 2008.

Duniway, Abigail Scott. *Pathbreaking: An Autobiographical History of the Equal Suffrage Movement in the Pacific Coast States.* Portland, Oregon: James, Kerns, & Abbott Co., 1914.

Eastman, Crystal. *On Women and Revolution.* Edited by Blanche Weisen Cook. New York: Oxford University Press, 1978.

Gage, Matilda Joslyn. *Woman, Church and State.* 1893. Reprint, New York: Arno Press, 1972.

Gilman, Charlotte Perkins Stetson. *Women and Economics.* Boston: Small, Maynard and Co., 1898.

Hallowell, Anna Davis. *James and Lucretia Mott.* Boston: Houghton, Mifflin and Co., 1884.

Harper, Ida Husted, ed. *History of Woman Suffrage,* vols. 5–6. New York: National American Woman Suffrage Association, 1922.

———. *The Life and Work of Susan B. Anthony*. 3 vols. Indianapolis: Hollenbeck Press, 1898–1908.

Howe, Julia Ward. *Reminiscences.* Boston: Houghton Mifflin Co., 1899.

Irwin, Inez Haynes. *The Story of the Woman's Party.* New York: Harcourt, Brace, & Co., 1921.

Jacobi, Mary Putnam. *"Common Sense" Applied to Woman Suffrage*. New York: G.P. Putnam's Sons, 1894.

Pankhurst, Emmeline. *My Own Story.* New York: Hearts International Library Co., 1914.

Park, Maud Wood, ed. *Victory, How Women Won It: A Centennial Symposium, 1840–1940.*New York: H. W. Wilson, 1940.

Sanger, Margaret. *My Fight for Birth Control.* New York: Oxford, 1931.

Shaw, Anna Howard. *The Story of a Pioneer.* 1915. Reprint, New York: Kraus Reprint Co, 1970.

Stanton, Elizabeth Cady, Susan B. Anthony, and Matilda Joslyn Gage, eds. *History of Woman Suffrage,* vols. 1–3. 1881–1886. Reprint, New York: Arno Press, 1969.

Stanton, Elizabeth Cady. *Eighty Years and More.* New York: European Publishing Company, 1898.

Stanton, Theodore, and Harriot Stanton Blatch, eds. *Elizabeth Cady Stanton As Revealed in Her Letters, Diary and Reminiscences.* New York: Harper & Brothers, 1922.

Stevens, Doris. *Jailed for Freedom.* New York: Boni & Liveright, 1920.

Stowe, Harriet Beecher. *Life of Harriet Beecher Stowe.* Boston: Houghton Mifflin Co., 1891.

Terrell, Mary Church. *A Colored Woman in a White World.* 1940. Reprint, New York: Arno Press, 1980.

Wells-Barnett, Ida. *Crusade for Justice: The Autobiography of Ida B. Wells.* Edited by Alfreda M. Duster. Chicago: University of Chicago, 1970.

Willard, Frances E., and Mary Livermore, eds. *A Woman of the Century: Leading American Women.* 1893. Reprint, Detroit: Gale Research, 1967.

Woodhull, Victoria; edited by Carl M. Carpenter. *Selected Writings of Victoria Woodhull: Suffrage, Free Love, and Eugenics.* Lincoln: University of Nebraska Press, 2015.

Secondary Sources

Adams, Katherine H. *Alice Paul and the American Suffrage Campaign.* Urbana: University of Illinois, 2008.

Anderson, Kristi. *After Suffrage: Women in Partisan and Electoral Politics Before the New Deal.* Chicago: University of Chicago Press, 1996.

Anthony, Katharine. *Susan B. Anthony: Her Personal History and Her Era.* New York: Doubleday, 1954.

Baer, Judith A. *Historical and Multicultural Encyclopedia of Women's Reproductive Rights in the United States.* Westport, CT: Greenwood Press, 2002.

Banner, Lois W. *Women in Modern America: A Brief History.* New York: Harcourt Brace Jovanovich, 1974.

Baker, Jean H. *Votes for Women: The Struggle for Suffrage Revisited.* New York. Oxford University Press, 2002.

Baxandall, Rosalyn, Linda Gordon, and Susan Reverby. *America's Working Women: A Documentary History, 1600 to the Present.* New York: Vintage Books, 1976.

Becker, Susan D. *The Origins of the Equal Rights Amendment: American Feminism between the Wars.* Westport, CT: Greenwood Press, 1981.

Beeton, Beverly. *Women Vote in the West: The Woman Suffrage Movement, 1869–1896.* New York: Garland Publishers, 1986.

Beisel, Nicola. *Imperialed Innocents: Anthony Comstock and Family Reproduction in Victorian America.* Princeton, NJ: Princeton University Press, 1997.

Berkin, Carol Ruth, and Mary Beth Norton, eds. *Women of America: A History.* Boston: Houghton Mifflin, l979.

Berry, Mary Frances. *Why ERA Failed: Politics, Women's Rights, and the Amending Process of the Constitution.* Bloomington: Indiana University Press, 1986.

Boisseau, TJ, and Abigail Markwyn: *Gendering the Fair: Histories of Women and Gender at World Fairs.* Urbana: University of Illinois, 2010.

Boles, Janet K. *The Politics of the Equal Rights Amendment: Conflict and the Decision Process.* New York: Longman, 1979.

Brant, Allan M. *No Magic Bullet: A Social History of Venereal Disease in the United States since 1880.* New York: Oxford University Press, 1987.

Briggs, Laura. *How All Politics Became Reproductive Politics.* Oakland: University of California Press, 2017.

Byrne, Pamela R., and Susan K. Kinnell. *Women in North America.* Santa Barbara, CA: ABC-CLIO, 1988.

Camhi, Jane Jerome. *Women against Women: American Anti-Suffragism, 1880–1920.* Brooklyn, NY: Carlson Publishers, 1994.

Caron, Simone. *Who Chooses? American Reproductive History since 1820.* Gainesville: University Press of Florida, 2008.

Carpenter, Angelica Shirley. *Born Criminal: Matilda Joslyn Gage, Radical Feminist.* Pierre: South Dakota Historical Society Press, 2018.

Chafe, William. *Women and Equality: Changing Patterns in American Culture.* New York: Oxford University Press, 1977.

Cooney, Robert P.J., Jr. *Winning the Vote: The Triumph of the American Woman Suffrage Movement.* Santa Cruz, CA: American Graphic Press, 2005.

Corder, J. Kevin. *Counting Women's Ballots: Female Voters from Suffrage through the New Deal.* Cambridge, UK: Cambridge University Press, 2016.

Cott, Nancy. *The Grounding of Modern Feminism.* New Haven: Yale University Press, 1987.

Degler, Carl. *At Odds: Women and the Family in America.* New York: Oxford University Press, l981.

DiFonzo, J. Herbie. *Beneath the Fault Line: The Popular and Legal Culture of Divorce in the Twentieth Century.* Charlottesville: University Press of Virginia, 1997.

Dorr, Rheta Child. *Susan B. Anthony.* 1928. Reprint, New York: AMS Press, 1970.

DuBois, Ellen Carol. *Feminism and Suffrage: The Emergence of an Independent Women's Movement in America, 1848–1869.* Ithaca, NY: Cornell University Press, 1978.

Dudden, Faye E. *Fighting Chance: The Struggle over Woman Suffrage and Black Suffrage in Reconstruction America.* New York: Oxford University Press, 2011.

Evans, Sara M. *Born for Liberty: A History of Women in America.* New York: The Free Press, 1989.

Felder, Deborah G. *A Century of Women: The Most Influential Events in Twentieth Century Women's History.* Secaucus, NJ: Carol Publishing Group, 1999.

Flavin, Jeanne. *Our Bodies, Our Crimes: The Policing of Women's Reproduction in America.* New York: New York University Press, 2009.

Flexner, Eleanor. *Century of Struggle.* New York: Atheneum, 1974.

Ford, Linda G. *Iron-Jawed Angels: The Suffrage Militancy of the National Woman's Party.* Lanham, MD: University Press of America, 1987.

Franzen, Monika, and Nancy Ethiel, with Nicole Hollander. *Make Way! 200 Years of American Women in Cartoons*. Chicago: Chicago Review Press, 1988.

Frost, Elizabeth, and Kathryn Cullen-Dupont. *Woman's Suffrage in America: An Eyewitness History*. New York: Facts on File, 1992.

George, Carol V. R., ed. *"Remember the Ladies": New Perspectives on Women in American History*. Syracuse, NY: Syracuse University Press, l975.

Gilmore, Glenda. *Gender and Jim Crow: Women and the Politics of White Supremacy in North Carolina*. Chapel Hill: University of North Carolina, 1996.

Gluck, Sherna. *From Parlor to Prison: Five American Suffragists Talk About Their Lives*. New York: Random House, 1976.

Goodier, Susan. *No Votes for Women: The New York State Anti-Suffrage Movement*. Urbana: University of Illinois Press, 2012.

Gordon, Ann D. and Bettye Collier-Thomas, eds. *African American Women and the Vote, 1837–1965*. Amherst: University of Massachusetts, 1997.

Goss, Kristin. *The Paradox of Gender Equality: How American Women's Groups Gained and Lost their Public Voice*. Ann Arbor: University of Michigan, 2012.

Gurko, Miriam. *The Ladies of Seneca Falls*. New York: Macmillan, 1974.

Haber, Barbara. *Women in America: A Guide to Books*. New York: G.K. Hall, 1978.

Halberstam, Malvina and Elizabeth Defeis. *Women's Legal Rights: International Covenants as an Alternative to ERA?* Dobbs Ferry, NY: Transnational Publishers, 1987.

Harvey, Sheridan, ed. *American Women: A Library of Congress Guide for the Study of Women's History and Culture in the United States*. Washington: Library of Congress, 2001.

Hewitt, Nancy A. *Women's Activism and Social Change in Rochester, New York*. Ithaca, NY: Cornell University Press, 1984.

Hine, Darlene Clark, ed. *Black Women in United States History*. 16 vols. Brooklyn, NY: Carlson Publishing, 1990.

James, Edward T., Janet Wilson James, and Paul S. Boyer, eds. *Notable American Women*. 3 vols. Cambridge, MA: Harvard University Press, 1971.

Janeway, Elizabeth. *Between Myth and Morning: Women Awakening*. New York: Morrow, 1974.

Johnson, John W. *Griswold v. Connecticut: Birth Control and the Constitutional Right of Privacy*. Lawrence: University of Kansas, 2005.

Joshi, S.T., ed. *A Documentary History of Prejudice against Women*. Amherst: Prometheus Books, 2006.

Katz, Esther, and Anita Rapone, eds. *Women's Experience in America: An Historical Anthology*. New Brunswick, NJ: Transaction Books, l980.

Kennedy, David M. *Birth Control in America: The Career of Margaret Sanger*. New Haven, CT: Yale University, 1970.

Kerber, Linda K., Alice Kessler-Harris, and Kathryn Kish Sklar. *U.S. History as Women's History*. Chapel Hill, NC: University of North Carolina Press, 1995.

Kern, Kathi. *Mrs. Stanton's Bible*. Ithaca, NY: Cornell University Press, 2001.

Kinnard, Cynthia D. *Antifeminism in America: An Annotated Bibliography*. Boston: G.K. Hall, 1986.

Klepp, Susan E. *Revolutionary Conceptions: Women, Fertility, and Family Limitation in America, 1760–1820*. Chapel Hill: University of North Carolina, 2009.

Laughlin, Kathleen and Jacqueline L. Castledine. *Breaking the Wave: Women, Their* Organizations, *and Feminism, 1945–1985*. New York: Routledge, 2011.

Lerner, Gerda. *The Woman in American History*. Menlo Park, CA: Addison-Wesley, 1971.

Levine, Susan. *Degrees of Equality: The American Association of University Women and the Challenge of Twentieth-Century Feminism*. Philadelphia: Temple University Press, 1995.

Lumsden, Linda J. *Inez: The Life and Times of Inez Milholland*. Bloomingdale: Indiana University Press, 2004.

Lunardini, Christine A. *Alice Paul: Equality for Women*. Philadelphia: Westview Press, 2013.

Lutz, Alma. *Susan B. Anthony: Rebel, Crusader, Humanitarian*. Boston: Beacon Press, 1959.

Mansbridge, Jane J. *Why We Lost the ERA*. Chicago: University of Chicago Press, 1986.

Martin, Theodora Penny. *The Sound of Their Own Voices: Women's Study Clubs, 1860–1910*. Boston: Beacon Press, 1987.

Mathews, Donald G. and Jane Sherron De Hart. *Sex, Gender, and the Politics of ERA: A State and the Nation*. New York: Oxford University Press, 1990.

McDonagh, Eileen. *Breaking the Abortion Debate: From Choice to Consent*. New York: Oxford University Press, 1996.

McKinley, A.E. *Suffrage Franchise in the Thirteen Colonies*. New York: B. Franklin, 1969.

Merkel, Richard. *"Save the Babies:" American Public Health Reform and the Prevention of Infant Mortality*. Baltimore: Johns Hopkins University, 1990.

Mohr, James C. *Abortion in America: The Origins and Evolution of National Policy, 1800–1900*. New York: Oxford University Press, 1978.

Morgan, David. *Suffragists and Democrats*. East Lansing: Michigan State University Press, 1972.

O'Dea, Suzanne Schenken. *From Suffrage to the Senate: An Encyclopedia of American Women in Politics*. Santa Barbara, CA: ABC-CLIO, 1999.

O'Neill, William L. *Everyone Was Brave: A History of Feminism in America.* Chicago: Quadrangle Books, 1971.

Page, Christina. *How the Pro-Choice Movement Saved America: Freedom, Politics, and the War on Sex.* New York: Basic Books, 2006.

Redfern, Bernice. *Women of Color in the U.S.* New York: Garland Publishers, 1989.

Roessner, Lori Amber and Jodi Rightler-McDaniels. *Political Power of the Press: Ida B. Wells-Barnett and Her Transnational Crusade for Social Justice.* New York: Lexington Books, 2018.

Roosevelt, Eleanor, and Lorena Hickok. *Ladies of Courage.* New York: G.P. Putnam's Sons, 1954.

Ross, Ishbel. *Sons of Adam; Daughters of Eve.* New York: Harper & Row, 1969.

Ross, Loretta J. and Rickie Solinger. *Reproductive Justice: An Introduction.* Oakland: University of California, 2017.

Rossi, Alice, ed. *Feminist Papers.* New York: Bantam Books, 1973.

Rothman, Sheila M. *Woman's Proper Place: A History of Changing Ideals and Practices, 1870 to the Present.* New York: Basic Books, 1978.

Ryan, Mary P. *Womanhood in America: From Colonial Times to the Present,* 2nd ed. New York: New Viewpoints, l979.

Rymph, Catherine E. *Feminism and Conservatism from Suffrage through the Rise of the New Right.* Chapel Hill: University of North Carolina Press, 2006.

Schneider, Dorothy and Carl J. *American Women in the Progressive Era.* New York: Facts on File, 1993.

Schwarzenbach, Sibyl B. and Patricia Smith, eds. *Women and the United States Constitution: History, Interpretation, and Practice.* New York: Columbia University Press, 2003.

Scott, Anne F., and Andrew M. Scott. *One Half the People: The Fight for Woman Suffrage.* Philadelphia: J.B. Lippincott Company, 1975.

Sicherman, Barbara, and Carol Hurd Green, eds. *Notable American Women,* vol 4. Cambridge, MA: Harvard University Press, 1980.

Sinclair, Andrew. *The Better Half: The Emancipation of the American Woman.* New York: Harper & Row, 1965.

Sklar, Kathryn Kish. *Who Won the Debate Over the Equal Rights Amendment in the 1920s?* Binghamton, NY: State University of New York, 2000.

Smith, Jessie Carney, ed. *Notable Black American Women.* Detroit: Gale Research, 1992.

Solomon, Barbara Miller. *In the Company of Educated Women.* New Haven, CT: Yale University Press, 1985.

Solomon, Martha M. *A Voice of their Own: The Woman Suffrage Press, 1840–1910.* Tuscaloosa: University of Alabama, 1991.

Steiner, Gilbert Y. *Constitutional Inequality: The Political Fortunes of the Equal Rights Amendment.* Washington: Brookings Institution, 1985.

Sterling, Dorothy, ed. *We Are Your Sisters: Black Women in the Nineteenth Century*. New York: W.W. Norton, 1984.

Strauss, Sylvia. *Traitors to the Masculine Cause: The Men's Campaigns for Women's Rights.* Westport, CT: Greenwood Press, 1982.

Stuhler, Barbara. *For the Public Record: A Documentary History of the League of Women Voters.* Westport, CT: Greenwood Press, 2000.

Terborg-Penn, Rosalyn. *African American Women in the Struggle for the Vote, 1850-1920.* Bloomington: Indiana University Press, 1998.

Turner, Edward R. "Women's Suffrage in New Jersey: 1790–1807." *Smith College Studies in History,* October, 1915–July, 1916.

Vacca, Carolyn Summers. *A Reform against Nature: Woman Suffrage and the Rethinking of American Citizenship.* New York: Peter Lang, 2004.

Ware, Susan. *Beyond Suffrage: Women in the New Deal.* Cambridge, MA: Harvard University Press, 1981.

Washington, Margaret. *Sojourner Truth's America.* Urbana: University of Illinois, 2009.

Weimann, Jeanne Madeline. *The Fair Women.* Chicago: Academy, 1981.

Weiss, Elaine. *The Woman's Hour: The Great Fight to Win the Vote*. New York: Penguin, 2018.

Wertheimer, Barbara Mayer. *We Were There: The Story of Working Women in America.* New York: Pantheon, 1977.

Wheeler, Marjorie Spruill. *One Woman, One Vote: Rediscovering the Woman Suffrage Movement.* Troutdale, OR: New Sage Press, 1995.

Wortman, Marlene Stein. *Woman in American Law: From Colonial Times to the New Deal.* New York: Holmes & Meier, 1985.

Young, Louise M. *In the Public Interest: The League of Women Voters, 1920–1970.* New York: Greenwood Press, 1989.

Zahniser, J.D. *Alice Paul: Claiming Power.* New York: Oxford University Press, 2014.

Ziegler, Mary. *After Roe: The Lost History of the Abortion Debate.* Cambridge, MA: Harvard University Press, 2015.

Index

Italic page numbers indicate images.

About the Author

Author Doris Weatherford is active in the political arena and has been extensively recognized for her contributions to the field of women's history. Affiliated with the University of South Florida, she was editor-in-chief and major contributor to the monumental reference work, *A History of Women in the United States: State-by-State Reference* (Grolier Academic Reference, 2004), which offers detailed and engaging histories of women in each of the fifty states. She also authored a two-volume work for CQ Press with a foreword by Congresswoman Debbie Wasserman Schultz, *Women in American Politics: History and Milestones* (2012), which was honored by the American Library Association as an Outstanding Reference Source and by *Booklist* with an Editor's Choice citation. Her other publications include, among others, *Foreign and Female: Immigrant Women in America, 1840-1920* (Facts On File, 1986) and *American Women during World War II* (Routledge, 2009).

Mango Publishing, established in 2014, publishes an eclectic list of books by diverse authors—both new and established voices—on topics ranging from business, personal growth, women's empowerment, LGBTQ studies, health, and spirituality to history, popular culture, time management, decluttering, lifestyle, mental wellness, aging, and sustainable living. We were recently named 2019's #1 fastest growing independent publisher by *Publishers Weekly*. Our success is driven by our main goal, which is to publish high quality books that will entertain readers as well as make a positive difference in their lives. Our readers are our most important resource; we value your input, suggestions, and ideas. We'd love to hear from you—after all, we are publishing books for you!

Please stay in touch with us and follow us at:
Facebook: Mango Publishing
Twitter: @MangoPublishing
Instagram: @MangoPublishing
LinkedIn: Mango Publishing
Pinterest: Mango Publishing

Sign up for our newsletter at www.mangopublishinggroup.com and receive a free book!

Join us on Mango's journey to reinvent publishing, one book at a time.

3 1333 04901 1081